Nationalism

___

Theories and Cases

Erika Harris

EDINBURGH UNIVERSITY PRESS

Edinburgh University Press Ltd
22 George Square, Edinburgh
www.euppublishing.com

Reprinted 2012

Typeset in 11/12.5 Sabon by
Servis Filmsetting Ltd, Stockport, Cheshire, and
printed and bound in Great Britain by
CPI Antony Rowe, Chippenham and Eastbourne

A CIP record for this book is available from the British Library

ISBN 978 0 7486 1558 2 (hardback)
ISBN 978 0 7486 1559 9 (paperback)

Contents

Preface

This book presents nationalism as an omnipresent thought in politics, in the minds of ordinary people, politicians and observers of politics, and in international relations. I began my study of nationalism with the exploration of post-communist transitions when it struck me that nationalism was at least as important as were the economy and democratisation, if not mutually dependent. When, as a doctoral student, I presented my proposal to explore the close relationship between democracy and nationalism, I was told by a member of the committee who were to approve it, that I was too sanguine about nationalism. Later, at some conference, I was told by a distinguished scholar that I did not understand the poetry of ethnicity. After another few years of studying and writing about nationalism and following the developments not only in Eastern and Central Europe but elsewhere, and researching into the relationship between nationalism and European integration, I have become less sanguine about nationalism and guardedly acknowledge the meaning of poetry that ethnicity may offer to people.

When in the early 1990s I visited a village on the Slovak–Ukrainian border, I found sun-bleached somewhat battered remnants of the communist era in the form of a hammer and sickle and the Soviet flag on top of the community hall, alongside the new bright Slovak flag. When I asked an old man why they don't take them down, he looked up, shrugged his shoulders, waved his hand and sighed in resignation. They used to tell a joke in the sub-Carpathian region about an old man telling a story of his life to a young western journalist. After mentioning that he went to school in Austro-Hungary, worked for Czechs, got married in Hungary, fought in Russia, worked in Czechoslovakia and is now retired in Slovakia, the journalist said that he must have travelled a lot in his life. 'No, said the old man, I never left this village.' The old man I met could have probably told the same story because he too spoke in the local Rusin dialect, was fluent in Russian and Hungarian and Slovak and hardly noticed that his village was part of a new state – again, about the fifth time since he was born there. Nationalism was everywhere in post-communist Europe; some people did not care, some cared too much, the countries were falling apart, and people's lives were chaotic in a frenzy of new borders and recriminations for the past and even the future. War was raging in the beautiful Yugoslavia, its cities and its charismatic people were being destroyed. The past rose out of every page of every newspaper, rehashed and altered to suit the new dawn of the newly established states. Rehashed again, that is, because rehashing history is considered a duty of all new regimes and states. Nationalism affects people's lifes, sometimes dramatically and beyond their control or their beliefs, but mostly it affects politics and ordinary daily lives in a less dramatic fashion. I do not believe that cultural identity leads to hostility to others, but I do believe that it matters enough to be easily exploited. I also believe that nationalism pertains to the political realm and that its role in human existence is therefore paramount. This is not because everyone is a nationalist but because everyone is endowed with a national label whether they wish to be or not – this is a political reality of our world, not a human characteristic.

This book is a result of my observations that many academic debates about nationalism are somehow devoid of the impact their subject has on the everyday lives of people. We academics tend to seek categorisations and typologies, but nationalism does not seem to fit easily to any pigeonholes we devise for it. Does it matter when the nation came into existence, when children in Israel are being escorted from one building to another by soldiers with guns? Does it matter whether nationalism is civic when there are thousands of immigrants in fear of being deported back to countries that they left having to sell every belonging they owned to pay for the passage to a better future? How good is an ethnically proportionate constitution in a post-conflict zone, when old ladies are being escorted to church by peacekeepers they do not understand and when the local policeman is the man whom they know burned down their houses? Why do people who have lived happily somewhere for decades support a militant movement in a far away country they hardly know because of their roots? How long does it take not to feel a foreigner and does everything we know about nationalism give us any indication? Can we really believe that fear and insecurity can be removed from a world of states whose legitimacy is rooted in a national idea? Which approach to nationalism should we look to for peace and equity?

I am not proposing that the reader will find all the answers in my book. My intention has been to deal with nationalism as a political ideology and to provide links between its historical roots and contemporary manifestations. I look to continuities but emphasise discontinuities in classical approaches to nationalism when explored through the prism of its contemporary manifestation in the world politics. My aim is to provide a number of suggestions through which to approach nationalism in our time when the role of the state and our expectations of it are changing. It is an ambitious idea and I am aware that my objectives may not be fully satisfied. I am hoping, however, that this book will be helpful to students who seek the application of the theories of nationalism in world politics and will possibly interest those who seek answers to some political developments that are clearly identity related. I hope that the case studies I use will demonstrate the role of nationalism as integral to political changes and democracy in the past and at present.

With the exceptions of some case studies and considerations which are a result of my own research, I have relied mostly on secondary sources and the work of other scholars for which I am very grateful and which often fill me with a great sense of humility. The conclusions and information I draw from their work, if erroneous, are my own fault, however. I thank my department and my colleagues for allowing me a sabbatical in order to write this book. Moreover, I want to thank many friends and colleagues with whom I have discussed various nationalism-related topics over the years in personal correspondence or at various gatherings. They will recognise our conversations in references and arguments. I want to thank my husband Julian for his endless support for everything I do and for his many useful comments. Finally, I wish that the many members of my family, who did not survive the worse excesses of nationalism in the former Czechoslovakia during World War II, could read this book and perhaps find some answers. This book is dedicated to them.

Erika Harris
December 2008

Introduction: The Nation Then and Now

But in all this great array of elaborate, statistically supported serious futurology mingled with free fantasy, there took place one movement which dominated much of the nineteenth century for which no significant future was predicted, a movement so familiar to us now, so decisive both within, and in relationships between, nations that it is only by some effort of imagination that one can conceive of a world in which it played no part. Its existence and its power (especially outside the English-speaking world) seem to us so self-evident today that it appears strange to have to draw attention to it as a phenomenon the prophets before our day, and in our time too, virtually ignored; in the case of the latter, at times with fatal consequences to themselves and those who believed them. This movement is nationalism.[1]

The story of nationalism mirrors history and modern history mirrors the story of nationalism; since about the mid-nineteenth century no place in the world remained untouched by its impact. This book is about nationalism, its beginnings and its very contemporary manifestations. It explores similarities and differences in nationalist politics across a number of states, and political processes taking place within and beyond the states, and by doing so critically assesses how nationalism and its theories developed and what is their significance today. The book contains a number of illustrative case studies but let me begin with the example of the former Czechoslovakia. The establishment and disintegration of this country reflect the last century in the eastern part of the European continent, starting with the fall of the Austro-Hungarian and Ottoman Empires and closing with the fall of the Berlin Wall. Each fall of a regime and each rise of another regime was accompanied by shifting borders, the changing status of national groups and some form of nationalism ranging from the emancipation of the people to their destruction. This is the story of Europe; it is the story of the former Yugoslavia; a similar story can be told about the contemporary Middle East and many other regions in the world.

Czechoslovakia, the state predominantly for Slovaks and Czechs, was founded in 1918 by Tomáš Garrigue Masaryk (1850–1937) who believed in multinationality as a principle of democracy and was endorsed by the Wilsonian national self-determination doctrine of the first hopeful 'new world order' of the twentieth century. Two decades later, Czechoslovakia, which was slightly less democratic and more nationally fragmented than Masaryk had perhaps envisaged, fell prey to that other doctrine that grew in intensity and ferocity parallel to the lofty ideas of the League of Nations – fascism. Fascism, argues Nairn, tells us far more about nationalism than any other episode.[2] Czechoslovakia was divided into two fascist entities, its Czech part annexed and occupied by Nazi Germany and its Slovak part which was naively and tragically lulled into co-operation with the Nazis by a promise of national independence. At the end of the cataclysmic war, the reunited country, its population reduced by the vanished Jews, the declared 'collectively guilty' and the deported Sudeten Germans and repatriated Hungarians, found itself on the Soviet side of the post-1945 world order. The communist Czechoslovakia tried briefly to make sense of its communism in 1968, but the invading Soviet tanks legitimised by yet another doctrine – the Brezhnev's doctrine[3] – while crushing through the national sovereignty barrier crushed also any hope of 'communism with a human face'. The period of bitter disappointment that followed was cynically named 'normalisation' by the new leadership which implemented only one of the many reforms demanded by the 1968 liberalisation Action Programme: the federalisation of the state into the Slovak and the Czech federal republics. The fall of communism (1989–91) ushered in the latest 'new world order' and, indeed, the new map of Europe. Czechoslovakia followed the other two communist federal states

– the Soviet Union and Yugoslavia – and disintegrated. Instead of resolving the accumulated national, political and economic divisions, the democratisation process reinforced them and gave rise to nationalist mobilisation which, in the absence of faith in the common state, could succeed only in breaking it up along its major ethnic lines. The successor states, the Czech Republic and Slovakia, have joined the European Union separately but under the same label: the eastward enlargement (2004). The new united Europe is hoping to prevent the repetition of its own past by curbing the role of the nation and its sovereignty as the primary line of division among European peoples. The history of Europe, so torn by nationalist struggles, suggests that as ideological experiments go, the European Union may be a truly worthwhile attempt. And yet, the peoples of Europe remain reluctant for the fear of losing their national sovereignties, contaminating their purportedly historical national identities, and hence the real obstacle to European unity remains nationalism.

Many people have died in the name of the nation they belonged to, defended or were excluded from. And still, the struggle for autonomy over what a nation considers its territory continues. The change is mostly in vocabulary: the old civil wars are called ethnic conflicts and the international influence comes in the form of a peace process policed by a new type of a warrior – a peacekeeper. The post-Cold War world is dotted with ethnic conflicts, redrawn by peace treaties, crowded with peacekeeping troops spread over the globe and bursting at the seams with refugee camps and asylum seekers' centres. History has not 'ended'; on the contrary, the global belief in democracy seems to have revived nationalism. Its success rests on a paradox. While politics and ideologies are changing and while the ultimate object of nationalism's desire, the nation state, is changing too, nationalism's core theme – the political recognition and dignity for a supposedly culturally unique nation they helped to create – remains unchanged. As we are rethinking our understanding of the world organised into nation states in a different era, and as we are pondering the puzzles emerging from the political and economic globalisation and unprecedented movement of people around the globe, we need to re-examine our thinking about nationalism. This is the main theme of this book.

Nationalism can be a doctrine, it can direct the vision for the future, it can be and is politics, and it can aid other ideologies or compete with them. The past is its inspiration, the future its aim.

Between, it creates and destroys, all in equal measures. The first questions must be when and why did the nation assume the relevance that can be, at best, considered important to human existence and, at worst, set against it? The answers to these questions will be sought in historical and theoretical terms in the first two chapters of this book, while the remainder of the book illustrates the contemporary manifestations of 'the nation' in the politics of nation states and beyond them.

Despite the conceptual controversy surrounding the origins and the meaning of the nation, nationalism is always understood as relating to individual and/or collective identities and carrying a degree of ideological consequence. There may have been times in history when that consequence meant merely a sense of awareness of belonging to a certain grouping characterised by the place, the language and the custom which derived from a certain historical experience. In the modern world, however, there can be little doubt that consequences are political and that nationalism reflects the relationship between two significant elements of human existence: culture and politics. This is how nationalism is viewed throughout this book.

The events of the last two decades have removed any trace of doubt that identity in our world could be apolitical: the Yugoslav conflict, the Rwandan genocide, the ongoing Israeli–Palestinian conflict, the attack on the twin towers on 11 September 2001, the continuing communal struggle in Iraq, the threat of terrorism, the genocide in Darfur, the conflict in Northern Ireland until only very recently, and European governments in pursuit of the most effective (that is, restrictive) policies on asylum seekers, and so on. All these illustrate that identity-related conflicts which fall under the broad umbrella of nationalism are not easily rivalled when it comes to arousing the passions of the masses and vote seeking of political elites.

Aims and definitions

Nationalist rhetoric articulates demands on behalf of and for the national group. Demands may vary in content, gravity and urgency but the claim is always in the name of justice (redressed or not yet addressed) and the 'right of the people'. The general aim of nationalism is that 'the people' be in charge of their collective destiny.

Being in charge entails the protection of the identity and dignity of the group and the maintenance of its unity which is thought to be best safeguarded through government by its own people, either in its own state or through a substantial degree of autonomy within any one state.[4] Thus, nationalism is, as it were, a programme for the nation's survival and future: at the very least, nationalism focuses on the articulation and the promotion of political aims in the name of, and on behalf of, a nation or national group[5] but, mostly, nationalism's actions are 'designed to render the boundaries of the nation congruent with those of its governance unit'.[6] The last is the variation on the very well-known definition of nationalism by Gellner as 'primarily a political principle which holds that the political and the national unit should be congruent'.[7] The congruence between a form of self-rule and the group of people that identifies itself as the nation is the clue to nationalism but, as will become clear throughout, this aim should not be taken to mean that 'the nation' is preordained and exists as a cohesive unit, nor should it mean that the political unit it seeks the congruence with is necessarily a state. The nation is as much a result of nationalist endeavour as it is its object, and the governance unit can be a state, a federal unit or any other form of political autonomy which allows the thus construed nation to be in control of its national programme. As I will argue, there are too many different forms of nationalism to assume that the national unit and the form of political unit that each seeks can be so easily defined.[8] But that is getting too far ahead of this introduction. The basic message of nationalism is that belonging to a nation, its existence and its survival are of supreme importance to its members and the right they share as members of humanity.[9] The explicit and implicit thread throughout this book is that, if nationalism is to be understood in its origins and in our time, its appeal must be sought in this democratic notion of 'the people' and their freedom and emancipation.

If nationalism was only about the beauty of one's mother tongue, the stories of stolen or improbable victories of one's nation, the passion for one's homeland and compassion for its people, we would probably relish nationalism without too many critical considerations. Once out of the hands of poets and admirers of local customs, however, and in the hands of political leaders, nationalism becomes a much-used strategy for the attainment and preservation of political legitimacy. The strategy employed depends on the combination of cultural and political conditions which, indeed,

can pervert its course and its ideals but this is not how nationalism entered the historical stage,[10] as will be argued in the first
chapter. According to nationalist strategy, the nation is the source
of legitimacy. Its values and interests become the primary objectives and therefore all actions necessary to attain these objectives
are assumed to be legitimate. Throughout history some of the most
reprehensible politics have been justified by appeals to national
interest – the prefix 'national' is the great justifier of human wrongs
– and hence, nationalism's bad name. This, however, is only a part
of the complex story of people, their personal and collective aspirations, their homelands and their states which can be vehicles for the
fulfilment of, or the barrier to, those aspirations in a world divided
into nation states.

The object of all nationalist endeavours is, of course, the nation
but its existence would not be enough to legitimate any action in
the name of its promotion or protection if it were not for the first
claim of nationalism, that the nation is culturally and historically
distinctive and therefore possesses moral authority to exist as a
separate territorial and political entity. The fact that there are
hardly any nations that can make a claim to such distinctiveness
is a different argument and will be expanded further throughout
this book. The universal appeal of nationalism is in its claim to
particularity of its nation, a claim that doesn't appear to diminish
in its significance despite the purportedly diminishing significance
of its object. Indeed, it would seem that 'particularity is a potent
universality'.[11]

The nation is a community of commonality, but so are many
other communities. The specificity of this larger social grouping is
in the emotional investment that it can extract from its members
and in the solidarity that it can inspire. This ability of the nation to
mark one's identity in such a significant way rests on a combination
of the objective commonalities, such as territory, language, history,
economy, politics and culture, and on their subjective reflection
in collective consciousness.[12] Is there a hierarchy of importance
among these commonalities? What constitutes a sufficient combination? Is one objective commonality and a strong affinity
with it enough to call it a nation? There are no simple answers to
these. If we had answers to these questions, there would be fewer
books about nationalism. More importantly, if we had a conclu-
sive answer to the question of what makes a nation there would
be fewer conflicts between recognition-seeking and recognition-

denying peoples in the world. Therefore, as a type of action and despite its many variations, nationalism is easier to define than the nations. On the other hand, the topic of this book is the phenomenon of nationalism and we should be careful to take it at its word by which it legitimises its own actions on behalf of a group it has already declared to be a nation[13] – preferably with ancient roots and dramatic past and deserving of a glorious future – but which actually may be only in the process of formation. In the section on diasporic nationalism, it will become obvious how intangible a nation can be. There are, however, certain attributes which we can assume to apply to a nation, such as sense of common historical experience based on common territory, or language or some other cultural commonality from which this experience derived and the intention to maintain these commonalities in future and unify under the same political system. So, one of the most comprehensive definitions of the nation that combines the past, the sense of belonging together and the daily affirmation of its existence comes from Ernest Renan (1823–92):

A nation is a soul, a spiritual principle. Two things which in truth are but one, constitute this soul or spiritual principle. One lies in the past, one in the present. One is the possession in common of a rich legacy of memories; the other is present-day consent, the desire to live together, the will to perpetuate the value of the heritage that one has received in an individual form.[14]

One of the major debates in the study of nationalism concerns the modernity versus ancientness of the nation. The more detailed discussion of the 'age' of nations will provide the basis of the discussion in the second chapter which tackles the classical theories of nationalism (I use theories and approaches interchangeably for reasons explained in the introduction to the second chapter). Here, it suffices to say that the nation as we know it – to which national sovereignty is attached – is a relatively modern construction. The date is less important than the fact that the formation of nations was an historical process in which changing societies sought answers to the relationships between ruled and rulers and in which people sought answers to the breakdown of the traditional societies in which they lived and the new ideas of enlightenment that were emerging. Throughout the sixteenth to seventeenth centuries the endless wars between the existing states produced a need for international law which was rooted in the sovereignty of states. It is only later that the nation becomes the subject of sovereignty, and later still that the political organisation of the state became wedded to and endorsed by the spiritual meaning of the nation. It can be argued that the legal concept of the state which emerged from the Peace of Westphalia (1648) predates modern nations as political entities. This Westphalian state and its international legitimacy have only later been enhanced by the principle of popular sovereignty (of which more in the first chapter) and by the doctrine of self-determination, both of which provided the moral principles for the political and territorial state, thus creating a nation state. The near marriage of the nation with the state was of unforeseen significance because, as will become apparent throughout, not only are there no perfectly married nations and states, but the imperfection of this union remains a continuous struggle between national groups within and beyond the states.

Ideas of nationalism reveal strong interdependence between politics and culture, whereby culture is thought to be best safeguarded through self-governance. The claim to self-governance which is nationalism per se is, however, conditioned on the existence of unique culture. Whether one believes, as most nationalists do, that nationalism emerges from cultural identity, or that cultural identity is strengthened by the politics of nationalism, as I believe, the fact is that nationalism seeks to answer whatever challenges society faces at a given time. As such, nationalism is attached to all political systems but to various degrees, depending on the prevalent ideology of the time, which equally seeks to answer society's challenges. The second question then that this book is asking is whether the challenges faced by societies in our time can be found in the classical nation state. The limitations of the nation state as the political organisation of our world are known and witnessed in numerous conflicts around the world but I am suggesting that it may be the time to acknowledge, not merely the limits of the nation state but the whole design.

The ideas that a group of people has in common a set of shared interests and that these people should be allowed to express their wishes about how these interests are best promoted,[15] and that that group should be culturally homogeneous and therefore united under 'a government to themselves apart', and that 'free institutions are next to impossible in a country made up of different nationalities',[16] expressed what were clearly becoming two dominating and rather contradictory ideologies – democracy and nationalism. It was the case in the nineteenth century and it is the case now. Some two hundred years later we are still preoccupied with the same set of interrelated challenges: legitimacy of the nation state, democracy, political unity and nationalism, cultural diversity and self-determination, and how they interact. The following chapters turn to each of these challenges separately, adding another theme to the assessment of nationalism in our time: the international and transnational dimension. My argument is that, while about states, nations and nationalism are not necessarily contained within them, not in our world, and that the state-centricity of nationalism has pervaded the studies of nationalism to the detriment of our understanding of processes connected to nationalism. It is never advisable to take the phenomenon one seeks to analyse at its premise. The politics of nations and nationalisms have moved beyond the states. Thus, the main argument advanced in this book is that, if theories of nationalism are to cover the actual cases of national and ethnic mobilisation, we need to look across the boundaries as much as within them.

The early political units were not defined by culture and certainly not by language. With the exceptions of Britain (not including Ireland) and France, most people belonged to multicultural empires and were ruled by foreign and often remote rulers. It was not until the nineteenth century that the Habsburg, Ottoman and Russian empires faced the threat of disintegration from linguistic groups demanding autonomy on the basis of their ethnic (that is, territorial) and historical distinctiveness. That process continued in fits and starts, and some historians may argue that the emergence of post-communist successor states in Eastern/Central Europe in 1991–3 (as will be discussed in Chapter 4) was the culmination of that process when finally all former empires disintegrated into their rightful national units.[17] Obviously, in the intervening years too many borders were drawn purportedly along the rightful lines, but hardly any of those Eastern and Central European states can call themselves true nation states, in the sense of a state of and for a particular national group – all states of the former empires consist of a dominant (titular) nationality, whose name the state carries, and a differing number of ethnic groups.

The nations surfaced in modern Europe and America from about the eighteenth century (some authors, for example Liah Greenfeld, prefer the seventeenth century),[18] then elsewhere, but their conception took place a little earlier, depending on the multitude of developments and mostly a combination of them. One was the rise of literacy attached to a wider availability of printed material (mostly of a religious character) which increased the possibility of a larger number of people becoming aware of either themselves or of others. The by now famed description of the nation as an 'imagined community'[19] may not have existed at that time when identity was very local, in the sense that people did not move much and hardly ever came into contact with strangers, let alone be aware that they could be bound to 'strangers' through historical and cultural ties they had no concrete experience of. Nevertheless, literacy and imagination are the necessary ingredients in the formation of a community of language and history, the interests of which, once identified, can be promoted. The technological advances, the spread of commerce and the militaristic expansion of states throughout the seventeenth century accelerated the shift from local, and at most regional, ethnic communities to a nation. This process is still in evidence in some parts of the world but Europe has possibly seen the end of it; it could be argued that the reverse is happening in Europe, in the form of the European Union (Chapter 6) and that we are reverting to a larger political unit divided into smaller administrative and cultural regions through which we conduct and experience our daily lives.

Michael Mann identifies three phases in this process: militarist, industrial and modernist,[20] stretching through the eighteenth to the twentieth centuries, all of which affected the character of nations, their size and their nationalism. The British and the French nations were almost coterminous with their states so that the idea of the nation reinforced the state. The nations within the federal Austrian, Ottoman and Russian empires had to subvert the state were they to become their own states. The Hungarian nation succeeded, almost, with the Austro-Hungarian Compromise (1867) but that meant that other movements, such as Slovak and Croatian, were subordinated even further as they became the subject of the nationalising policies of the new Hungarian state competing for supremacy within the Austro-Hungarian Empire. The different sequences and conditions in which each nation rose to its current status are responsible for the most employed, and I shall argue, misguided, distinction of nationalism – the civic (Western) and the ethnic (Eastern). For the moment, it is enough to say that geography is not the place from which to evaluate the politics of nationalism. Nationalism and territory are tightly connected, but that is a different argument and will be elaborated in Chapter 5.

There was also a third kind of nation, represented by the German and Italian nations which were spread over various states and principalities. Thus, the creation of German and Italian states also happened along the ethnic principle but, instead of extrication, they sought unification (state-creating nationalism). It is important to note in the introduction to this book about nationalism that, despite being better recognised for its particularistic and fragmentary character, nationalism has a capacity to integrate and to unify. Many political leaders in the new post-communist states employ what would be considered to be a nationalistic rhetoric were it not for the purpose of European integration; national prestige has many disguises depending on national aspirations of the time. It is futile, even while critically assessing nationalism, to deny its creativity and its ability to respond to the aspirations of the people. Whatever will emerge by the way of a critique of the politics of nationalism, it is not my intention to deny its inspirational qualities.

With states come taxes, administration, public office and armies (and throughout the eighteenth and nineteenth centuries states did little more than fight wars) and with armies come conscription and stories of conquests and defeats, more centralisation, and more mobilisation of popular sentiments. At the same time, nobility from linguistic regions (Britain's experience of it was only with Ireland), discontented with their limited upward mobility, engaged clergy and peasantry and mobilised them on the basis of regional ethnic sentiments. The language assumed a major importance: as much as the 1848 revolutionaries claimed that it was their language that stopped them getting the top jobs in public service in Budapest or Vienna, language also became the main tool of their revolt. This is the time of the codification of languages (some of the official Central and Eastern European languages date precisely to that time; prior to that people spoke only local dialects, and if they were educated at all it was in the language of the ruling aristocracy) which were then taught in elementary schools.

Thus, the picture of cultural identity entering the political arena, aided by the technological, commercial, military and state expansion, emerged more clearly throughout nineteenth-century Europe. Had democratic intentions of early nationalists been rewarded with the federalisation of states within empires, there is no telling how modern history would have evolved. The disregard and hostility for national movements tend to have disastrous consequences – then and now. The powers of that time, however, could not have known that because nations may have existed already, but the darker side of nationalism in the making escaped the attention of political thinkers. We have inherited the world of nations and nationalism in which the consequences of aggressive nationalism somewhere in the world greet us daily from the pages of newspapers and television screens, but it is important to reiterate that terror, genocide, war and expulsion (chapters 3, 5 and 7) were not associated with nationalism in the nineteenth century.

Nationalism came hand in hand with liberal aspirations. Owing to contingency rather than design, however, somewhere along the road of human progress, unpredicted, unplanned and almost unnoticed, a major historical event took place – the concept of 'the nation' was established. This new nation was equipped with a whole series of new meanings: it had a past and destiny and political future. Its members belonged to a particular group which automatically allowed them to participate in the 'great drama of history'[21] – if not in the past, if not in the present, then in the near future – for such a nation could inspire greatness and sacrifice. If circumstances required it, the nation could resort to defensive action and intolerance of others because 'peace', wrote the founding thinker of the sovereign nation, Jean Jacques Rousseau (1712–78), can be 'incompatible with freedom' and 'one must choose'.[22] So, the nation escaped the confines of culture and joined power politics. The principles by which its politics would be conducted, thus nationalism, entered international relations; they altered international law and grew to provide the moral justification for human endeavour and struggle until the present day.

I want to conclude this introduction by clarifying the crucial difference between the nation and the state. Nationalism refers to political sovereignty, or to a degree of it within a given territory. Hence, nationalism is not limited to actions and policies of the nation in charge of the nation state, but could be policies and actions of other national groups living in the territory of the state and challenging its legitimacy, or merely seeking autonomy which the dominant nation refuses to offer. I shall argue that the perceived congruence between the nation and the state produces the majority of conflicts in our world. These conflicts derive from the mobilisation of ethnic groups vis-à-vis each other or vis-à-vis the state, and are identified in this book as ethnic politics. Ethnicity refers to a social bond based on the belonging to an ethnic group which defines itself, or is defined by others, as sharing common descent and culture. The nation is then a similar group, defining itself as sharing a common culture and history which are less deterministic than descent, and which also possesses or claims to possess 'its own homeland and the exercise of political rights therein'.[23] The difference between ethnic group and the nation is important because, first, ethnicity is strictly a cultural trait in which the binding issue is primarily a common ancestry, and second, because ethnicity is not necessarily attached to any particular legal structure of the state as will be well illustrated in the section on diasporas (Chapter 6). Another explanation of the distinction between the ethnic group and the nation would be that, while ethnicity may be construed as a fact of one's cultural heritage, the nation comes with certain values and norms that accompany a more political and territorial discourse. Nevertheless, our world is one of frequent repositioning of borders which directly affects inter-ethnic relations within the relevant regions and indirectly beyond them. It is a world in which immigration, globalisation, Europeanisation and the internationalisation of interstate and inter-ethnic relations substantially reduce the 'sacredness' of the nation state and consequently create a fluidity of spaces and affiliations in which ethnic identity is no longer subordinated to national identity attached to a state, but increasingly rivals the official cultures of states. The state, on the other hand, is a legal concept; it describes a definite territory and denotes the aggregation of political and administrative institutions. The difference between the nation and the state is a consequence of the historical evolution of the state into a nation state but, for a critical assessment of nationalism, it is politically and analytically crucial to maintain this difference, as I will do throughout.

Structure of the book

The book is divided into three parts: I Nationalism from an historical perspective; II Contemporary debates about nationalism and cultural identities; III Assessing theories of nationalism. Having already sketched briefly the history of nationalism in this introduction, Chapter 1 traces its ideological foundations and provides analytical tools with which to underpin the contemporary debates in the study of nationalism. Following the chronological structure of this book from history to the present, Chapter 2 investigates the classical approaches to nationalism and divides them into fairly conservative but well-established rival schools of thought, primordial and modernist. The former is represented by Anthony D. Smith, the latter by Ernest Gellner. I discuss the work of Liah Greenfeld as the challenge to both primordialists and modernists. In the subsection on 'other theories', I include Tom Nairn's economic approach and John Breuilly's very convincing political approach. Staying with modernists, I then move to the 'invented' and 'imagined' nations as represented by Eric Hobsbawm and Benedict Anderson respectively. Giving the ideas of nationalism possibly more credit than is currently fashionable with the modernists, among whom I would like to count myself, I discuss how these ideas spread, according to Elie Kedourie and Miroslav Hroch, and then conclude with a moderate ethno-symbolist approach of John Hutchinson.

Part II, about contemporary debates in nationalism, seeks to show that its present manifestations are challenging to traditional approaches which are better equipped to account for the rise of nations and nationalism in the nineteenth century and possibly in the first half of the twentieth century than at the present. It opens with Chapter 3, at the heart of which is possibly the most important issue in the study of nationalism today: how to reconcile cultural diversity with political unity within the state. After ascertaining the reality that there are no states for and of one nation, I continue with the discussion about ethnic and national identity and various forms of accommodation of minorities in contemporary states, and conclude this chapter with debates surrounding multiculturalism in western societies. Chapter 4 is about the rise of nationalism in post-communist societies. I believe that post-communism, with its unexpected rise of 'the nation', offers valuable lessons about the relationship between nationalism and democratisation and about the conditions in which ethnic nationalism rises, and that these lessons are applicable everywhere where states and regimes are collapsing or have been dismantled (for example, in Iraq). The institutionalisation of ethnic identity in the form of the nation state allows for the appropriation of state power by dominant ethnic groups which in turn leads to strained relations between ethnic groups and the consequent occurrence of ethnic conflict. This dynamic is the subject of Chapter 5. Everything we need to know about nationalism, the relationship between ethnicity and territory, and the empowerment of a people either protected by the state or bereft of political power and seeking it through armed resistance, is encompassed in the title of this fifth chapter – 'ethnic violence'. The most disturbing aspect of contemporary nationalism is the rise of ethnic violence which finds no explanation in any theory of nationalism. Chapter 6 the last in this section about contemporary debates in the studies of nationalism, moves to diasporas. Diasporic identity, more than any other, illustrates the emerging questions about the fluidity of spaces and ethno-political affiliations in our world in which the traditional relationship between the nation, its territory and the state has been disrupted. Again, there is little in approaches to nationalism that captures these important issues represented in international politics by diasporas and other forms of transnationalism.

Part III assesses theories of nationalism in the light of the foregoing discussions. It starts with the role of the nation in international relations (Chapter 7). The discussion commences with dilemmas of the national self-determination doctrine which concern not only the lack of clarity, how and when should it be implemented, but also the selectiveness with which the international community chooses to support the creation of new states for reasons that bear more relation to the geopolitical situation than to the strength of national movements or even to the righteousness of their claims. Included in this chapter is 'Constructivism' as the only theory of international relations that conceptualises identity and its relation to nationhood and statehood. This section concludes with challenges to the nation state arising from cosmopolitan discourses and the international character of religious and ethnic violence.

The last chapter is the conclusion. It elaborates a number of arguments which will have emerged throughout the text.

1. There is an inherent tension between nationalism and democracy which is exemplified by the national self-determination doctrine as the fundamental principle of nationalist endeavour. Nationalism makes democratic claims but its actions are exclusivist. There is no answer to this dilemma within the classical nation state which is based on the national self-determination of the dominant national group.

2. The nation state has not been very successful in reconciling the two main tenants of the reality in contemporary states: the need for political unity and the fact of cultural diversity. Policies of nation

states, including liberal states, tend towards a preferential treatment of the dominant nation which leaves minorities having to seek special measures to protect their identity and interests. Classical approaches to nationalism are inattentive to this dynamic.

3. The approaches to nationalism stress either the modernity of the nation or the durability of the ethnic affiliation. The former blinds us to the power of ethnicity, the latter to the political consequences of ethnic mobilisation which is on the increase in the otherwise globalising world.

4. The studies of nationalisms suffer from too many binary concepts, such as ethnic and civic nationalism, modern and primordial, national and ethnic identity, homogeneity, multiculturalism, accommodation, conflict and so on, which only obscure the fact that nationalism thrives on ambiguities and dilemmas.[24] Nationalism is simultaneously modern and pre-modern, ethnic with some civic features, democratic and exclusivist, and despite the continued relevance of the nation state, increasingly more international.

5. Contemporary nationalism cannot be understood through traditional approaches because its manifestations have escaped the confines of the traditional nation state for which these approaches have been developed. 'New' nationalism is not new in the claims it is making; in fact, it is increasingly more atavistic but it is new in the strategies it employs, its geopolitical scope and its global significance. This is where we ought to look for some answers to Islamic terrorism.

6. Democratisation and the internationalisation of inter-ethnic relations are the most important aspects in analysis of contemporary nationalisms. Therefore, solutions to some ethnic conflicts have to be sought in the combination of measures above and beyond the politics of the state, such as regional settlements and international agreements.

7. There is no traditional approach nor a theory of nationalism that is wrong and does not explain one or two aspects of all nationalisms. On the other hand, there is not one approach that encompasses the emerging issues in contemporary nationalism which appears to have adapted better to shifting geographies and complexities of our simultaneously fracturing and globalising world than approaches to it. We are living in a transitional period between the classical nineteenth-century nation state to something yet unformed; this 'new' nation state cannot be subject to similar theorising in the way that the classical nation state is.

Case studies

My theoretical argument is illustrated by a number of case studies; the larger case studies constitute separate sections in the relevant chapters, while a number of smaller case studies, predominantly from Europe and the Middle East as well as examples from around the world, are incorporated in the text. The main case studies are: The national question in the Austro-Hungarian Empire (Chapter 1); A movement for unity: a case study of Arab nationalism (Chapter 2); Multicultural Britain (Chapter 3); Post-communism and the collapse of Yugoslavia (Chapter 4); Dominant ethnos: the case of Israel (Chapter 5); Ethnic kin across the border: the Hungarian minority in Central Europe (Chapter 6) and finally, Kosovo: a state in waiting? (Chapter 7).

Reading

Each chapter is concluded by relatively extensive notes which identify the relevant sources that were either used or deal with a similar argument (the full bibliographical references of these notes are in the bibliography). I am convinced that my references are only a fraction of the literature that I should have mentioned. I apologise to all authors who are not included and probably should have been. The omissions are not a reflection of their scholarship, however, but are due to the lack of time and space. I suggest a few more sources (books only and in alphabetical order) that come into my mind: Appiah, K. A. (2005), *The Ethics of Identity*, Princeton: Princeton University Press; Beiner, R. (1999), *Theorizing Nationalism*, Albany: SUNY Press; Billig, M. (1995), *Banal Nationalism*, London: Sage; Berezin, M. and Schain, M. (2003), *Europe Without Borders*, Baltimore: The Johns Hopkins University Press; Brown, D. (2000), *Contemporary Nationalism: Civic, Ethnocultural and Multicultural Politics*, London: Routledge; Calhoun, C. (1997), *Nationalism*, Minneapolis: University of Minnesota Press; Chatterjee, P. (1993), *The Nation and its Fragments*, Princeton: Princeton University Press; Delanty, G. (2006), *Europe and Asia Beyond East and West: Towards a New Cosmopolitanism*, London Routledge; Eatwell, R. (2003), *Fascism: a history*, London: Pimlico; Laitin, D. (1998), *Identity in Formation*, Ithaca: Cornell University Press. Mayall, J. (1990), *Nationalism and International Society*, Cambridge: Cambridge University Press; Nimni, E. (2005), *National Autonomy and its Critics*, London: Routledge; Poole, R. (1999), *Nation and Identity*, London: Routledge; Taylor, C. (1994), *Multiculturalism: Examining the politics of recognition*, Princeton: Princeton University Press; Tilly, C. (1975), *The Formation of National States in Western Europe*, Princeton: Princeton University Press; Weber, E. (1976), *Peasants into Frenchmen: the modernization of rural France*, Stanford: Stanford University Press.

Notes

1. Berlin (1972), 'The bent twig', p. 15
2. Nairn (1975) in 'The modern Janus', p. 17.
3. 'the sovereignty of independent socialist countries can not be set against the interests of world socialism and the world revolutionary movement', cited in. Linz and Stepan, *Problems of Democratic Transition and Consolidation*, p. 236.
4. Anthony D. Smith (1991), defines nationalism to be a movement for attainment and preservation of 'the autonomy, unity and identity of a nation', *National Identity*, p. 74.
5. Harris (2002), *Nationalism and Democratisation*, p. 2.
6. Hechter (2000), *Containing Nationalism*, p. 7.
7. Gellner (1994 [1983]), *Nations and Nationalism*, p. 1.
8. Behar, (2005), 'Do Comparative and Regional Studies of Nationalism Intersect?', p. 590.
9. Harris, *Nationalism and Democratisation*, p. 51.
10. See also Mann (1995), 'A political theory of nationalism and its excesses' in S. Periwal (ed.), *Notions of Nationalism*, pp. 45–63.
11. Hardt and Negri (2000), *Empire*, p. 105.
12. Hroch (1993), 'From national movement to the fully-formed nation', p. 4.
13. See also Bauman, (1992), 'Soil, blood and identity', p. 677.
14. Renan [1882], 'What Is a Nation?' in Eley and Suny (1996), *Becoming National*, p. 52.
15. Halliday (2005), 'Nationalism' in *The Globalization of World Politics*, p. 525.
16. Mill (1991), *On Liberty and other essays,* pp. 427–8.
17. Harris, *Nationalism and Democratisation*, p. 32; Mann 'A political theory of Nationalism and its Excesses', p. 51.
18. Greenfeld (1992), *Nationalism: Five Roads to Modernity*.
19. Anderson (1983), *Imagined Communities*.
20. Mann, 'A political theory of Nationalism and its Excesses', p. 46.
21. Berlin, 'The bent twig', p. 19.
22. Rouseau, J.-J. [1772], *The Government of Poland*, cited in Benner (2001), 'Is there a core national doctrine?', p. 168.
23. Mann (2001), 'Explaining murderous ethnic cleansing: the macro-level' in Guibernau and Hutchinson, *Understanding Nationalism*, p. 209.
24. Roshwald (2006), *The Endurance of Nationalism*, pp. 1–2.

Part I

Nationalism from an historical perspective

CHAPTER ONE

Ideological Foundations of Nations and Nationalism

The aim of this first chapter is to set out the broad theoretical background to nationalism as a political ideology by tracing its ideological foundations in order to assess the impact of the historical evolution of nationalism on its contemporary forms and expressions. Simply put, the chapter seeks the signs and foreshadowing of what has come to pass and seeks the analytical tools with which to underpin the contemporary debates in the study of nationalism. The priority here is to extract the origins of nationalism from the accumulation of historical and conceptual debris that surrounds it.

From a political community to a 'political nation'

The principle of sovereignty resides essentially in the Nation. No body, no individual can exercise any authority which does not explicitly emanate from it.[1]

When did the nation become an important political player? where is one to look for the beginnings of nationalism and when was its main ideological pillar – national self-determination – erected to the universal specification which holds that any self differentiating people has the right, should it so desire, to rule itself?[2] The culture and history are central to nationalist rhetoric but no amount of cultural heritage could have ever given 'the nation' the authority were it not expressed in political terms, had this particular community not been invested with a legitimacy which rested on the premise of freedom of 'the people' themselves.

The idea of the democratic (political) nation is rooted in the Enlightenment and based on the ideas of the French political thinker Jean-Jacques Rousseau (1712–78)[3] who can be credited with the concepts of participation and citizenship as the principles of a political community. Despite the general academic consensus about the advent of the modern usage of the word 'nation' being associated with Rousseau, one should not overstate his contribution to the nationalist doctrine. Rousseau's thinking is better considered as the main influence on one stream in the political ideology of the nation – the democratic and political conception of 'nation'. Rousseau's contribution is a major one in the conceptualisation of the early notion of democracy as a community of citizens with equal rights regardless of their socio-economic position. This does not necessarily suggest a particular cultural community but could, in principle, be any grouping based on some kind of shared interests, such as class. Given the fact, however, that humanity is organised along cultural lines, however ill-defined or artificial they may be, a united community of equal citizens in a struggle for political rights became the basis of the national self-determination doctrine. How this happened and why are the subjects of this chapter but an early example of Rousseau's notion of the nation as the bearer of political and legal rights was well illustrated by the slogan of the French Revolution (1789) – 'Liberty, Equality, Fraternity'. This is not strictly nationalism as we think of it now but the ideas of unity of the people, political equality and freedom are similar to the aspirations and claims of all national struggles, inspired by the French Revolution.[4] It will become apparent throughout this book that the tight link between the national self-determination doctrine and democracy remains the key to the tension between democracy and nationalism and to conflicts among national groups. Democracy and nationalism are mutually challenging ideologies but their nearly simultaneous birth – historically and ideologically – allows for a degree of compatibility which in turn leads to confusing and rival interpretations about the objectives of nationalism and the aims of democracy.

To Rousseau, citizenship equates with mutual interdependence of fellow citizens and that with a community of 'general will' rather than a community of selfish individuals[5] given to the 'tyranny' of his fellow citizens and not restricted by laws. Notable in Rousseau's thinking is the distinction between patriotism and citizenship, the former an 'unmediated given', a passion spontaneously arising from the love of one's country, while citizenship is an 'artificial and mediated creation'.[6] If, however, one is to seek nationalism in our time, that is national identity as a constitutive element of political power (to maintain, reform or attain a political system), in Rousseau's writing, it is his advice to *The Government of Poland* (1772).[7] First, there is the idea that national awareness has a power, if not to resist domination then to resist the destruction of the nation by unifying it behind one overarching aim, and second that such an awareness can be manufactured. The manufacture of national identity requires, of course, a certain cultural distinctiveness to start from, but that must be enhanced by a more deliberate 'effort to construct an overarching collective identity based on a putative common national sentiment, mostly ethnic sentiment'.[8] In our political vocabulary such a deliberate effort stands for nation building. If state building is a complementary project which aims at unifying a political community behind the loyalty to the state, its institutions and its interests,[9] thus citizenship in Rousseau's mediated, but not spontaneous sense, then paradoxically, Rousseau, when faced with a political conflict, put more faith into culture than into citizenship. Many political leaders of varied ideological persuasions have followed a similar strategy ever since. Politicians are often unwittingly aided by political theorists who, in their attempt to theorise and, I shall argue below, accommodate the evident force of nationalism tend to emphasise its emancipating and unifying qualities, despite historical evidence which is rather on the less positive side if not, at times, catastrophic. I would argue that the assessment of nationalism depends on the balance between nationalism and other ideologies present in a particular society, and that it is thus rather the resistance to nationalism than compliance with it that defines nationalism in a particular society.

Seeking 'the soul' of the nation

Although Rousseau has been credited with investing 'the people' with political legitimacy, thus producing a political nation, the discourse of nationalism, as we recognise it today, drew further inspiration from another source – nation as a community of descent with its identity steeped in history and tradition. This notion owes its origins to German romanticism, exemplified in the writings of Johann Gottfried Herder (1744–1803) and Johann Gottlieb Fichte (1762–1814). The German romantic idea claimed that the identity of a distinctive cultural community can be explored, discovered and investigated, and that humanity was divided into nations with specific characteristics of which the language was the most important marker. It is the combination of Rousseau's political nation with the romantic's cultural one that contemporary nationalisms promote. The cultural element of nationalism provides a better platform from which to analyse its frequent descent from the celebration of the nation into an aggressive assertion of the national supremacy of a particular group.

Nationalism is often accused of not producing any great thinkers and therefore of being less than a real ideology.[10] This lack of great thought does not undermine the relevance of nationalism; on the contrary, it adds to its flexibility and ability to reformulate its claims according to the context and fit with a variety of other ideologies. Nationalism has a vision of the society whose interests it purports to represent but this vision, unlike other ideologies, is dominated by 'who' the participants are rather than by 'how' the society should be governed. Nationalism possesses a popular thought (in contemporary political language, it could be called a great 'spin') which can address everyone across historical, ideological, moral, ethical and physical boundaries. Over and above Rousseau's political legitimacy, that thought is that the nation has a soul, it has perpetuity and it requires love and nourishment to fulfil its destiny, and in return makes us who we are. Nationalism is perhaps thin in terms of a great thought but it is rich in terms of the opportunistic possibilities that it offers. By this I mean that nationalism is a specific kind of political ideology, rather a political strategy without emphasis on one particular agency (as are, for example, class in Marxism, or an individual in liberalism) whose objective is the relationship between 'the people' and the state. The strategy may change depending on history and circumstances – ideologies also come and go – but paradoxically, the core objective of nationalism remains. That alone qualifies nationalism to be considered an ideology of a kind and gives it a unique character of continuity and legitimacy. Political systems can be liberal, democratic, socialist, fascist, theocratic or any other hybrid, but none is non-national. The reason is twofold. First, the political unit, as we know it, is national, and second, the national doctrine has persuasive qualities that political elites find difficult to ignore.

The origins of this less political idea of nationalism – that national identity is something more than the mere membership in any existing state – are also rooted in the Enlightenment, but particularly in the rejection of its all-encompassing 'reason' as a mode of explaining all human affairs. Each society was unique, therefore one rational explanation could not be taken as an ideal as how to explain the existing social order or how to construct a desired political order,[11] as was the claim of the French Revolutionary thinkers. Nationalism may not have its own great thinkers but it takes inspiration from many. This is illustrated by the fact that Herder, who is credited with the paternity of the cultural nationalist doctrine, was not actually what we would now consider a nationalist; not a nationalist that would have given nationalism and his native Germany the bad name for their excesses later (and not unconnectedly) acquired, but something of a historian of the nation. He resisted the idea that many German principalities and little states were inferior – by implication the people were inferior – to the big states surrounding them and should become uniform in the name of progress (with reference to conquest by the Prussia of Frederick the Great [R. 1740–80]). The resistance to progress, or straight-out resentment of societies not considered progressive in comparison to others, ought to be kept in mind as important sources of nationalism – then and now.

Herder's key idea of the defence of each nation's individuality that language makes us human[12] and that meaning and thought are synonymous with language (crudely put, we know what we feel only when we know how to express it to ourselves) does not seem so startling now but it was novel in his time. Consequently, he argued that language can be learnt only in a community and that those who share the language 'constitute the rudiments of a nation'; by implication, a nation is the natural extension of the family because the family is the earliest group with shared linguistic meanings.[13] Herder's emphasis on language was meant to underline the human capacity for culture because, following his thoughts, humans are who they are because they were brought up within a particular culture, within a people (*Volk*). It then follows that each community has its own language which expresses a community's unique values and ideas. While such exaltation of the uniqueness of a community puts obvious limits on the spread of universal ideas, to Herder, each culture, each community was of equal value. There is little of concern here but let us extrapolate: it is then difficult to impose any system which would constrain the development of this unique culture and, if the community is deterministic of the culture, then it is the ordinary people who are the primary carriers of their own uniqueness. It does not take much imagination to see how such poetry of the spirit of the nation can be construed into something much less poetic and more dangerous. Every populist nationalist leader relies on the 'ordinary people' and their values; all exultation of ethnicity claims its uniqueness. History has taught us that, far from celebrating the plurality and individuality of cultures, Herder's ideas served also as the ideological foundation for the supremacy of a particular culture at the peril of those who happen not to share it.

Herder's philosophy became a principal source of inspiration for nationalist intellectuals of small nationalities within the Austro-Hungarian and Ottoman empires. An example is a leading Czech nationalist, František Palacký (1798–1876) who, in his struggle for Czech autonomy, inspired and defended the struggle for national rights of all Slav nationalities who were oppressed by Magyars and Germans within the Empire. By the nineteenth century, the reassertion of national political rights became conditional on the existence of an historical national entity and accompanied by the intellectual efforts to create a sense of national awareness in order to justify the demands. The revolutionary year of 1848, often referred to as the 'spring of the nations', became the embodiment of Herder's cultural nation seeking Rousseau's political roof. I will return to the case of the Austro-Hungarian Empire at the end of this chapter in order to illustrate this point. To this day, nationalism has not changed this fundamental dynamic where the cultural and political interpretations of the nation seek one another in order to strengthen the meaning of both.

Sentiment versus reason

Herder's cultural nationalisms inhabiting a world divided into diverse cultures without competition or a hierarchy of more cultured and, therefore, more deserving of more protection and entitled to more respect, admiration or territory, may have lacked the political astuteness at that time. The foreshadowing, however, of a more sinister interpretation of Herder's overall innocent ideas can be gleaned already in the writing of Fichte.[14] To a contemporary reader, equipped with historical hindsight, German romanticism of the early nineteenth century looks increasingly less romantic. The culturally determined nation becomes an all-encompassing entity; the language, the nation/ *Volk* and the state all merge into one and, in the process, absorb the individual in the quest for the 'higher purpose' which is 'the steadily progressing development of pure humanity in the nation'.[15] The future incarnation of these ideas, the thus formulated superior nation and its relationship to German fascism, is not too hard to guess at.

For the purpose of this chapter, the relevant question is where is one to seek the origins of such passionate and rather irrational claims. The inspiration of romantic thought is in the rejection of 'reason' as the inspiration of the Enlightenment. If humanity was the agency of progress to the Enlightenment thinkers, to romantics human nature, rooted in tradition and culture, should not be changed according to some universal model, but remain unique. 'Unique', however, is meaningless without a measure against which it can be compared and from which it can be protected. Sentiments and emotions were set against reason. Reason and universalism, which 'applied to all men at all times',[16] came with the French Revolution but also with Napoleon's victories and German defeats. The best protection against the corruption of the German culture was the aggressive assertion of the existing, even if less progressive, culture. The military humiliation and economic and political inferiority of the present were being assuaged by the glories of the past and the celebration of the simplicity uncorrupted by the empty sophistication of riches and power. It then follows that there is more glory in store for the uncorrupted than for the soulless victors of the moment. Whether the sense of national inferiority is camouflaged by the elevation of it as a free and pure spirit of the *Volksgeist*, as the proponents of that type of messianic theme really believed, is not that relevant. The German romantics set a tone for a certain national discourse which was later followed by the Russian Slavophiles, by the Poles and by many other nationalist leaders of small nationalities who had, indeed, little more than myths of the past to offer and with which to inspire their people. This type of rhetoric, which only thinly disguises the resentment[17] at being patronised by the greater and the larger, or the fear of being overwhelmed by changes, can be discerned in the contemporary populist discourses of national leaders everywhere: in the Balkans and Eastern/Central Europe, in the Middle East and in Africa. The combination of the accumulated resentment and historical fear forms the basis of the downward spiral of ethnic violence in today's world, as will be discussed in Chapter 5.

Far from being a relic of the nineteenth century, the cultural component of nationalist ideology has not lost its relevance for contemporary nationalism. If anything, its relevance has increased. The overwhelming reason for this is that cultural identity and politics, having had a long and successful marriage, are not easily divorced. Cultural identity has an added normative appeal which is particularly empowering now, in the age of rights and democracy, and, in times of the extreme movement of peoples and ideas, across boundaries of increasingly more porous and less confident states. First, cultural identity empowers weaker groups to seek a degree of autonomy which is in tune with the overall democratisation and increased communication across the globe. Second, where the state is dysfunctional or crumbling under societal pressures, cultural identity can provide a social solidarity necessary to sustain the population. The third reason is connected to the relative loss of a nation state's influence on its own political processes, due to the strong internationalisation of national politics. Nationalist sentiments, thus bruised by the erosion of control over their state, have become, understandably, very protective of culture as their remaining bastion of purpose. Related to this is the evident fact that imagining the 'global village' has not affected the imagining of one's own community in a way that may have been expected; while national cultures are bracing themselves to survive the onslaught of the purported cultural globalisation, the latter is not yet much in evidence but the former are ready for mobilisation. Lastly, mass communication and mass participation have increased the number of politicians seeking support through populist rhetoric which assumes, rightly so it seems, that cultural identity – particularly that of others – has a good mobilising potential. All of those aspects of the old notion of cultural identity and its contemporary demonstration will be discussed in the following chapters.

Civic and ethnic nationalism: an old dichotomy for our time

Nationalism has been built on the interplay of two highly persuasive but also contradictory principles: traditionalism and rationality.[18]

That interplay touches on the fundamental tension between individuals and communities. It is a tension between tradition and moral reason, between one's self-image as a free and rational individual and one's self-consciousness as a member of a community, a community which is at once a cultural and a political creation.

The intellectual response to this simultaneity of appeals has been an attempt to theorise and categorise nationalism, thus making sense of the positive and negative impacts it so obviously exercises over human affairs. Moreover, it is often assumed that the evidence of differentiation between good and bad nationalism – the latter leading to the domination and intolerance of others – is also the explanation of the phenomenon itself. This is to ignore that nationalism derives from one core idea of merging the cultural and political unit, and that it is the context within which and to which nationalism responds that alters its manifestations. The historical foundations of nationalism have provided us with the most commonly used distinction in the characterisation of nationalism: civic and ethnic. The argument that follows contends that the distinction is a useful academic tool but obscures more than it adds to the understanding of contemporary political processes because it is the politics of nationalism, not its characterisation, that are in fact being evaluated.

Nations vary in the way they define the basis of their unity and in the way they justify their identity. The literature on nationalism is replete with suggestions that, by defining its group as a community of descent, ethnic nationalism is inherently collectivist, illiberal and contradictory to democratic citizenship.[19] Civic nationalism, then, is antithetical in character, inclined towards an inclusive definition of the nation as a community of equal citizens, hence its benign character which, provided it maintains this inclusive character, can be complementary to democracy. In other words, whatever the objectives of ethnic nationalism may be (improvement of political or cultural conditions or dominance within the state), their achievement seeks to accommodate only one particular group whose membership is defined by their ethnicity and not open to 'others', whereas civic nationalism can extend the membership of the group to all people inhabiting a given territory. In the terms of the above discussion: political nationalism meets cultural nationalism, Herder, or more abrasive Fichtean, version meets Rousseau.

Liah Greenfeld[20] makes the distinction clear by saying that the idea of the nation, which originally implied sovereignty of the people, emerged as individualistic but later emphasised the people's uniqueness. She goes so far as to suggest that 'these two dissimilar interpretations of popular sovereignty', individualistic/libertarian versus collectivistic/authoritarian, underlie the basic types of nationalism which may be either 'civic' (volunteristic), that is identical with citizenship, or 'ethnic' which implies particularism and is necessarily collectivistic. Finally, collectivistic ideologies are inherently authoritarian, argues Greenfeld.

A closely related distinction is that between Eastern and Western nationalism, according to which civic nationalism developed in Western Europe (and the United States) and ethnic nationalism in Eastern Europe. This conventional dichotomy served for a while as a ready-made theory through which the rise of nationalism in post-communist Europe could be easily explained. 'Easily' is an operative word here because there were other processes connected to the rise of post-communist nationalism[21] which, when analysed carefully, show that the distinction between ethnic and civic nationalism is not so easily drawn. I will return to this point in Chapter 4 on post-communist nationalism.

The civic/Western and ethnic/Eastern distinction has been initially articulated by Hans Kohn[22] on the basis of their origins and characterisation. In the West (the United States, Britain and its dominions, France, the Netherlands, Switzerland), Kohn argued, nationalism arose as a result of political and social processes which were taking place within established states or coincided with the development of those states. This nationalism was of a political character and inspired by ideas of the Enlightenment in the struggle against dynastic rulers; it equated nation with citizenship. In the East (Eastern Europe, Middle East and Asia) nationalism arose within empires (for example, Austro-Hungarian, Russian and Ottoman) and national demands sought to redraw the political boundaries along ethno-geographic boundaries. The notion of the nation could not consolidate around citizenship but had to assume a more '*volk*-ish' character. The East/West distinction appears to be actually a question of 'sequence',[23] that is, what comes first; in the West, state precedes the nation whereas in the East, the nation precedes the state. I would argue that there is more merit to this 'sequence' distinction than to the ideological one, for it connects to history in countries where national development has been arrested by hostile empires and associated with conflicts between national groups. It also provides a better explanation for contemporary processes. The added complication in post-communist Europe is that the nationalities of these former empires often constitute minorities within the new states which seems to carry the supposedly more 'ethnic' nationalism of these societies into contemporary politics. The same can be argued about the Middle East.

There are many reasons why these dichotomies should be questioned. The first reason to stress is that of citizenship. Citizenship is a valued commodity and has civic attributes; it is an official stamp (a passport) that confirms that an individual is a member of a political community, of a nation state. It carries rights and obligations and, in our world, considerable social provisions. A person without citizenship has a limited access to the protection of law, to benefits and to decisions that may affect his or her life. This is why awarding citizenship to foreigners (naturalisation process) is a lengthy legal process, subject to strict laws in all countries of the world, including the most civic ones. The regulations for naturalisation are mostly based on presumed exclusion, and it is up to the applicant to convince authorities that he/she is worthy of inclusion; hence, the principle of citizenship is based on exclusivity, even in its most civic form.

The second point to consider is the principle of national self-determination which, throughout the twentieth century, has been often hailed as a principle of justice and progress and the basis of political reorganisation following major systemic changes and the collapse of multinational empires. National self-determination is a normative principle but it is not necessarily a peaceful one; the Yugoslav conflict is a tragic example of disenchantment with the national self-determination principle. There are at least three points to make in reference to national self-determination. The first concerns the issue of the principle itself: what is it we are supporting when we are supporting, for example, the independence of Kosovo, of which more in Chapter 7? If it is the principle of national self-determination of Kosovo, which is an ethnic Albanian enclave within post-Yugoslav Serbia, then why not support the independence of Republika Srpska which is also an ethnic enclave but of Serbs in the new Bosnia and Herzegovina? If we are concerned that the creation of mini-statelets will pose a dangerous precedent for minorities in other states[24] and endanger the territorial integrity of states, then the independence of Kosovo should be questioned too. The point I am making is that, if we accept that Kosovo should gain independence from oppressive Serbian rule on humanitarian grounds, as many countries round the world do, then we must also accept that ethnic nationalism is not incompatible with humanism and democracy. Why? Because, what other nationalism could have evolved in Kosovo under the circumstances – which is rather a pragmatic argument? If, however, we are then also expecting independent Kosovo to comply with all principles of a democratic state and treat the Serb minority accordingly, thus jettisoning the ethnic principle on which their plight is founded and adopting a civic one, it is less pragmatic, if not naive. The case of Kosovo is clearly a combination of ethnic and civic demands, and neither is a matter of conscious choice but an unavoidable situation arising from the self-determination of an ethnic group.

The second and related point in reference to national self-determination is that nationalism does not finish when a self-determining group has achieved statehood. There are many examples where nationalist mobilisation increases after the attainment of independence. The new state is a vehicle for the nation[25] and its elites to construct a justification for its existence which logically is sought in the historical injustices committed against its nation. The result of national self-determination is more ethnic determination by the dominant national group within the newly formed states. Nationalism can be both: a cause of the break up of a multinational state, but also a consequence. This was the situation that arose after the break-up of Czechoslovakia, which was in no way underpinned by national movements but happened as a consequence of political elite manoeuvres in the post-communist chaos. While the Czech leaders could blame the Slovak nationalism, with its history of autonomist aspirations, the Slovak leadership resorted to the well-rehearsed story of historical injustices committed by the more numerous Czechs against its nation. The anti-Czech rhetoric rose, and all small resentments gained in weight and historical consequence but, soon after the split, the anti-Czech nationalist rhetoric no longer captured the public's imagination and quickly moved to a different target – the Hungarian minority. The Hungarian oppression of Slovak lands during the Austro-Hungarian era was a more tangible story, and there was a large Hungarian minority in Slovakia which could be seen as the direct extension of a historically hostile Hungary and thus Slovak ethnic mobilisation, while hardly present at the beginning of democratisation, grew in intensity after independence.

The third point refers to the extent to which a national self-determination can be civic? The boundaries and the content of the state are historically determined by national self-determination of a particular group whose national 'self' cannot be determined externally. National self-determination is based on the right of the oppressed peoples to achieve self-rule, a political unit which, in terms of democratic theory, should be civic. The problem, however, is that the solidarity of all citizens, based on a civic principle of belonging to nation state, is hardly ever the main inspiration – no national liberation movement has ever declared to fight on behalf of all ethnic groups that may be living in the territory, and the liberators expect to be the future state of and for their nation. It takes complex negotiation and effort to create a civic and inclusive constitution (as we are observing in Iraq) and these are usually a result of political process and, therefore, can hardly be a precondition. Hence, the civic or ethnic distinction is a useful academic tool for distinguishing varied conceptions of nationhood, but these conceptions are not predetermined. All nationalisms are civic and ethnic to a greater or lesser degree at different times.

Nationalism is a way of seeing the world. It is fundamentally about identifying the group, its place and its interests.[26] Far from just articulating identity, nationalism articulates political aims and promotes interests in the name of and on behalf of a group it helped to constitute as a national group. It is a truism that culture and polity seldom converge and that nearly all polities are 'multicultural', or multi-ethnic or multinational. All those terms suggest that there is a number of ethno-cultural groups sharing the state. The evaluation of nationalism thus depends, not so much on how the group is identified, but rather on the extent to which the interests of other groups are respected. If suppression occurs, it is not because nationalism is inherently incompatible with rights, but because it has an inherent tendency to favour its own group to the detriment of others – all nationalisms, whether ethnic or civic, are at different times guilty of this. The difference is that civic nationalisms are more likely to be found in more democratic states, so that other mechanisms through which civil and other liberties are protected are established more effectively. The normative condemnation of ethnic nationalism in the cases where minority nationalism could not develop a civic form for whatever reason (for example, the Baltic states in the Soviet Union, Palestinians in occupied territories, the Kurds everywhere, minorities in newly independent, post-communist states and so on) means that these groups would not be given the opportunity ever to do so.

Rather than getting involved in labelling nationalism as 'civic'/ good and 'ethic'/bad, it seems more appropriate to evaluate the political aims nationalism promotes and the form through which it pursues these aims. What is invariably meant by ethnic nationalism is what I would prefer to term ethnic politics. By ethnic politics is meant the politicisation of ethnicity for the purpose of political gain of one ethnic group over the others, and therefore the conflictual claims of different ethnic groups, either vis-à-vis each other or vis-à-vis the state. Such politics can take a form of irreconcilable ends leading to aggression and domination but, more often, it involves an attempt to maximise the influence and conditions for one's own national group. Many policies, such as language laws, immigration policies, citizenship laws, land reforms etc. can be viewed as ethnic politics, even in 'civic' states, because invariably they entail the promotion of interests by one ethnic group – usually the dominant nationality within the state.

'The people', identity and democracy

Most conflicts around the globe, in the past and at present, in one way or other involve national groups in a struggle for independence, more autonomy, a more just distribution of resources, more recognition, readjustment or revenge for historical wrongs, protection of resources, security and protection of territory. And so the list of national grievances and conflicts continues. This is before we even consider the unscrupulous exploitation of national feelings for the attainment of political gains in which case any of the above reasons can be used, regardless their genuineness. It is clear that the underestimation of the power of nationalism is politically naive at best and, at worst, it can be disastrous. Academic concerns about ethnic and civic nationalism, let alone whether nationalism is an ideology or merely a political practice, do not address the main point of nationalism's enduring relevance: nationalism lives in the political and social world where perceptions are more important than objective facts and where political legitimacy may be purchased through an emphasis on national rather than on any other identity.

Hence, the ideological foundations of nationalism discussed thus far can be summed up as follows:

1. Culturally and historically distinct 'people' should be in charge of their collective destiny, preferably through their own

government either in its own state or through a substantial degree of autonomy within a state.

2. Belonging to a nation, and that nation's existence and its survival are of supreme importance to its members and the right they share as members of humanity, hence the principle of national self-determination as the moral validation of nation's existence as a separate territorial and political entity.

3. This entity is presented in national narrative as a culmination of a long and ongoing process – the process may stagnate or be accelerated at times but, whatever the fortunes and misfortunes of the national project, it has a destiny. Being part of this ongoing historical process is the most significant principle of national identity.

As long as the nation state is the main framework – and it is difficult to think about political community outside its frame – for solidarity, sovereignty and the exercise of political ideologies, nationalism, often by violent means, furnishes the political unit and its system with legitimacy. Individuals perceive of their future within the confines of the state; even in our time of the increased displacement of people(s), acclaim of cosmopolitan virtues and transnational organizations, there is no effective political participation across boundaries, so that the nation state remains the main protector of cultural and physical security of people as well as the main distributor of cultural rewards and material resources.

All political ideologies claim to speak in the name of 'the people', but none as persuasively as nationalism and democracy which has earned them a pivotal place among the ideologies of modernity. The already mentioned paradox here is that, despite their historical and ideological congruence in the French Revolution, there is a constant tension between them. Both nationalism and democracy are associated with popular sovereignty and participation from below, meaning rights, beliefs, expectations and interests; in short, both are rooted in the idea that all political authority stems from the people. I wish to argue that the understanding of the tension between democracy and nationalism is the most important challenge of our time: how to reconcile political unity with the immense cultural diversity when the right to foster one's culture[27] has become synonymous with democracy. I shall elaborate on citizenship in Chapter 3, where I discuss the challenge of national self-determination and the rights of minorities, but here I wish to sketch the theoretical framework that underlies these challenges.

Vesting political legitimacy in 'the people' is the key to democracy and nationalism but there is a crucial difference between them. Democracy is a system of rule that, at its minimum, is based on 'public control with political legitimacy';[28] this political legitimacy rests on explicitly defined political principles about participation, inclusion and political equality. Nationalism, on the other hand, bases its legitimacy on one principle – the rule of 'the people', thus 'the nation'. The fundamental tension between democracy and nationalism is rooted in legitimacy and 'the people', whereby both aspects are pivotal to both nationalism and democracy. The problem is with the ambiguity of 'the people', because 'whilst nationalism tells us who they are, democracy is less concerned with the addressee and more with delivery'.[29]

The experience of democratisation processes suggests that the preservation of a democratic regime is arguably more difficult than its establishment, precisely because the premise of legitimate rule means different things to different people. The fragility of democracy, for example in post-communist Europe, only partially derived from the disagreement about the rules of political competition. One of the greater obstacles to democratic consolidation arose from the fundamental misconceptions about democracy as something to do with the majority (expressed in national terms), rather than the substance. The distinction is crucial because, while the implementation of popular rule is one of the core democratic principles, in our time, democracy understood as liberal democracy must be checked against the arbitrary exercise of power by the majority.[30]

The crux of the matter is that the exercise of democracy requires a prior legitimate political unit because neither competition nor co-operation can take place without a clear definition of who is in the game and where the physical boundaries of the 'playing field'[31] are. The predominant principle for defining those boundaries in modern times is 'nationality' which provides the criteria for the identification of 'the players' who determine their political destiny (*demos*).[32] Thus, the decision about who and what constitutes the 'nation' is not only an integral part of national self-determination but of democracy too. This is why in the world of increased democratic ambitions, when we should be expecting less nationalism and more democracy, the opposite appears to be true. As has been already suggested, the 'nation' can be an aggregation of citizens in the state, united by the attachment to its institutions and the legitimacy of the regime (in this case a democratic one), or the 'nation' can claim to be a political expression of an ethnic group, thus based on common culture and descent (*ethnos*). The assumptions about 'civic' and 'ethnic' nationalism, the former more compatible with democracy than the latter, are therefore partially right except that the establishment of states and the prevalence of either 'ethnic' or 'civic' principles for the definition of the 'nation' are characterised by a degree of historical contingency and political development to which democratic theory provides little solution.

It can be argued that the legal concept of the state which emerged from the Peace of Westphalia (1648) predates nations as political entities, and that the legitimacy of this Westphalian state has only later been enhanced by the principle of popular sovereignty and by the doctrine of national self-determination. To nineteenth-century political thinkers, such as John Stuart Mill (1806–73), the state and its cultural homogeneity must have appeared to have been a precondition for democracy, otherwise he could not have claimed that 'free institutions are next to impossible in a country made up of different nationalities'.[33] We know that cultural homogeneity is not an option, and that the aim of democracy is to reconcile different nationalities within one state, because there are no states of and for one nationality only. Thus, legitimacy of the nation state has always been entangled with two contradictory principles, civic (democracy) and ethnic/national (self-determination). We have to concede that, first, nationalism and democracy may go hand in hand, may have some commonalities and may even at times support a common goal, but their actual long-term compatibility is fraught with mutual contradictions.

The principle of national self-determination establishes the right of nations to claim their own states with a corresponding notion that states are legitimate because they embody self-determining nations. This principle has considerable implications for internal and external legitimacy of states[34] and international relations, of which more later (Chapter 7). In the world of nation-states, 'the nation' is considered an important source of personal identity.[35] Even if one was to dispute how important a source it is, one would have to concede that nationality provides one with a place (a home?) in the world and hence exercises a considerable influence over one's opportunities and choices in life. Obviously, one's life is largely influenced by more immediate groupings and relationships than 'the nation' (that is, gender, status, religion) but national culture provides an important moral and practical resource in an individual's existence. The main reason for favouring national self-determination derives from these assumptions and rests on the belief that national cultures are worth protecting and that the distribution and management of a community's resources and decisions about its future are best served by more autonomy. In a contemporary world, where so many national groups are demanding political representation, national self-determination also stands for the establishment of a preferred form of government for a national group that may be a component of a multinational state, but I shall say more on this subject in Chapter 3.

History does not offer much comfort when it comes to the treatment of weaker national groups within multinational states: from attempts at assimilation by force or social policies to social engineering, oppression and ethnic cleansing, the states have tried all these methods to homogenise the population, so that empirically there is enough evidence to assume that the best protection against the erosion of one's culture and resources is to share decisions with like-minded people, thus keeping them within one's own state. That, however, does not stop a particular political or economic grouping from exploiting its co-nationals so, strictly speaking, only a democratic state would be able to ensure that the national self-determination truly reflects the will of 'the people' and therefore, in theory, national self-determination is linked to democratic consent and citizenship and the development of a modern state, itself the guarantor of the nation.

The state and the nation: a complementary or contradictory relationship?

The emphasis upon culture and identity is possibly useful in understanding a type of nationalist development in a particular country, but too much emphasis on the particularity of nationalism is to neglect the fact that the controversy of nationalism comes from its innate tendency towards the appropriation of the state's authority and the exercise of power. Despite the much propagated view that the state has sacrificed its predominance to global economic interdependence, political power is still about significant control of the national state; hence, the relationship between the state and the nation is deeply involved. On the one hand, national leaders cannot impose any desired relationship with 'the people' without a significant control of the state which, in order to increase or maintain its legitimacy, then reinforces the nation. On the other hand, the national culture, along with national education and the physical protection of citizens, rely on the state.

I want to conclude this theoretical chapter by clarifying the crucial difference between the nation and the state. The conflation of those two fundamentally different concepts has already given us the nation state which, as will be argued in this book, has not been very successful in reconciling the two main tenants of the contemporary state's reality: the need for political unity and the fact of cultural diversity. Nationalism refers to political sovereignty, or to a degree of it within a given territory. Hence, nationalism is not limited to actions and policies of a nation in charge of the nation state, but could be policies and actions of other national groups living in the territory of the state, as is discussed in detail in Chapter 3. Ethnicity refers to a social bond based on the belonging to an ethnic group which defines itself, or is defined by others, as sharing common descent and culture. The nation is a similar group, defining itself as sharing a common culture and history (history is less deterministic than descent) and which also possesses or claims to possess 'its own homeland and the exercise of political rights therein'.[36] The difference between ethnic group and the nation lies in the fact that ethnicity is strictly a cultural trait in which the binding issue is primarily a common ancestry and which is not necessarily attached to any particular legal structure of the state, as will be well illustrated in the section on diasporas. Another explanation of the distinction between the ethnic group and the nation would be that, while ethnicity may be construed as a fact of one's cultural heritage, the nation comes with certain values and norms that accompany a more political and territorial discourse. The state, on the other hand, is a legal concept. It describes a definite territory and denotes the aggregation of political and administrative institutions. The difference is politically crucial and will be maintained throughout this book. While emphasising the difference between the nation and the state, it is equally important to stress the distinction between the culturally dominated nation building and institutionally underpinned state building.

Nation building stands for a deliberate effort to construct an overarching collective identity which can bind the political community in a more meaningful way. The focus of this effort is the construction or promotion of a national narrative which is based on the language, history, literature, and other cultural traditions that together form what we call national identity. State building should be understood as a complementary project, aiming at the establishment of a political community of citizens, a forging of social solidarity, and respect and loyalty to state institutions. This is fundamentally a different process, not necessarily culturally inspired – one does not need to be born into citizenship, one can acquire it and with it adopt a sense of belonging to the state. Obviously, the clash between the administrative and the political thrust of state building and the culturally preoccupied nation building is less relevant where there is a congruence between the polity and cultural nation but, in the cotemporary world, ethnic homogeneity is less and less possible to achieve, if it ever was. Thus, the compatibility of those two processes depends on many variables, such as whether national elites conceive of the state as for and of dominant nation, historical contingencies and the legacy of the interrelationship between national groups, international relations and so on. I am reiterating the distinction between those two processes for the same reason I have emphasised the distinction between the state and the nation. My concern throughout this book is to assess critically how nationalism and its theories developed, and how nationalism is now playing in our world. One among a number of political consequences of the history of nationalism has been the conflation of the nation and the state in both practice and theory.

The national question in the Austro-Hungarian Empire

I begin this very brief case study of the national question within the Austro-Hungarian Empire with a statement by a leading Hungarian politician who, in order to defend the 'magyarisation' policies against the non-Magyar-speaking ethnic groups within the Hungarian half of the Austro-Hungarian Empire, argued: 'we want a legitimate state, but we will build it after we have secured the national state. The interests of the Hungarian nation demand that the national state be built on a highly chauvinistic principle.'[37] This statement, which appears in a historical essay about the Slovak national (under)development under Hungarian rule, illustrates a number of dilemmas that the empire was facing in the second half of the nineteenth century. First, the political loyalty of the Magyars came to be identified exclusively with the Hungarian-Magyar state and not with the Habsburg Empire. Second, there was a growing assumption that a modern state – particularly one that seeks to rival the imperial power, as was the case with the Hungarian state – must be a national state. Third, political legitimacy and the national conception of the state are directly linked, and, fourthly, the interests of other nationalities therefore can be and must be subordinated to the interests of the dominant nation. We also know that the growing political demands of ethnic groups in the multi-ethnic empire undermined the idea of the 'Habsburg' state which the latter could not resolve and not withstand.

The 'revolutions' of 1948–9, inspired by the French Revolution, led not only to the abolishment of serfdom and social reforms, but these new democratic ideas also brought 'the nation' to the fore as an actor, though not directly, however. It was the radicalised aristocracy of the culturally more dominant groups who could claim historic rights in the first place and only later, as a reaction, the smaller ethnic groups developed national movements of their own led by a lesser gentry and by educated elites.[38] Such a dominant group was the Hungarians, but also Germans and, to a lesser extent, Croats and Czechs. Unlike Slovaks, the last had some nobility and a semblance of recognition as a historical entity, while Slovaks had none of those and were simply considered Slav-speaking peasants of upper (northern) Hungary. While under Habsburg control, Hungary had high nobility, its own constitution and proposed its own legislation (diet). Hungarian nationalism developed not as a reaction to oppression, but rather as a reaction to progressive reforms proposed by the monarchy in Vienna which indicated the loss of privileges for the Hungarian nobility vis-à-vis the peasant population and the monarchy. Nationalism of the nineteenth century carried progressive thought within it and very soon the idea of a more independent, democratic (not for non-Magyars who were expected simply to assimilate), modernising and reforming Magyars was propagated by the Hungarian leading nationalist Lajos Kossúth who found wider support among lesser nobility and among urban intelligentsia, of which he was a part, in Buda and Pest. It is important to stress that the Hungarian nationalism, which was stimulated by the French Revolution in the name of 'national freedom', developed in a relatively backward and feudal society and built on a longer history of anti-Habsburg feeling and even uprisings going back to the eighteenth century.

Trying to deflect the revolutionary zeal spreading among Hungarians and other nationalities in 1848, the monarchy proposed a number of laws which would, in principle, establish Hungary as a constitutional version of the historic kingdom of Hungary, tied to Vienna in a vague form of union.[39] Thus, the unofficially formed Hungarian state, now enforcing Magyar as the official language and central government, faced national demands from non-Magyar groups[40] and divisions among its own elites, some of whom felt partially satisfied and others who pushed for more autonomy; in the end, the Magyars mounted the most successful armed revolutionary movement of 1848 against Austrian imperial power. The imperial victory was necessarily followed by considerable centralisation and repression of the Hungarian national movement, but only for a while, because the monarchy was challenged from the every corner of the Empire.

The Hungarian nationalism was not stifled by the partial compromises and continued to seek more and more independence from Vienna. The Czech (Bohemia and Moravia) national movement led by František Palacký, and resting on undisputed rights as a historical and national entity, sought the federalisation of the empire, but initially based on historical–national principle, and only later framed its demands in ethnic terms. At the Slav Congress held in Prague in 1848, the Slovak nationalists joined the Czechs in demands for the federalisation but, unable to provide a reasonable claim as a historical entity, they were abandoned by the Czechs.[41] Let me stress that, while the development of the Czech national movement must be viewed from the perspective of the new Czech middle classes trying to resist the domination of German speakers in the western half of the empire, the national movements of the nineteenth century were generally seeking a degree of national emancipation within the empire and not its destruction.

The point of this case study is to trace the rise of nationalism in the nineteenth century when political awareness and cultural uniqueness were joined in the struggle for emancipation of the people. The next chapter will deal with the theorising of nationalism and the rest of the book with its political consequences in our time but, at this stage, it is important to emphasise two points: by the second half of nineteenth century all grievances within the Habsburg monarchy, whether faced by peasantry, middle and professional classes or nobility, became expressed in ethnic terms (as did the domination) and that this precedent of an ethnic form of nationalism associated with a national struggle marked the politics in Eastern and Central Europe until the present day.

After another military defeat by Prussia (1866), the Austro-Hungarian relations arrived at the Compromise in 1867 in which momentous constitutional changes split the Habsburg Empire into the Dual Austro-Hungarian Empire. The Hungarians achieved even greater autonomy over the eastern part while the influence of Germans in the western half was reduced by a degree of national protection awarded to other national groups. Dualism had a significant impact on the national development of Eastern and Central European nationalities because, while the western half was semi-federalised, the eastern half fell under an increasingly centralistic Hungarian state. The federalisation should not be seen as official recognition of national groups, but the basic State Law (Article 19, 1867) provided that 'all national groups have equal rights' to 'cultivate its nationality and language', that customary languages in the crown lands, in schools, government agencies and public life are recognised, and that in lands 'inhabited by several national groups', every one of those national groups 'receives the necessary means of training in its own language without compulsion to learn a second language of the land'.[42] The Czechs, Slovenes, Italians (Istria), Serbs and others could express their opinions in their own language in the Viennese parliament which may have enhanced their national self-respect but achieved little because nobody in the central government, under whose control the crown lands remained, could or wished to understand them. Compared to the Hungarian state where nationality laws were never put into practice, where Magyar remained the only official language and where eventually all other languages ceased to be taught at secondary schools, the western half of the dual empire appeared more liberal while the eastern half was modernising under the strong nationalising policies of Hungary.

Nationalism was rife in the empire because the modernising elites agitated the people and the people saw all political struggles, including the right to vote (men only), in terms of national liberation. In Hungary the street demonstrations for universal suffrage failed because Hungarian nationalism feared the numerical domination of the non-Magyar-speaking nationalities whose political rights would almost certainly have affected Hungarian hegemony in the eastern half of the empire. The monarchy faced an impossible task in maintaining respect for the state and the loyalty of nations where national aspirations of one precluded the national aspirations of others. It is possible to argue that the federalisation of the empire could have been an answer but that was not an option in the eastern half where the Hungarian state considered federalisation on an ethnic principle to be the enemy of the state.[43]

The idea of the national state produced an irresolvable national conflict within the empire, already weakened by its own federalisation into two constitutionally different entities. Even the Austrian Germans contributed to the weakening of the central authority: under the influence of language as the identity marker, they demanded more German influence (and the more radical elements even wanted unification with Germany) which was becoming increasingly less possible, and that at a time when the ideas of the unification of southern Slavs under the Serbian leadership was rising. Politically, the nationalism of all ethnic groups led to the formation of new ethnic political parties and to the fragmentation of existing political parties, also along national lines. Again, I must stress that democratisation and nationalism, both understood as mutually co-dependent, dominated the Austro-Hungarian Empire at the end of the nineteenth century and beyond. The end began with the assassination of the Archduke Franz Ferdinand by a Serbian nationalist in Sarajevo in 1914 in an attempt to separate the south Slav provinces from the empire. The external pressures of World War I aside, it is doubtful that the Austro-Hungarian Empire could have been saved because the national aspirations of its peoples were no longer compatible with the aspirations of the empire.

Notes

1. The French Revolution's Declaration of the Rights of Man and Citizen in Schwarzmantel (1991), *Socialism and the Idea of the Nation*, p. 31. See also Greenfeld (1992), 'The three identities of France' in *Nationalism: Five Roads to Modernity*, pp. 89–188.
2. Connor (1972), 'Nation-Building or Nation-Destroying?' p. 331.
3. Özkirimli (2000), *Theories of Nationalism*, pp. 20–1; Breuilly (1993), *Nationalism and the State*, pp. 54–64. For Rousseau's contribution to the formulation of democratic nation which is a standard reading of ideology of nationalism, see also Schwarzmantel (1991), *Socialism and the Idea of the Nation*, pp. 25–33.
4. Halliday (2005), 'Nationalism' in Baylis and Smith, eds, *The Globalization of World Politics*, p. 525. asserts that the early examples of 'national' struggle against foreign domination were in the Americas; in the North against British rule and in the South (1776–83) against the Spanish (1820–28).
5. Barnard (1984), 'Patriotism and Citizenship in Rousseau: A dual Theory of Public Willing', pp. 244–65;
6. Özkirimli, *Theories of Nationalism*, p. 21.
7. Rouseau, J.-J. [1772], *The Government of Poland*, cited in Benner (2001), 'Is there a core national doctrine?', p. 167.
8. Harris (2002), *Nationalism and Democratisation*, p. 3.
9. Ibid. p. 3.
10. Anderson (1983), *Imagined Communities*, p. 5; Gellner (1994), *Nations and Nationalism*, pp. 124–5; Benner, 'Is there a core national doctrine?', p. 157.
11. Breuilly, *Nationalism and the State*, p. 56.
12. Barnard (1983), 'National culture and political legitimacy: Herder and Rousseau', pp. 231–53.
13. Ibid. p. 243.
14. Breuilly, *Nationalism and the State*, chapters 2 and 4; Greenfeld, *Nationalism: Five Roads to Modernity*, pp. 322–52; Schwarzmantel, *Socialism and the Idea of the Nation*, chapter 2.
15. Cited in Schwarzmantel, *Socialism and the Idea of the Nation*, p. 38 (note 430).
16. Berlin (1972), 'The bent twig', p. 16
17. For the notion of *ressentiment* see Greenfeld, *Nationalism*, pp. 15–17.
18. Barnard, 'National culture and political legitimacy', p. 252.
19. Brubaker (1998), 'Myths and misconceptions in the study of nationalism' in J. Hall, *The State of the Nation*, pp. 272–306.
20. Greenfeld, *Nationalism*, p. 11.
21. For various hypotheses about the crisis of identity in post communism see Harris, *Nationalism and Democratisation*, chapter 1, and Brubaker in Hall, *State of the Nation*.
22. Kohn (2005), *The Idea of Nationalism*; Özkirimli, *Theories of Nationalism*, pp. 41–3; Shulman (2002), 'Challenging the civic/ethnic and West/East dichotomies in the study of nationalism'.
23. Harris, *Nationalism and Democratisation*, p. 19.

24. Kaldor, Mary (2008), 'Sovereignty, status and the humanitarian perspective', *Open democracy*, http://www.opendemocracy.net/article/sovereignty-status-and-the-humanitarian-perspective, accessed 26 September 2008.
25. Shulman, 'Challenging the civic/ethnic and West/East dichotomies in the study of nationalism', p. 581.
26. Brubaker in *State of the Nation*, p. 292.
27. Soysal (1998), 'Toward a postnational model of membership' in Shafir, G., *The Citizenship Debates*, pp. 189–220.
28. Lord and Harris (2006), *Democracy in the New Europe*, p. 2, citing Albert Weale.
29. Lord and Harris, *Democracy in the New Europe*, p. 32.
30. Sartori (1995), 'How Far Can Free Government Travel?' p. 102.
31. Lord and Harris, *Democracy in the New Europe*, p. 32, citing Schmitter, Philippe.
32. Diamond and Plattner (1994), *Nationalism, Ethnic Conflict, and Democracy*, Introduction, xi.
33. Mill (1991), *On Liberty and Other Essays*, p. 428.
34. Keitner (1999), 'The False Premise of Civic Nationalism', p. 341.
35. Miller (1995), *On Nationality*, p. 82.
36. Mann (2001), 'Explaining murderous ethnic cleansing: the macro-level', in Guibernau and Hutchinson, *Understanding Nationalism*, p. 209.
37. Baron Desiderius Bánffy, cited in Lipták (1998), *Slovensko v 20.storočí*, p. 44.
38. Breuilly, *Nationalism and the State*, p. 124.
39. Breuilly, *Nationalism and the State*, pp. 128–9.
40. Croatia was awarded a degree of autonomy. Romania, largely peasant population with no institutional and historical claims to speak of, was not. Slovaks, with even less political organisation, were ignored and for a while even supported Vienna against Hungary, with some devastating results for their hardly born national movement.
41. Harris, *Nationalism and Democratisation*, p. 77.
42. Kann (1973), *The Habsburg Empire*, p. 86.
43. Kováč (2005), 'Nacionalizmus a politická kultúra v Rakúsko-Uhorsku v období dualizmu', p. 51.

CHAPTER TWO

Theories of Nations and Nationalism

If nations and nationalism are mutually reinforcing social and political phenomena, then there are many questions to clarify: how do nations and nationalism come about? how recent are they? is there a theory that can predict the rise of nations? who are the people who inspire a group to understand itself as a culturally distinct group? does nationalism emanate from the existence of such a group or is it the other way round? when and under what conditions does the sense of cultural understanding become a political movement? Lastly, how important is any of it for our understanding of the behaviour of nations? These debates have been continuing for at least forty years, and our fascination with the theories of nationalism continues too. As each decade brings new identity-related conflicts (and some remedies, for example, Northern Ireland) we remain baffled, appalled and fascinated by the power of nationalism.

In this complex and contested field of study of nationalism, the two main rival schools of thought are the 'primordialists',[1] who are rather on the side of the antiquity of nations or at least their essential ethnic cores, and the 'modernists'[2] who view the nation as being a result of modernity and its processes in both the construction of the idea of the nation and the actual nation formation. This classification is most widely accepted in literature and therefore is employed throughout this book; some scholars refer to the primordial approach as 'essentialist' and to the modernist approach as 'instrumentalist' (or 'constructivist', which I avoid using so as not to confuse it with Constructivism, an approach to international relations to be discussed in Chapter 7). Somewhere not quite between the two opposites, are 'ethno-symbolists' who adopt a more moderate primordialist approach that stresses the durability of pre-modern ethnic ties in order to argue the importance of ethnicity in elite attempts to forge nations. [3] As with all polarities, this one is also less strident in the actual analysis than it would appear. Particularly since the war in Yugoslavia, both sides are now complemented by thoughts less convinced about the relevance of the chronology of nation formation and more interested in the ways collective identities shape, and are shaped by, politics and the international system, and thus, ultimately, how they affect people's lives today. This is the theme of this book too. I, like the majority of students of nationalism, subscribe to the modernist school of thought, which can be summed up by saying that 'nations do not make states and nationalism, but the other way round'.[4]

Before I continue, some clarifications about the structure and purpose of this chapter are in order. The main concern of this book is the role of nationalism in all its forms in contemporary politics within nations and beyond them. This means all political expressions of cultural identity over and above the state and nation formation. The aim in this chapter, however, is to move the debate about the ideological foundations of nationalism from the previous chapter to classical theories of nation formation which is the very focus of nationalism. I want to convey these ideal forms of modernist and primordial schools for two reasons: (a) because both positions, and particularly any critique of them, offer important insights into nationalism; and (b) because, after having discussed the manifestations of nationalism in our time in the following chapters – which is the main theme of this book – my argument will suggest that the developments among nations and ethnic groups do not fit neatly into the existing theories. The use of the term 'theories' in the title is somewhat misleading because all schools of thought about how nations came to be, when and what the role of nationalism in their formation was are actually approaches rather than theories. In a concession to the wide use of the latter in the literature, I will use both terms interchangeably. John Breuilly argues that we are dealing with concepts that lack clarity of definition, that the evidence against which we could test hypotheses is retrospective, and that more often than not we tend to apply definitions which were not known at the time.[5] Thus, the theories of nations and nationalism are actually attempts to explain a phenomenon within a certain framework of thoughts which can then be categorised under similar 'umbrellas' depending on which aspects of the history of nationalism authors tend to stress. I continue by conveying the main arguments for and against the primordial and modernist approaches as represented by Anthony Smith and Ernest Gellner respectively. Then, before I conclude with a suggestion in favour of seeking a whole new approach, I will bring in other theories, mostly within the modernist argument, and a brief ethno-symbolic example. I will conclude with a case study of Arab nationalism which, in its complexity, touches on many approaches but cannot be explained by any one of them in its entirety.

Historical mission: from '*ethnie*' to a modern nation?

'Primordialists' are best represented by Anthony Smith who must be considered one of the most prolific and influential scholars in the study of nationalism.[6] The basic idea behind Smith's theory of nations is that, even if nationalism is a modern phenomenon connected to the emergence of the Enlightenment and the political ideas of the French Revolution, nations themselves are not modern but are the continuations of earlier forms of cultural identity – *ethnies*.[7] In that sense Smith, particularly in his later work, represents also the ethno-symbolic approach, of which more later. An *ethnie* is a 'named human population with shared ancestry myths, histories and cultures, having an association with a specific territory, and a sense of solidarity'.[8] In other words, it is an ethnic group, members of which experience a sense of solidarity as a commitment that may, in times of need, transcend any other forms of belonging such as gender, class, profession or region. The most important characteristic of *ethnie* is that it is an enduring community throughout time and that the story of misfortunes, threats, defeats and victories contributes to the sense of uniqueness and continuity.

In view of what has been said so far and will be said later in this book, I would like to stress the durability of ethnic affiliation, which is one of the most convincing arguments in Smith's work. In ancient and medieval times, ethnicity played an important role because societies were less complex, less mobile, less aware of the wider world and therefore more reliant on the immediacy of their group for help and for understanding of the world around them. Oddly, the conditions may have changed, but ethnic affiliation remains an important aspect of human identity. Obviously, it would be historically wrong to conflate ancient ethnic communities with modern nations as we know them, but Smith has never argued that they were the same entities. His central argument is that modernity created the structural conditions in which nationalism could become an ideology of modern nations built round this ancient ethnic core.[9] We cannot observe modern nationalisms without conceding that the most called-for resource in the struggle for historical justice is rooted in old ethno-histories. When nationalist leaders refer to the 'blood of our ancestors', what they are appealing to is the shared past which should then imply a shared destiny. Smith explains: '*ethnies* are constituted, not by lines of physical descent, but by the sense of continuity, shared memory and collective destiny, i.e. lines of cultural affinity embodied in myths, memories, symbols and values retained by a given cultural unit of population'.[10]

Ethno-histories, with their arsenal of ethnic symbols (flags, hymns, monuments, costumes, iconic landscapes), play an important role in the mobilisation of 'nation-to-be' for political action, including violence that could not be justified on any other grounds. They provide a 'cognitive map', 'public moralities'[11] and the cultural landscape to navigate the group throughout history. Two ideas emerge from this all-too-brief account of Smith's theory of the nation: (1) implicitly, the interpretation of the story is unique to each group and, by implication, must be defined in relation to other groups (which in a less theoretical analysis is a standard reading of ethnic nationalism); and (2) there is a linearity – an *ethnie* evolves into a nation.

I want to elaborate on the second point, which ultimately suggests that there is no nation without ethnic essence and that nations maybe modern but their cores go a long way back. How then does *ethnie* become a nation? Smith suggests three routes.[12] First, there is the bureaucratic incorporation of loose *ethnies* into a territorial nation. This is largely a story of the competition between various monarchs and their successful incorporation of middle classes, aristocracy and clergy, together with their wealth, in order to wage wars to maintain the territories, which become territorialised and politicised national cultures that later were devolved downwards to 'the people'. The result has been a formation of territorial states in Western Europe, often labelled as having formed through 'civic nationalism' because territorial, not ethnic, aims dominated the aspirations of these bureaucratic states which, centuries later, forged 'the nation'. Nevertheless, the ethnic core is strongly present in the civic nations such as France, Spain, Britain, etc. The second route to nationhood is through the transformation of *ethnie* (*vernacular* mobilisation) into an ethnic nation. In Eastern Europe, the Middle and Far East and parts of Africa, the intelligentsia reappropriated ethno-histories of 'the people' and 'edited' them into usable ethno-histories that could inspire the national struggle in the face of hostile empires and later serve as the authentic foundation of national identity. The nationhood, thus rationalised on the basis of language, myths and symbols, is logically ethnic in its conception. The third route is the formation of a nation from immigrants of a number of *ethnies*: examples include Canada, the United States, Australia and other settlers' societies. A point of interest here is that, while nationalism of these new nations celebrates the new territory, the national narrative tends to exclude the native *ethnies* and eulogise the pioneering spirit of the new and selected ones.

It is perhaps interesting to digress and return to the distinction between 'western' and 'eastern' notions of nationalism, already made in the first chapter, because the assumptions attached to this dichotomy may obscure the historical contingency in which nationalism evolved. Liah Greenfeld, in her majestic work *Nationalism: Five Roads to Modernity*, poses something of a difficulty for both modernists and primordialists: first by placing the birth of a nation in sixteenth-century England – too early for a modernists – and secondly, by connecting the nation to 'sovereign' people and nationalism to democracy, thus putting the emphasis on the interpretation of the nation, she reduces the importance of ethnicity, too. Greenfeld argues that the original idea of the nation emerged as sovereign individuals, and only later and in different conditions, the nation became identified with 'a unique sovereign people'. This 'uniqueness', however, does not need to be ethnic, as for example in the United States where the population is not an ethnic community, but a national one. The extent to which 'the criteria for the membership in the national collectivity' are correlated with ethnicity gives an indication of the type of nationalism that has evolved in that particular national community.[13] It is either 'civic', that is, open and voluntaristic and can be acquired (in principle), or it is 'ethnic' and believed to be inherent (one cannot acquire it nor change it); ethnic is not dependent on individual will but on genetic characteristics. Finally, collectivism is more likely to lead to ethnic nationalism while individualistic nationalism is likely to be civic. It is argued throughout that, in reality, all nationalisms will be mixed.

When combining the two non-modernist approaches of Smith and Greenfeld, it becomes obvious that the distinction between the Western/civic nationalism and Eastern/ethnic one is, indeed, a question of the sequence of historic developments, as has been argued in the previous chapter, rather than an inherent trait of certain *ethnies*. *Ethnie* does not figure large in Greenfeld's approach but it is clear that she places the emergence of nations well before the modern era and, therefore, nationalism, too, cannot be defined by its modernity only.

The main theme in Smith's theory of nations and nationalism is that, even if nations are a creation of modernity and nationalism is an ideology rooted in modernity, it is only half the story[14] in which the other, ethnic half, remains important because 'the nation' is, if not politically then historically, embedded in antiquity. The move from a simple traditional ethnic community to a modern omnipresent dynamic social and political organisation is historically predetermined by the existence of *ethnie*. In the final analysis, then, *ethnies* are linked directly to nations, thus modernity. The process of evolution may stagnate, be diverted or sabotaged but there is no getting away from the historical mission of *ethnies* as precursors of modern nations. This is also largely the view held by another primordial theorist, John Armstrong, with a difference though: ethnic identity in pre-modern times is different from modern nations which are political structures formed on the basis of pre-existing ethnic identities. Armstrong contends that the force of the ethnic group produced nations in pre-modern times and that there are pre-1800 nations and modern nations inspired by nationalist identities. Identities go through a long evolutionary cycle and nationalism, as we understand it, is a form of national identity connected to the modern era. This identity may be a continuation of a pre-modern ethnic identity (for example, Jews and other diaspora communities) but it can be transformed so dramatically that Armstrong suggests that ethnic identity is rather more a recurrent phenomenon than a continuous one.[15]

The consequences of this ethnically deterministic interpretation of the rise of nations are numerous: (1) modern nations must be furnished with an ethnic myth – whether it be virtual or real is less relevant; (2) nations are inevitable – if the essence of the people is ethnic then the dominant ethnicity should have a privileged position within its nation state; (3) attempts at creating a modern collective identity without ethno-history are futile (hence, Smith's less than optimistic view of the future of European identity).[16] This is not very reassuring in our time of ethnic conflicts, rising religious fundamentalism and attempts at a less national understanding of humanity and its needs. Many questions remain unanswered in this largely historically accurate account of nation formation. If *ethnies* have a historical role to play in the formation of nations, what comes after nations? Should their relevance decline as some observers would argue is already in evidence? If *ethnie* will inevitably become a nation, is the process of disintegration of multi-ethnic states (nearly all states) endless? What is the role of external factors in this ethnically essentialist account? The relevance of these questions will become more apparent throughout chapters 3 to 7.

A constructed nation? The modernist approach

Smith provides us with one of the most comprehensive definitions of nationalism as 'an ideological movement for the attainment and maintenance of self-government and independence on behalf of a group, some of whose members conceive it to constitute an actual or potential 'nation''.[17] In reluctant acceptance of modernity, or rather the relevance of the political element in the rise of nations, the nation, is defined by Smith as 'a group of human beings, possessing common and distinctive elements of culture, a unified economic system, citizenship rights for all members, a sentiment of solidarity arising out of common experience, and occupying a common territory'.[18]

Smith was a student of Ernest Gellner who personifies the modernist school of nationalism. Gellner's best-known maxim asserts that 'nationalism is not the awakening of nations to self-consciousness: it invents nations where they do not exist'.[19] If nationalism 'engenders nations'[20] and nationalism is a modern ideology that can be dated only as far back as the French Revolution, then nations are novel and not the culmination of the existence of *ethnie*. A considerable space has been given to the role of *ethnie* in this chapter for reasons that will become obvious in the subsequent chapters, but it is time to turn to the modernist school of thought that views the nation as a construction of modernity with a clearly defined function to answer the changing needs of societies converting from the pre-industrial to industrial eras.

Gellner's work is too great in volume and intellectual rigour to be related fully here but the principal thought can be summed up as follows. There is nothing natural about nationalism. Nationalities are not God-given and it is not a self-evident fact that people of the same nationality should, and want, to live in the political unit, let alone be ruled by people of the same nationality. For most of human history, people lived in various political units (tribal, city states, dynastic empires, etc.) where political legitimacy, if sought at all, was certainly not inspired by 'culture'. Nationalism as a principle of political legitimacy is a modern phenomenon, strongly connected to the erosion of traditional social structures and the emergence of industrialisation and political modernisation. Thus, from a contemporary perspective of nationalism, Gellner's theory is actually a theory of political legitimacy which 'holds that political and national unit should be congruent', hence ethnic boundaries should not separate the power holders 'from the rest'.[21] Whatever the forthcoming criticisms of Gellner's account of the rise of nations, the connection between political legitimacy and nationalism is not one of them, and the account remains a relevant and enduring explanation of national(ist) aspirations to this day.

So, what function did nationalism perform in the time of the great 'tidal wave' of modernisation spreading from Western Europe unevenly to other parts of the world to become the dominant solidarity and cohesion-forging ideology? The main function hinges on language.[22] Industrialisation created new, mostly impoverished urban populations, lost in the new world in which traditional rules and relationships no longer applied and new ones were not yet available. Language and culture could rebuild communities to replace the old ones and make sense of the new settings. Fast-rising cities, the large-scale economies and increased bureaucracy required literate citizenry and that required mass education. With mass education, society could stratify; a citizen could become a 'clerk', or even a member of the rising intelligentsia. Mass education in turn required standardised schooling and the state to fund it.

This new society, however, was full of social conflicts – between the educated and illiterate, between the employed and unemployed, between the newcomers and the old population. Where these social conflicts could be expressed in ethnic terms, a new divide was created; where the ambitions of new elites were curtailed by their ethnicity and could be improved by nationalist movements, they demanded secession from the larger political unit. Demands expressed in national terms need the nation and its story to be told to the masses. Gellner explains:

> Political and economic forces, the aspirations of governments for greater power and of individuals for greater wealth, have in certain circumstances produced a world in which the division of labour is very advanced, the occupational structure highly unstable, and most work is semantic and communicative rather than physical. This situation in turn leads to the adoption of a standard and codified, literacy-linked ('high') idiom, requires business of all kinds to be conducted in its terms, and reduces persons who are not masters of that idiom (or not acceptable to its practitioners) to the status of humiliated second-class members, a condition from which one plausible and much-frequented escape route led through nationalist politics.[23]

Indeed, in this account, nationalism invented the nation, but it did so with 'some pre-existing differentiating marks to work on, even if, as indicated, these were purely negative'.[24] While Gellner explained that needs do not engender reality and while this modernist account is very persuasive, it is also somewhat too neat in its premise that society in need of a solution finds one and thus the phenomenon can be explained. There are some problems with this functionalist explanation because:

1. Not all language groups in the world have managed to produce a 'nation'. Gellner claims that there are some 8,000 language groups in the world, but there are just under two hundred states and possibly a further six hundred groups which are seeking a state.[25] Can a 10 per cent success rate be an adequate explanation of the phenomenon?

2. Nationalism, or at least the sense of community, strong enough to bind people into a structure, the destruction of which would cause societal distress, is present in non-industrial societies where the majority of the population has limited access to

education. We know this is the case because many ethnic conflicts in our time are located in non-industrial societies (for example, African states). Moreover, in the nineteenth century, when some Eastern European languages were codified (for example, Slovak, Croat) for the purpose of nationalist struggle in the non-industrial Austro-Hungarian empire, the bases of those languages were rural dialects and the celebrated culture was the 'low', pre-industrial culture of villages. As the case study will show, a similar argument can be made about the rise of nationalism in the pre-industrial Ottoman Empire.

3. Industrialisation and modernisation are definitely contributing factors in the production of nations, but they can also create resentment of national ideology among groups whose religious beliefs contradict any other form of social integration except the religious (for example, the tension between certain interpretations of Islam and political forms of nationalism, as will be shown below). The destruction of traditional societies and the influx of non-traditional, non-religious influences often spark off attempts to revert to a more traditional and religious past (the 'ethnic revivals' in post-communist Eastern Europe and ethnically inspired nationalisms in Western Europe serve as examples of modernisation stimulating ethnicity as much as diminishing it).

The persuasiveness of Gellner's 'modernisation' theory is, however, more seriously dented by the following three considerations:

4. A social group and its will is not enough to sustain a culture. As the plight of many minorities in oppressive states demonstrates (see mainly chapters 3 to 5), a culture, no matter how well established and how lovingly maintained by its group, needs institutional arrangements to sustain it in long term. The modern nation state has a long history of subordination of non-dominant ethnic groups (non-'high' cultures). Gellner accounts for the rise of a national culture but his theory does not stretch to the simultaneous attempts at the erosion of other national cultures.

5. Time after time, history shows that the attainment of nationhood depends on more than the strengths of its national movement, the intensity of patriotic fervour or even the level of industrialisation. I will show that the attainment of nationhood depends also on politics and on the constellation of power in the international system (Chapter 7). Nationalism is not, and cannot be, divorced from international politics because its very aim – the state – is a political structure, based on the principle of national

self-determination, and both the state and the national self-determination depend on international recognition.

6. After the collapse of communism, new states mushroomed into existence. Democracy, it seemed, came hand in hand with nationalism, and many scholars, including myself, tried to explain this phenomenon which will be elaborated in Chapter 4. Scholars, international observers and politicians were taken by surprise by this sudden salience of all things national when democracy was the main aspiration – or so we thought. With hindsight, it should not have been such a surprise because, in the short history of modernity, hardly any dramatic changes occurred without affecting 'the people' who were, if not the bearers of changes, than certainly the receivers. The collapsing states and discredited regimes lost any legitimacy and true, the legitimacy gap was filled by nationalism, but the collapse of communism and the subsequent national reawakening were both inspired by democracy. The complex interplay of two sometimes competing and at other times mutually complementing ideologies was discussed in Chapter 1. Thus, my remaining comment is that it is surprising that Gellner, who regarded nationalism as a principle of political legitimacy, failed to include democratisation in his modernisation approach. Industrialisation did not just modernise societies, it changed the expectations and structure of societies and necessarily brought democracy into the realm of politics. Hence, when analysing the post-communist nationalism, it was not Gellner to whom scholars turned, but primordialists because the ethnic revival appeared anachronistic when, in fact, we were observing political modernisation of a kind.

Whatever the critique of Gellner, the most valued and influential aspect of his contribution to social sciences ought to be his commitment to nationalism, because nationalism has structured our world with some magnificent results, but also some tragic consequences. Gellner convinces us that this structure has been erected fairly recently, that is within the last couple of centuries. On the other hand, Gellner's industrialisation tells us little about political modernisation, which makes his approach less persuasive in supposed post-modern and post-industrial times and offers little by way of solutions to the persistence of nationalism. When all's said and done, nationalism's modernity or a nation's antiquity does not affect its intensity and does not direct its political actions.

There are other theories . . .

The discussion so far has focused on the primordial and modernist schools of thought as the two best known, and has ignored a number of approaches that belong to either one or the other. The main distinction is that, while modernists emphasise one factor over other factors, the main thread of their arguments is looking to the novelty of the nation as an answer to new necessities of societies in the throws of modernisation processes and not to the durability of emotional attachments and commitments to traditions that may remain resistant to modernisation. The literature on 'when', 'how' and 'why' nationalism is too prolific, and I can not go into the whole gamut of this impressive scholarship here. I shall confine myself to three more variations within the *modernist* approach which I consider the most relevant to nationalism today: economic transformation, political transformation, and invention of traditions, and say something about ethno-symbolism at the end.

The economic transformation approach rose to prominence with the analysis of post-colonial national movements which were the harbingers of the struggle against imperialism and international capitalism.[26] These movements posed something of a dilemma for Marxist intellectuals because their natural sympathy had to rest with the fight against the exploitation of colonial peoples, but their intellectual commitment tended to disregard ethnicity as the form of solidarity in the struggle against the exploitation of capitalism. The solution to the ambivalence and the sympathy has been perhaps best outlined in Tom Nairn's *The Break-up of Britain: Crisis and Neo-Nationalism* with the theory of 'uneven development'. At its core, this is an attempt to redress 'Marxism's great historical failure' in addressing nationalism as, if not the main, then certainly one of the major, movers of history. Nationalism doesn't just accompany industrialisation and modernisation which spread unevenly round the globe leaving the peripheries dominated, invaded and exploited without perspectives of ever catching up on developed countries of the world. Nationalism then became a strategy of 'catching up', a way of social and political development in 'peripheric' nationalisms which, indeed, instrumentalised primordial identities, in the same way as in Europe.

This approach, while providing an explanation of some anti-colonial nationalisms and the establishment of some new post-colonial states in the remnants of the Ottoman Empire and in

Africa, remains deficient in accounting for nationalist movements in Europe, that is, in the Balkans or Central Europe, where backward small nations developed significant nationalist movements during the nineteenth century but which, nevertheless, did not succeed in gaining independence at the time (such as Serbs, Slovaks, Croats, and so on). As I argued in the previous chapter, the most significant nationalist movement in the region belonged to the Hungarians (*Magyar*) who were, relative to others, the least backward and the most privileged national group. The backwardness is relative to the aspirations, and Budapest sought comparison with Vienna, not Zagreb. While important in terms of post-colonialism, the theory of 'uneven development' doesn't quite fit the historical sequence or reflect the complexity of why some movements succeed and others fail, or even explain adequately how socio-economic interests link to the politics of nationalism.[27]

For a more political and, to my mind, the most convincing approach to nationalism, I turn to John Breuilly who refers to nationalism as 'political movements seeking or exercising state power and justifying such action with nationalist argument'.[28] This definition immediately strikes one as recognisable in nationalist politics everywhere, and I used this approach in my work on post-communist nationalism. I argued that the main objective of 'nationalist strategy is the promotion and protection of the nation and its interests' and that 'the basic message of nationalism is the conviction that belonging to a national group, its existence and survival are of supreme importance to its members' and that these interests can be 'best safeguarded through sovereign rule, or a degree of autonomy'. [29] This largely overlaps with Breuilly's main assertions about the nationalist argument which is further emphasised by a very important and evident fact that nationalism is about politics and politics is about power and 'power in the modern world is about control of the state'.[30] In my opinion, there is little to argue with Breuilly's assessment of the relevance of power relations within modern societies where the relationship between society and the state is institutionalised through citizenship in the form of the nation state. The individual, the state, the legitimacy of the state and the identity of the political community, and thus the ability to pursue the interests of the people and legitimise the actions on their behalf all merge into the politics of the nation state. This political approach can also explain better the success or failure of nationalist movements seeking greater autonomy within the state or even the separation from the state and the unification with the neighbouring kin state – once the sentiment is translated into political action, nationalism makes more sense in terms of its aspirations.[31] So, whether we are observing separation-seeking nationalisms of the former Yugoslav republics, or an autonomy-seeking Hungarian minority in post-communist Europe, or the Palestinian struggle for the extrication from Israeli occupation, nationalism is an action-orientated political movement seeking control of a territory. All of those movements will be discussed at greater length in the following chapters.

The tools of the nationalist trade, however, are not always forward looking. Nairn spoke of nationalism as being a 'modern Janus' – Janus was the Roman god with two faces, one looking forward and one back. The backward glances are looking into the past of the nation to seek joys of victories, recall pains of defeats and appeal to the wisdom of the people who have survived the past and must 'gather strength' for the struggle ahead.[32] This, of course, assumes that the story of the nation is a real one and that there is a past that can be tapped into in a constructive way for the task in hand.

I don't want to spend much time reminding the reader that the power of nationalist elites to spin a story is not limitless – it needs the audience to respond and to respond with a sense of recognition and emotiveness which reinforces a sense of common destiny, and therefore a common future. A successful nationalist discourse invokes memories by retelling an old story, the moral of which points to new challenges. While this memory-invoking discourse is the staple of nationalist discourse, often, even more effective is a memory-creating narrative. Distinctiveness of the group is the main asset in all nationalist endeavours and, if there is not enough distinctiveness, then it needs to be convincingly invented.

Eric Hobsbawm, in his *The Invention of Tradition* (co-edited with Terence Ranger, 1983) and in *Nations and Nationalism since 1780: Programme, Myth, Reality*, views the nation as an 'invented tradition'.[33] To a greater or lesser extent, all societies need to 'adapt their traditions and institutions to new situations'.[34] Hobsbawm is more concerned with a deliberate invention of traditions which are intended for a purpose to create a sense of continuity, a sense of cohesion, legitimation of a certain attitude and, in the most extreme cases, to engineer collective behaviour. It is increasingly clear that rapid social changes threaten established orders and fracture societies, and that nationalism is a successful strategy to re-establish the norms, values and boundaries of belonging and commitment. We have seen the invention of the antiquity of newly independent states in post-communist Europe where nearly all new constitutions make reference to 'centuries of struggle' when the nation as such may not have even existed (for example, Slovakia, looking into the eighth century for its precursor), and where new public holidays are declared, new history books are written, and new monuments are commissioned to justify the existence of the new nation state and clarify who its members are.

As a historian of modernity, Hobsbawm reminds us that citizenship, democracy and mass politics required novel methods of reinventing the relationship between ruled and rulers, and that the new societies emerging from the nineteenth century onwards had to be underpinned by some form of new identity with which the new more complex and much more class- and politically aware society could identify and by which it could be presented to the world, as it were. Nationalism becomes a 'new secular religion'.[35] The invention of tradition is a version of the Gellnerian model of the modern construction school of thought, but its added value is in the inclusion of 'people' as participants in the process of the construction rather than mere subjects of change beyond their awareness.

Nations emerge in the process of modernisation because a degree of technological and economic advance must be reached before school-books can be printed and read by the masses. There must be a degree of awareness of interests before they can be articulated in the newspapers and opposed. There must be, however limited, forms of communications before people know who they are. This brings me to the last influential approach which I mention briefly for its fame rather than for its intellectual distinctiveness: Benedict Anderson's 'imagined community'.[36] The nation is an 'imagined political community' whose members will never know all their fellow members who, despite the differences in class and wealth, are seen as comrades, imagined to offer freedom because they were born in the age of Enlightenment, and imagined as a new form of identity different from the great religiously imagined communities which were declining from the sixteenth century onwards when Latin ceased to be the 'European' language of the intelligentsia. Literacy and newspapers aided this secularisation of societies where people could gain knowledge about other people whom they were never to know directly but could imagine them being part of the same community and who spoke the same language and knew the same story. 'Print capitalism' was surely a contributing factor in the rise of the modern nation, infectiously termed as an 'imagined community', but Anderson's approach doesn't quite explain the rise of nations and certainly does not account for the huge political upheavals and loss of human life that nationalism has engendered. Moreover, many of those sacrifices continue to be in the name of the nation which, often far from abandoning religion as a form of communal identity, has taken religion, its myths and symbolism as its main identity markers[37] (for example, modern Israel, post-communist Poland or the contemporary Islamic states, such as Iran).

Nations maybe invented and imagined (have we any other nations to compare it with?) but, given the rise of ethnic nationalism around the world, it is prudent not to dismiss primordialists because they remind us all too well of the power of continuity, ancestry, emotional attachment to the past and other recurrent themes in the nationalist discourse.[38] These themes are about the power of ethnic affiliation, a building block of nationalism which remains a powerful concept. The main problem with the modernist approach is that it disregards the people who, when all is said and analysed, are the ones who are willing to kill and die for an idea of the nation. Surely, the emotiveness of identity must be touching something deeper than industrialisation, modernisation, communication and other ingredients of the top-down modernist approach. The politicisation of ethnic identity in our time is often precisely because some societies resent the modernisation. The past is more attractive because the present is trying to remove what is dear to people who may only have tradition to rely on for comfort and understanding of their lives. If elites are powerful enough to politicise ethnic separation, why are they not powerful enough to homogenise populations when they insist on doing so? When we do not like nationalism for its murderous track record, we are right but the underestimation of the depth of ethnic attachments will not make nationalism go away. What possibly will is the ability to imagine how others imagine their own nations – inventions and manipulation included.

This brings me to two further approaches to nationalism which must be included if we are to comprehend the sheer variety of historical contexts and sociopolitical conditions within which nationalism has arisen: the ideational (doctrinal) approach under the modernist umbrella and the historical approach under the ethno-symbolic label. The former is best represented by work of the late Elie Kedourie but also by that of the Czech historian, Miroslav Hroch. To Kedourie, nationalism is a 'doctrine invented in Europe',[39] but interestingly, the true relevance of his approach becomes obvious in non-European societies, as I will show below in the case study of Arab nationalism. The ideas of nationalism are 'diffused' downwards in two ways: from European intellectuals to Western-educated native intelligentsia and then, through and from this intelligentsia to the population at large (which may or may not be literate).[40] The important point here is that the spread of nationalism by these intellectuals who, by a large, were discriminated against by the colonial administrators and, in spite of their education, had limited career opportunities, carried also a strong sense of resentment. Resentment was already mentioned in the previous chapter as a potent element in the spread of nationalist rhetoric in less developed parts of the world. In the present context, we are looking at a combination of resentment, ideology, doctrine and 'uneven development' which surely should not be underestimated in connection with colonial societies. Interestingly though, Miroslav Hroch used a similar model in explaining the history of national movements in Eastern and Central Europe where non-dominant ethnic groups were dominated by exogenous ruling classes,[41] thus mirroring in part the colonial situation.

Hroch developed a 'phase' model of diffusion between the initial stage of growing national consciousness and its emergence in the ethnic group at large: Phase A – scholarly inquiry into historical attributes of the non-dominant group and whether such a group could develop into the nation; Phase B – the emergence of activists engaged in the patriotic 'awakening' of national consciousness; and finally, Phase C – a mass movement, when the major part of the population 'came to set a special store by their national identity'.[42] I believe that this model can be applied to other 'colonial' types of societies, too, because the transition from phase B to phase C is crucial and explains the relationship between the 'old' regime and the establishment of a 'new', if not constitutional order, then certainly the beginning of a mass national movement against the ruling administration. The resentment felt by the new university-educated intelligentsia of the non-dominant ethnic groups in Eastern and Central Europe at being excluded from leading positions is similar to that of the Western-educated intelligentsia in colonial situations.

Hroch expressed it as a 'nationally relevant conflict of interest'[43] and showed that this conflict of interest gave impetus to growing national movements. The case study of Arab nationalism at the end of this chapter will illustrate Kedourie's and Hroch's theories about the spread of nationalism among disenchanted intelligentsia in non-industrial and non-European societies.

We must concede that culture and history matter to politics, and John Hutchinson argues that *ethnie* is a reservoir of symbols.[44] According to Hutchinson 'long established cultural repertoires (myths, symbols and memories) are "carried" into the modern era by powerful institutions'.[45] The questions, of course, are which symbols? what memories? which myths? These are valid questions[46] and typical of the primordialists and ethno-symbolists versus modernists debate. The national narrative has many pasts and variations and many interpretations depending on whichever events are more suitable for the task of constructing the nation: threats, victories, defeats, oppression, justice, all can be emphasised with lesser or greater intensity, and memories are selected and deselected accordingly. Modern ethno-symbolists claim that they accept the conflictual nature of nations and that nationalists speak to their constituencies in 'languages the latter understand' but do not accept that nationalists have freedom to select whichever story in order to manufacture consent.[47] Human lives are relatively short but nations deal in generations; the histories of nations transcend the length of human life and that is what makes one's national story so appealing and politically useful because it presents national interest in more emotive terms than ordinary politics would otherwise do. To my mind, though, this is still more politics than a confirmation of *la longue durée* of *ethnie*, whether in a classical primordialist, or more modern and moderate ethno-symbolic, approach.

It would seem that neither the cynicism of modernists nor the romanticism of others can really provide answers for the rise of nations and the role of nationalism in our world. A possible way forward is to look at what nationalism does to humanity, as well as for humanity. Where in those approaches are emancipation and democratisation? Where do we find the explanation to the mistreatment of minorities, the ferocity of ethnic conflicts and the will to resolve them? What is the role of the international community in the formation of nations? In our societies, when nationalism and ethnic mobilisation are on the rise, it is perhaps wise to approach nationalism through first, its democratic thrust, and secondly, by recognising that the new challenges our societies face need new approaches to our forms of nationalisms. The following chapters turn to these challenges in order to seek what is relevant and what is less relevant in terms of theories of nations and nationalism – today. I say this because I believe that classical approaches to nationalism, as they have been conveyed thus far, just about explain nationalism in the nineteenth and twentieth centuries, but do not quite stretch to nationalism as a form of collective identity and action in our twenty-first century.

A movement for unity: a case study of Arab nationalism

> ... the Arab nation is that human collectivity which speaks the Arabic language, inhabits a territory called the Arab lands and has a voluntary and spontaneous feeling of belonging to that nation.
>
> Arab nationalism is the sum total of characteristics, qualities and hallmarks which are exclusive to the collectivity called Arab nation, [whereas] Arab unity is a modern notion, which stipulates that all disparate Arab countries should be formed into one single political system under one single state'.[48]

The representation of the Arab world is often contradictory: a fragmented region which, nevertheless, is assumed to be monolithic in its 'theologocentricism' by which all acts and thought are attributed to Islamic theology. While bemoaning the destruction of the historical 'cradle of our civilisation' sites in Iraq, the Western media kept stressing the civilisational 'clash' with the West. Arabs are meant to be people united by culture, history and religion but, while Arab unification is apparently a thing of the past, we are being warned about its dangers in the current form.[49] The reasons for including Arab nationalism in this chapter are: (1) it attests to the spread of a European idea of nations and nationalism in the Middle East; but (2) is a case in the study of nationalism in non-Western post-colonial societies. While some Arab scholars contest the importation of nationalism and stress the authenticity of the eternal Arab nation (*umma sarmadiyya*), Arab nationalism (3) was a response to the structural reality of the modern international system organised into nation states. Nationalism transformed the existing system of Westphalian states into a system of national states which was a challenge that the Ottoman Empire, just like the Austro-Hungarian Empire, could not withstand.[50]

Arab nationalism is an offspring of disillusion with, and dissolution of, the Ottoman Empire; its historical context is the ascent of the idea of a nation and nationalism in the second half of the nineteenth century, following the impact of liberal and democratising ideas of the French Revolution. In that sense, Arab nationalism follows the European model, similarly to all national movements that arose within the Austro-Hungarian Empire, and sought the establishment of national states. The story of the nations within the Ottoman Empire is, however, more complicated: Arab peoples went through a period of colonial rule by Western powers. The decolonisation of the Arab part of the world led to the creation of numerous nation states but not to a pan-Arab nation state which, given the cultural, religious and linguistic homogeneity of Arab peoples, could have been plausibly expected and certainly was desired by some Arab nationalists. The questions connected to when and how Arab nationalism emerged, its highs and lows and what unites Arabs now are equally complex and subject to many diverse opinions which cannot all be relayed here.

There seems to be a consensus that the first organisations seeking to politicise Arab culture took place within the Ottoman Empire, mostly by its Christian Arab and Muslim Arab officers. The western values of progress and democracy, increasingly more connected to the cultural realm, spread into the Arab world. Calls for local and cultural autonomy within the empire were expressed at the first congress of Arab nationalists in 1913 in Paris.[51] At the same time, the idea of nationalism was spreading among the Turks who proceeded with 'Turkicising' the empire which, in turn, led to a growing discontent with Ottoman rule and to Arab resistance movements during World War I (for example, Sharif Husayn's revolt in 1916). These movements later turned against the British and the French who went back on various promises they had made of political autonomy for Arabs, but the shift of emphasis from democratic concerns against Ottoman rule to concerns about Arab cultural identity and its political expression – thus nationalism – dates to the time of World War I and its aftermath.[52]

There are at least three stages of Arab nationalism. The first stage, as I have already identified, during and after World War I, was marked by a shift from the liberal French idea of a nation (which should have a state) to a more ethnic conception of a nation (which does not have a state) and therefore is united on the basis of culture, history and language. This shift conforms to everything that has been said in Chapter 1 about how the original liberal democratic ideas of nationalism, depending on conditions of the society in which they were spreading, often changed from universalism to particularism. The second stage was ushered in by the victory of the *Free Officers*, in Egypt in 1952, led by Nasser (Gamal Abdul, 1918–70), which ended the monarchy. Nasser is inextricably linked with the heyday of Arab nationalism which, under his mentorship, assumed a level of populism and political legitimacy in the Arab world. It came to an end with the defeat of the Arab armies in the 1967 war with Israel. This defeat marks the beginning of a new stage in Arab consciousness, rooted in self-questioning and very complex international relations in the region in reference to each other but mostly to Israeli military and territorial expansion and the Palestinian refugee issue. We are probably still in the midst of this third stage which, arguably, is being marked by renewed appeals to Arab unity; no longer a national unity in a pan-Arab state but unity through political Islam which also sees Arabs as a single entity.[53] Whether the Israeli–Palestinian conflict and the position of the Arab world vis-à-vis the West add to the sense of unification among Arabs, or are actually a pivotal unifying factor, are separate questions and well beyond this necessarily brief case study. Given the context of this chapter, the focus here will be on the rise of Arab nationalism.

There is little doubt that the idea of Arabness is, in the first place, ethnic before it is national. How did this idea spread and how did the idea translate into a political movement of considerable significance? I will confine myself to two schools of thought: the intellectual (ideational) approach and the political. The former looks to nationalism as fundamentally a 'doctrine invented in Europe' as Kedourie argued[54] which was then disseminated by Western-educated elites downwards to 'the people'. The latter, political approach, following Breuilly, looks to nationalism as a form of politics that responds to changes in the political and regional environment.

The most influential intellectuals of Arab nationalism, such as Sati' al-Husri and Michel Aflaq (the founder of the Arab Ba'th party, 1947) were much influenced by the writings of Fichte, Marx, Hegel and other European philosophers of the earlier era. The beginnings of Arab nationalism have to be sought among Arab, often Christian, intellectuals who were products of Western education within the Ottoman Empire. This Westernised intelligentsia was nevertheless working and living in an exploited and relatively backward society and faced discrimination by their alien rulers. This brings together a number of important aspects in the success of nationalist ideology: resentment, personal indignation at the humiliation of one's cultural group, and the ideas of progress and democracy. Thus, nationalism, combined with the growing discontent with the Ottomans, were seen as a means of political opposition. The 'intellectual' approach rests on the dissemination of ideas of nationalism which, when accepted by the population at large, provides a basis for collective national consciousness and eventually culminates in growing resistance movements.[55] There are considerable limits to this interpretation, as I will go on to argue, because, by putting its store in the spread of ideas by certain elites, it ignores all other processes. For the moment, though, it is important to realise that industrialisation and secular education were limited in the Arab world of that time, and that nationalism was spreading in the feudal system of alien administration and strong local loyalties. Ideas are powerful, and the question is about motivation and inspiration. Hence, there is a degree of merit in this approach in the early stages of Arab nationalism, possibly up to 1945.

Gershoni identifies two narratives, 'old' and 'new' in the studies of Arab nationalism.[56] The old narrative, which includes work of Kedourie and many others,[57] views nationalism as an idea which, when articulated, 'can have a life of its own'. Ideas have a life but their implementation requires much more. This is getting ahead of the 'old' narrative, however, in which the Arab nation is a linguistic and historically constituted entity. While the language is an objective fact, the history in such a narrative traces the past to some common 'golden' age from which a glorious nation arose and for which a similar glorious future awaits – the path of such a nation is full of traditions, symbols and heroes. This is a fairly standard foundation of most national narratives in pursuit of recognition of the nation. As I have already argued, nationalisms are particular but the rhetoric is universal which in no way suggests that the story is entirely manufactured or that its genuineness affects nationalism. Of great importance here is the distinction that this narrative had to make between 'an affinity for the Arab nation and Arab nationalism (*qawm*) and a patriotic affiliation with one's specific homeland (*watan*), because Arab nationalism sought unity (*wahda*) that had to be forged across many already existing narrower loyalties (for example, Egyptian–Pharaonic, Iraqi–Mesopotamian, etc.)'.[58] This is markedly different from a nationalism which seeks to forge a political nation in the less complex and narrower context such as, for example, nationalisms of nationalities within the Austro-Hungarian Empire whose loyalties were not tested by any other forms of affiliation between the crown and the strictly local (attempts of pan-Slovophiles never came anywhere near the coherence of early Arab nationalism, let alone to its full emergence after 1945). On the other hand, the fragmentation of the Arab world remains an obstacle to Arab unity then and now.

What of the relationship between Arab nationalism and Islam? Bassam Tibi, who also subscribes to the 'history of ideas' school of thought but tends plausibly to stress the globalisation of the international system, argues that the history of Arab nationalism can be looked at from two perspectives. (1) The Arab awareness of the European concept of 'nation' which changed, following the colonisation, from the liberal pre-1913 position to *Germanophilia* (organic, ethnic) form. (2) As a response of the evolving state system: from the royal state system of Arab rulers in the interwar period (the Hashemites in Iraq and Jordan, the Saudis in Arabia and Muhammad in Egypt) to Nasser's United Arab Republic (1958). The Arab defeat in 1967 plunged the regional state system into crisis and ended pan-Arabism.[59] Tibi also argues, though, that there is an inherent tension between the modern understanding of 'the nation' and the Islamic *umma* to which every Muslim belongs regardless of his or her ethnicity – *umma* is the universal community of believers and not a civic community. The Arab nationalists' concept *al-umma al-'Arabiyya* was an attempt to bridge the secularism of nationalism with the Islamic divine order.[60] Currently, though, the secularism is replaced by Islam as the unifying ideology which again does not fit the world of nation states, and the tension remains. Gershoni, too, argues that in the 'old' narrative, Islam was relegated to a 'component' of Arab national identity.[61]

The 'old' narrative thus viewed Arab nationalism as the reaction of Arab elites to the collapse of the Ottoman Empire, in the first instance, and secondly as a guest for unity in protest against colonial domination and the arbitrariness of artificial states. This narrative does not only rely on the texts written by leading ideologues of Arab nationalism, it is elitist in its neglect of the public reception of these ideas even if we were to assume that it was well received. Moreover, the 'old' narrative, which dates to the 1950s and 1960s when Arab nationalism was at its height, understandably is not reflective enough to analyse the sociopolitical changes on the ground and is too nationalistic in its neglect of external influences.

The 'new' narrative dates to the 1970s and 1980s, a period of reflection about the decline of Arab nationalism. Relying on the theoretical background emerging in studies of nationalism (for example, Gellner, Smith, Anderson, Hobsbawm), Arab nationalism came to be studied within the context of the disintegration of rural communities, of urbanisation and modernisation, of the invention of traditions, and the expansion of the middle classes. Thus, as I already identified in the work of Bassam Tibi, the 'new' narrative looks at nationalism not only as an anti-colonial response but also at social structures within which this ideology emerged.[62] Such a 'structural' approach offers more than an account of how the idea of the Arab nation arose. Importantly, it can account for its failure under the impact of external influences, local conditions and other parochial affiliations. The urban, educated middle classes (*effendiyya*) embraced nationalism not only because they were alienated but because the new ideology was a political strategy whereby to pursue their interests. The *effendiyya* were a product of an urban and sophisticated culture but nevertheless they struggled against various obstacles connected to the 'old hierarchical bureaucrats' as well as against the lack of access to positions given in preference by the colonial rulers to foreign professionals.[63] If it was to offer a political opposition, nationalism needs 'the people' and indeed, the protest is always in 'ethnic' identity and so it was the case of a radicalised Middle Eastern intelligentsia; the difference here is that 'ethnic' stood for the promotion of pan-Arabism. While more present in the 'new' narrative, however, the people are still largely recipients of nationalist rhetoric from above but their experiences, their poverty, their illiteracy, their exploitation, also at the hands of the indigenous elites, and their colonial experience are largely absent. Moreover, the experience of their colonial masters, the international system within which the Ottomans, and the British and French, and later the Arab states operated and which, too, was changing dramatically, is also rather absent.

So, I turn to the 'political' approach as elaborated by John Breuilly in his *Nationalism and the State*. The first question to ask is why did Arab nationalism, if inspired by nineteenth-century Europe (where the 'spring of nations' and the first pan-Slav Congress happened in 1848), appeared relatively late and certainly not until about 1914? The answer to this question must be sought first in Islam as the religion in the Ottoman Empire which 'tied the Arab subjects to their ruler', and 'nationalising' the religion, as was already argued, was in tension with the religious loyalty to the empire that embodied Islam. Secondly, the impulse to nationalism in the Ottoman Empire, as everywhere else throughout time and space, is in response to centralising pressures of the state. Here the state became increasingly Turkish, the pressures increasingly nationalist, which offended not only Islamic sentiments but also the traditional 'collaborators' who, in return for loyalty to the Ottomans, enjoyed a degree of local autonomy. The reforms, induced by the series of military defeats by the Ottomans, may have been welcomed, but not in their overwhelmingly Turkish form. After 1918, the region became subject to the British and French mandates and, because autonomies promised during World War I did not come to fruition, Arab nationalism became a logical response.[64]

Where did the next impulse come from, because it appears that Egypt, for example, remained aloof from Arab nationalism and, as a territorial state, grew its own? Breuilly looks to the post-1945 situation in the Middle East which was significantly affected by the events of World War II, namely the Holocaust of the European Jewry and the influx of Jewish refugees into Palestine, followed by the establishment of the state of Israel. I shall deal with the ensuing Israeli–Palestinian conflict in Chapter 5 but, for the present purpose, it is vital to acknowledge that the disregard for the rights of Palestinians outraged Arabs. The attacks against Israel in 1948, aimed at its destruction and co-ordinated by Arab armies – or, as it happened, not co-ordinated – failed. Arab nationalism became reinvigorated by the need for co-ordination and actions against this enemy. In an opportunistic bid for the leadership of the Arab world, Nasser and his 'revolutionary' regime in Egypt took up the challenge and combined the idea of Arab unity and Islam with anti-imperialism, socialism, and hostility towards Israel. In 1958 he formed the United Arab Republic with Syria, later joined by Yemen.[65] The Arab world was not united, however: Saudi Arabia resented Egypt for its leadership and also for its un-Islamic nationalism which, in fact, fought Muslim organisations in Egypt. Syria resented its inferior position within the Arab Republic, and left in 1961, and other Arab states pursued their own foreign policies. Finally, after defeats in the 1967 and 1973 wars with Israel, Arab nationalism lost its popular support.

In recent years, many different states have tried to assume the leading position in the Arab world but there are too many conflicts of interests among the contemporary Arab states, vis-à-vis one another and the United States, and these are now augmented by the salience of security issues in international politics. The remaining unifying factor for Arabs seems to be Israel and Palestine who are engaged in a bitter struggle deriving from their own mutually contradictory nationalisms. But that is not strictly the concern of this case study. Ideas do not die completely, and Arab nationalism as an idea may continue to exist and may even be resurrected in one form or other but, whatever form it takes, it will be a different nationalism. It will not be anti-colonial in the classical sense; it will face the same challenge as all nationalisms face in defining 'the nation'; it is likely to be more centred around Islam and less around liberalism and democracy; it will not need to draw inspiration from Europe; and it will most certainly, as all nationalism always do, respond to the political challenges of its time. If international relations in the Middle East at the moment are anything to go by, the likelihood of a single Arab state, as envisaged by the founding myth of Arab nationalism, is very remote.

Notes

1. Mainly Anthony D. Smith but also John Armstrong and Pierre van den Berghe.
2. Mainly Ernest Gellner, John Breuilly, Eric Hobsbawm and Benedict Anderson.
3. For an overall overview of the classification of theories of nationalism see Özkirimli (2000), *Theories of Nationalism*; for this particular topic, pp. 60–3.
4. Hobsbawm (1990), *Nations and Nationalism since1780: Programme, Myth and Reality*, p. 10.
5. Breuilly (1996), 'Approaches to Nationalism' in 'Balakrishnan, G., *Mapping the Nation*, p. 146.
6. There is a 'more primordialist' theory of nations formulated by Pierre van den Berghe (1979), *The Ethnic Phenomenon*, New York: Elsevier. His sociobiological perspective views nations as extensions of ethnic groups which are characterised by kinship – each as a kind of extended superfamily, based on kin ties. In this view a common ancestry is not merely cultural but, to a degree, biological – hence, diffusions or fusions with neighbouring groups, the manipulations of groups' myths, and other historical occurrences cannot detract from the fact that ethnic groups correlate to its original pre-existing population bound by kin selection.
7. Smith (1986), *The Ethnic Origins of Nations*, pp. 21–31. See also Malešević (2004), '"Divine ethnies" and "Sacred nations": Anthony D. Smith and neo-Durkhemian theory of nationalism', pp. 561–5.

8. Smith, *The Ethnic Origins of* Nations, p. 32; and Smith (1998), *Nationalism and Modernism*, p. 191.
9. Malešević, '"Divine ethnies" and "Sacred nations"', p. 565.
10. Smith, *Nationalism and Modernism*, p. 192.
11. Smith, *Nationalism and Modernism*, p. 195; or chapter 8 in *Ethnic Origins of Nations*.
12. Smith, *Nationalism and Modernism*, p. 194.
13. Greenfeld (1992), *Nationalism: Five Roads to Modernity*, pp. 8 and 11 respectively.
14. Smith, *Nationalism and Modernism*, p. 195.
15. Armstrong (1982), *Nations Before Nationalism*; and Smith, *Nationalism and Modernism*, pp. 167 and 181–7.
16. Smith, *Nationalism and Modernism*, p. 195.
17. Smith, *Theories of Nationalism*, p. 171.
18. Smith, *Theories of Nationalism*, p. 18.
19. Gellner (1964), *Thought and Change*, p. 168. For an in-depth exploration of Gellner's work see Hall (1998), *The State of the Nation*.
20. The most influential book on 'modernity' of nations is Gellner, *Nations and Nationalism*, p. 55.
21. Gellner, *Nations and Nationalism*, p. 1.
22. Gellner, *Thought and Change*, chapter 7.
23. Gellner, cited in Hall, *The State of the Nation*, pp. 9–10.
24. Gellner, *Thought and Change*, p. 168.
25. Gellner, *Nations and Nationalism*, p. 44.
26. Zubaida (1978), 'Theories of Nationalism', pp. 65–6.
27. For a broader review of critiques of Nairn's work: see Özkirimli (2000), *Theories of Nationalism*, pp. 88–96.
28. Breuilly (1993), *Nationalism and the State*, p. 2.
29. Harris (2002), *Nationalism and Democratisation: Politics of Slovakia and Slovenia*, p. 5.
30. Breuilly, *Nationalism and the State*, p. 1.
31. Breuilly (1996), 'Approaches to Nationalism' in 'Balakrishnan, *Mapping the Nation*, p. 166.
32. Nairn (1975), 'Modern Janus', p. 18.
33. Hobsbawm (1990), *Nations and Nationalism since 1780: Programme, Myth and Reality*; and Hobsbawm and Ranger (1983), *The Invention of Tradition*.
34. Özkirimli, *Theories of Nationalism*, p. 117.
35. Hobsbawm and Rengger, *The Invention of Tradition*, p. 303.
36. Anderson (1983), *Imagined Communities*.
37. Özkirimli, *Theories of Nationalism*, p. 153.
38. Hearn (2009), *Rethinking Nationalism*, p. 43.
39. Kedourie (1960), *Nationalism*, p. 9. See also Kedourie (1971), *Nationalism in Asia and Africa*, for a less Eurocentric approach.
40. Behar (2005), 'Do Comparative and Regional Studies of Nationalism Intersect?' p. 597.
41. Hroch (1993), 'From National Movement to the Fully-Formed Nation', p. 5.
42. Ibid., pp. 6–7.
43. Ibid., p. 11.
44. Kaufman (2008), in 'Debate on John Hutchinson's Nations as Zones of Conflict', p. 3.
45. Hutchinson (2005), *Nations as Zones of Conflict*, p. 41.
46. Özkirimli (2008) in 'Debate on John Hutchinson's Nations as Zones of Conflict', p. 6.
47. Hutchinson (2008), 'In defence of Transhistorical Ethno-Symbolism: A Reply to My Critics' in 'Debate on John Hutchinson's Nations as Zones of Conflict'.
48. Jalal al-Sayyid (1913–92), cited in Choueiri (2000), *Arab nationalism*, p. 24.
49. AbuKhalil, As'ad (1992), 'A new Arab ideology? The rejuvenation of Arab national-ism', pp. 22–9.

50. Tibi (1997), *Arab Nationalism*, pp. 1–13.
51. Ibid., p. 16
52. Breuilly, *Nationalism and the State*, p. 150; Choueiri, *Arab nationalism*, p. 54.
53. Tibi (1997), *Arab Nationalism*, p. 25.
54. Kedourie, *Nationalism*, p. 9; and Kedourie, *Nationalism in Asia and Africa*, p. 28.
55. Behar, 'Do Comparative and Regional Studies of Nationalism Intersect?', p. 597.
56. Gershoni (1997) 'Rethinking the Formation of Arab Nationalism in the Middle East, 1920–1945', in Jankowski and Gershoni, *Rethinking Nationalism in the Arab Middle East*, 4–25, p. 4.
57. Ibid., see notes 11 and 12, pp. 291–2.
58. Ibid., p. 8.
59. Tibi, *Arab Nationalism*, p. 203.
60. Ibid., p. 18.
61. Gershoni, 'Rethinking the Formation of Arab Nationalism in the Middle East, 1920–1945', p. 8.
62. Tibi, *Arab Nationalism*, pp. xi–xii.
63. Gershoni, 'Rethinking the Formation of Arab Nationalism in the Middle East, 1920–1945', pp. 16–17.
64. Breuilly, *Nationalism and the State*, p. 152.
65. Ibid., p. 284.

Part II

Contemporary debates about nationalism and cultural identities

CHAPTER THREE

A Multinational Condition and the Rights of Minorities

At the heart of this chapter is a paradox of the national self-determination doctrine: it creates states but it is also responsible for political and cultural challenges to the nation state by non-dominant ethnic groups. The most important issue in the study of nationalism today is how to reconcile cultural diversity and political unity within the state. Thus, the main theme of the present chapter comprises the people in the 'grey area'[1] where the cultural and political nation do not overlap. There were always these grey areas but the contemporary nation state is increasingly less capable of insulating its borders from the influx of immigrants and, therefore, now more than ever, the role of citizenship and national narratives need to be re-evaluated. I am suggesting that we find out more about nationalism when investigating the 'grey areas' than we do when focusing on the presumed congruence between the political and cultural nation, and that theories of nationalism tell us little about providing solutions to this very contemporary predicament of nation states and their peoples.

The chapter provides a theoretical framework for the rest of this section which depicts our world as one in which two simultaneous, but not necessarily complementary, processes are taking place: the increased awareness and protection of cultural identity, the cultural 'verticalisation' as it were of the world into ever smaller cultural units on the one hand, and political and economic 'horizontalisation', transgressing and ignoring cultural idiosyncrasies on the way to global markets and political integration. While the nation state traditionally assumed the right to homogenise the population to achieve political unity, the modern state's predicament of how to reconcile cultural diversity with political unity has been compounded by international institutions, international law which, in some cases, is less concerned with a state's sovereignty and more with its human rights protection (selectively, but that is another topic altogether), transnational movements, and technological and communications advances. The last have shrunk the physical distances and, while bringing people closer together, have also sharpened the differences and increased cultural confrontations. Cultural diversity is an irrefutable and permanent fact of our political and social reality. That is not a historical novelty; the novelty, however, is the challenge to the state and its cultural and political authority. If the state is losing its unassailable image, logically, the relationship between the state and society is changing, too, and we can safely say that the most visible among those changes is the relationship between majorities and minorities. I shall continue this chapter with the discussion of this relationship, firstly in theory and practice, and then I shall move on to the exploration of the multinational condition of contemporary states and the available normative and constitutional responses. Contemporary Britain serves as an example of a number of controversies reflected in this chapter which emphasise the distinction between the contemporary nation state and its nineteenth-century ideal.

The non-nation state

The main historical achievement of the state has been its ability to transform itself into a 'nation state' which implies much more than an administrative and legal unit than a state is; it implies a community of like-mindedness, cemented by a common past and driven by a common future, a community of allegiance, in which the sacrifice for the existence and the continuation of the state is offset against the protection and rewards of the official status of the citizen. There may never have been a common past; there is never like-mindedness; the state may abuse its own people; its future may be in doubt; the allegiance may be shaky; but who can say that its people have never felt a sense of pride at their 'national' treasures, whether in the form of natural beauty, sporting achievements, cuisine, architecture, literature, and so it goes on? We all like the idea of our state and, even as a critic of its limitations in terms of peaceful coexistence among national groups, I am willing to concede that the state has a role in human existence which is beyond strictly impersonal and legal matters. On the other hand, the state also has a role as an arbiter of relations among peoples within its boundaries and beyond, and that role constitutes one of the state's greatest weaknesses.

The principal idea behind the nation state lies in that 'eternal hyphen'[2] which, in all its innocuousness, carries the enormous weight of national unity and political legitimacy by linking two fundamental categories in political science: the nation and the state. The assumption is that there is a natural overlap between the two, that they belong together as a form of political community, the membership of which is citizenship. In a world divided into nation states, citizenship is not only a necessity (as all immigrants, asylum seekers and refugees who do not have it will attest), it is a legal status, it is a passport in a literal sense to rights and political participation, and a label offering an identity which comes with belonging to the nation state.[3] All these assumption are open to contestation. First, there are no nation states that are of and for one nation[4] because the overlap between the self-determining nation (*ethnos*) and the totality of the population that resides in the territory of the state is hardly ever as neat as nation-building elites would like – the overlap usually leaves some residual people who, even if citizens, are not members of the state-constituting group. These people are considered, and consider themselves, minorities – they do not belong fully and, depending on the state's policies and history, they may be prevented from full political participation or their loyalty may be questioned to the point where their contribution to the common good is not welcomed by the state. Second, the body of citizens (*demos*) is not united on all issues and is further 'internally' divided in terms of class and cultural and political dominance – and this is before we touch on gender which, despite its importance is not the subject of the discussion here.

Umut Özkirimli starts his book with a startling statement that 'nationalists have no country',[5] because there is no congruence between the nation and the state and there is no particularity of the nation because all claims that nation builders are making are the same for all nations; hence, the dream of the unique nation in charge of the state and its own destiny is never fulfilled. By the same token, there are no true nation states, only states that are home to one core national group 'which is understood as the legitimate "owner" of the state'[6] and a number of minorities. This does not mean that the nation state does not pursue the 'dream' of homogeneity; on the contrary, all states are guilty of homogenising tendencies in order to remedy this 'deficiency'. The clue to the relationship between majorities and minorities is actually in the intensity of these homogenising tendencies which range from mild attempts at the appropriation of state power by the dominant national group to the exclusion of minorities when taking a negative perspective, or the level of accommodation of minorities from a more positive position.[7]

The question of who constitutes the rightful nation which constitutes the state is fundamental to the relationship between the state and the nation and, by implication, to the relationship between majorities and minorities. So, when do we speak of a minority? A minority is an ethno-cultural group that perceives itself, and is perceived to be, different from the core group that has established the state. The mere existence of such a group, however – whether of a different language, or with different customs, different religion or skin colour – doesn't necessarily have political consequences, and it is the politics of the minority–majority relationship that interest us here. Minorities that enter the political arena, wittingly or unwittingly, demand a state's recognition as a minority group and, these days, increasingly assert rights based on such recognition which involves certain collective rights, cultural and/or political. In sum, a minority is not given by virtue of existing but by virtue of a decision to represent itself as such. This represents a challenge to both the state and the minority because the self-representation as outside 'the nation' is akin to a degree of mistrust connected to a lack of affiliation while it also spells difficulty for the state and its typical efforts to homogenise the population.

Depending on the history between national groups, a minority may be accused of historical injustice committed against the core group (and vice versa), the injustice that the new state considers its duty to redress. If a minority resides anywhere near a contested border, their demands are soon translated as attempts to secede. Hence, nowhere is the issue of the 'ownership' of the state and the relationship between national groups as blatantly played out as in the newly independent states (this topic I discuss in the following chapter, too). I have argued elsewhere that the new state has to undergo certain processes such as writing a new constitution, establishing criteria for citizenship, recasting some institutions and filling them with new personnel (often as rewards for the support of new nationalising elites), carving out a new position in the international community and seeking to homogenise around the ideal of this new state.[8]

While these processes are necessarily connected to state formation, they are also threatening to minorities, particularly when the core nationality treats the new state as if owned by it without giving enough consideration to issues which are important to minorities and without making constitutional provisions for them. It could be argued that state formation should be an opportunity to set the precedent of good majority and minority relations but evidence shows that this is precisely the time when precedent for bad relations is set.[9]

Joel Migdal uses the Israeli case to illustrate the fragmentation of society between Jews and Palestinians where the latter, despite having been granted Israeli citizenship at the beginning of independence, have never been fully incorporated into the society at a time when conditions were set by the Israeli state so that Palestinians could be excluded and segregated.[10] Given the further developments in the Israeli–Palestine relationship, this precedent has not only prevented the integration of Palestinians into society but continues to jeopardise the security of the state within and beyond its already much fought-over borders. An interesting facet of this case (which will be discussed in greater detail in Chapter 5) is that it confirms that new states tend to care more about the assertion of who constitutes the state-forming nation than about long-term harmony and democratic credentials which were at the heart of the national self-determination efforts. Israel is a relatively new state, and its troubled inter-ethnic relationship with its main Palestinian minority and its neighbours is comparable to what we have observed in Eastern and Central Europe in the early 1990s. I shall discuss post-communist Europe in the following chapter but, for the moment, I would like to bring in another example of the presumed ownership of the state which brings into question citizenship and its many unofficial forms, namely the case of the newly independent Slovakia.

In the period 1989–92, Slovak political elites tried to assert the position of Slovakia within the Czechoslovak federation which would be based on the 'new understanding' as the federation of the 'two sovereign national state-forming republics'.[11] The inability of the Czech and Slovak elites to agree on the form of this new federation resulted in the disintegration of Czechoslovakia. The newly independent Slovakia came about as a result of (failed) elite negotiations between the Czech and Slovak sides and without a national referendum. Thus, it was a surprise to its population who found themselves in possession of a state they had not really struggled for. Consequently, while it is assumed that the struggle for independence contributes to uniting a society, in Slovakia, independence became a divisive issue. The combination of a relatively high degree of ethnic heterogeneity and the circumstances under which the new state was established contributed significantly to the formation of a nationalist elite who never really elaborated the concept of the future state, except for the notion of a state for Slovaks on which their legitimacy was based. This particularity of Slovakia, where nationalist mobilisation has significantly increased after independence (as it were, justifying the fact after the event) is very damaging to finding a consensus among the political elites because it suggests that only certain people deserve the right to act or even to argue on behalf of the nation. The division was not merely ethnic, between Slovak and non-Slovak, but was further compounded by 'good' (pro-separation) and 'bad' (pro-federal) Slovaks whereby the latter, following this logic, by not having contributed to the existence of the state had no right to govern it.[12] What we observed was the fragmentation of society not only between the majority and its main Hungarian minority but also among Slovaks themselves. The forging of political unity behind the intended democratic project became subordinated to the forging of national solidarity in conditions of extreme societal and political fragmentation. The Slovak nation was poorly prepared for that statehood and for the responsibilities that the 'state-forming' nation carries towards the minorities living within its territory.

Moreover, the largest and the most politically active minority in Slovakia, the Hungarian, carries an enormous weight in Slovak national consciousness which is synonymous with the suppression of the Slovak language and all things national during the Austro-Hungarian rule and with territorial annexation during World War II. Thus, in its attempts to homogenise national culture and redress its historical position, and perceived to be weak compared to its Czech and Hungarian neighbours, the nationalising state set out to assert the ownership of the state by the dominant group. Slovakia extends the full citizenship rights to all her citizens regardless of their ethnic affiliation but the tension was not about citizenship, it was about the 'ethnicisation'[13] of political life in which the Slovak government in the period 1992–8 tried all but to exclude Hungarians. If citizenship implies membership of a political community, then in Slovakia one could not speak of formal exclusion from citizenship as was the case with ethnic Russians in the Baltic states (Estonia and Latvia mainly). It was rather an implicit and informal division between Slovaks, who perceive themselves to be the state-forming group and the owners of a self-determining state, and 'the others', who are seen as less deserving of control in that state. Citizenship in this case takes on a different meaning; the 'price' for membership of the national community is expected to be paid, usually in the form of conforming to the dominant culture. That is where such measures as the Language Laws, disputes about street signs, territorial and electoral reforms to reduce the control of local authorities in all-Hungarian districts, reduced budgets for cultural activities, quarrels about what language school reports should be written in, and so on come in – all in order to distinguish the real 'nation builders', the ones who gave the name to the new state, from other citizens. In principle, the demands of the Hungarian minority, which constitutes the majority in southern Slovakia, are based on a similar idea of self-determination, that is control over their region, and that is precisely the point of the continuing tension – the control over the territory and the preservation of the 'immediate' identity.[14] I shall return to the Hungarian minority in Chapter 6 where I discuss diasporic identity which constitutes a somewhat different form of minority, but the fundamental issues associated with 'ownership' of the state by the dominant nationality and the meaning of citizenship where they do not overlap remain the same.

Ethnic labelling

A further elaboration on the concept of identity appears necessary for two reasons. First, this book is largely concerned with a critical assessment of nationalism which is ultimately a political agenda of and for a 'nation', and a nation is a form of collective identity. In fact, my concern, as previous chapters illustrate, is not so much with whether nations actually exist or the extent to which there is a shared identity and for how long they may have existed but with the far-reaching consequences of the emergence of this particular category of collective identity. Enough has been said about nationalism thus far to warrant this present chapter about minorities who also comprise a form of collective identity. Second, identity maybe a powerful and necessary part of the human condition but its ubiquity requires further clarification if analysis based on its presumed existence as a sociopolitical category is to make sense. In an article which should inspire some soul-searching in all of us working with 'identity', Brubaker and Cooper say, 'if identity is everywhere, it is nowhere'. As my objective here is to come to grips with the 'power and pathos'[15] of contemporary identity politics, it seems appropriate that I make clear what identity lies at the heart of 'my' identity politics. Brubaker and Cooper further argue that the concept of identity is too 'ambiguous' and 'riddled with contradictory meanings and encumbered by reifying connotation' to perform successfully as an analytical concept.[16]

Hence, following Brubaker and Cooper, identity stands for a collective self-understanding of a group characterised by 'sameness' and a solidarity based on some shared attributes which can be objectively observed, but also characterised by their subjective reflection in a group's consciousness. Obviously there are many groups that fit this description (gender, class, sexual orientation, political affiliation, religion, profession and so on) but, in the present context, I am referring to ethnic groups, and by shared attributes I mean common ancestry and/or a shared historical past, religion, or even just the language. I stress the language because, for example in Eastern and Central Europe, it would be very difficult to find other distinguishing attributes among national groups who have shared the same territory, the same history, the same customs, political regimes and often the same religion for generations within multinational empires and later within what were the communist multinational federations, the Soviet Union, Yugoslavia and Czechoslovakia. What distinguishes these groups is the language and their different status related to their position vis-à-vis the state (or the crown). Certain of these groups had, at one time, been conquerors and rulers; their rule had been overthrown,[17] and they became, if not subjects of new rulers, then minorities in new states. The status, past and present, largely determines the interethnic relations everywhere, but particularly where borders, rulers and regimes were often changing. The examples from Eastern and Central Europe and the Middle East throughout this text confirm this assertion.

People feel differently about their ethnic affiliation, some very strongly and some less so, but inter-ethnic relations reflect more than the intensity of affiliation among the members of a given group. They also reflect the intensity of feeling among other groups towards this given group. Following the Holocaust, many Jewish people have tried to change their idiosyncratic Jewish surnames and even officially change their religion only to find out that, if they stayed in the same place, they were as much a target of anti-Semitism as the Jews who have maintained an open and strong Jewish identity. Ethnic labels enjoy longer life than the situations in which they were created – how one identifies oneself is at least as important as how one is identified, and both aspects are 'fundamentally situational and contextual'.[18] Ethnic identities change in the intensity of affiliation and in importance for one's daily existence, depending on personal self-understanding of who one is and on external factors, but 'groupness', in the sense of belonging to a distinct cultural entity, thus an ethnic identity, remains a category of a collective identity through which certain political processes and social dynamics should be analysed.

Hence, in the present context, under identity politics I understand the promotion and articulation of cultural distinctiveness vis-à-vis other cultural groups. When the focus of identity is ethnic identity and when the definition of a group's interests becomes dominated by ethnic distinctiveness, and political solidarity becomes based on the 'sameness', therefore 'otherness', often to the point of an exaggerated preference for one's group and even hostility to others, we are talking of ethnic politics. This shifts a gear from identity politics, which do not necessarily signal a conflict of interest among ethnic groups, to ethnic politics, which invariably do. The latter refers to the conflictual claims of different ethnic groups, either vis-à-vis each other, or vis-à-vis the state, which can take the form of politics of irreconcilable ends, but more often involves a struggle to maximise the influence and conditions for one's own ethnic group.

Ethnic labelling has many problems. First, collective identities, no matter how weak, ambiguous, fluid or constructed, nevertheless refer to a group as a whole which inevitably affects one's sense of safety, opportunity, prestige and esteem. All those aspects of one's identity are emotive and therefore open to exploitation, misinterpretation and mobilisation, and hence ethnic groups are ready-made constituencies for political elites who often unscrupulously exploit the identities of their groups for purposes of political gain. Second, when it comes to a political solution of sociopolitical problem, too much focus on ethnicity can be limiting to finding a solution. Different minorities face different problems. The maintenance of identity is perhaps the main concern of many minorities but identity, for all its glory, will not substitute the basic sociopolitical conditions that are equally, if not more, constitutive of satisfactory human existence. Take, for example, the position of the Roma in Eastern and Central Europe. The discrimination they suffer is a result of a whole people historically being labelled by their ethnicity which is associated with criminality, lawlessness and the inability to socialise within the norms and values of the dominant culture. This to the point where, in Slovakia (and the Czech Republic), Roma children are sent to segregated schools and often even to schools for educationally disabled children. Whole generations of Roma have grown up without a proper education (http://www.eumap.org/journal/announcements/roma_slovakia_brussels) only to be accused later of having lesser abilities and a lack of contribution to society. This deplorable state of affairs would not be tolerated if these children were not labelled by their ethnicity but viewed as children from an extremely deprived background which is what de facto they are. It has always been the case that stereotyping and discrimination are mutually reinforcing, and that these dynamics are less than conducive to finding solutions to the problems that may arise.

Identity and the state

The modern state is largely responsible for the importance ethnic identity has assumed in modern times. It is clear that not only does it endow people with their politically and economically most consequential identity – national identity – but the state possesses authority and resources and its government the political will to determine what happens within its borders and who is 'in' and who is 'out', that is, degrees of inclusion, favouritism and exclusion. The state is the owner of the civic affiliation and the owner of cultural norms and rewards, and therefore all minorities in one form or another seek the ability to share in the government of the state in order to safeguard their own interests. The relationship between the state and identity is very involved. As an administrative and legislative unit, the state seeks as much information as it can gather about its citizens with – depending on the type of regime – the intension of improving the efficacy of the government, or increasing control over the population. All states, whether democratic, less democratic or dictatorships, seek to unify the population behind its goals, and the general assumptions of a vast array of literature on this subject is that more cultural unity equals more effective governing.[19]

The state's pursuit of cultural unity and the production and continuous maintenance of identity for all to cohere under (national identity) labour under one principle idea, that shared identity is a political condition, if not a precondition, to more easily agreed grounds for compromise necessary for the politics of equality, common good and social justice.[20] All these assumptions are particularly relevant to liberal democracies because non-liberal and non-democratic states (and various other 'hybrids' of lesser democracies), while still seeking a coherent national identity, tend to forge ahead with political agendas with less concern for social justice. On the other hand, it is also naive to argue that ostensibly liberal democracies do not, in the name of national identity, engage in unjust policies against national groups not willing or not wanting to conform.

Given this background, and before I move on to the various forms of political organisation of diversity within the contemporary state, a few words on identity that holds a premise for political unity are in order. To some scholars, national identity should be such a political identity. David Miller[21] distinguishes three kinds of social divisions: ethnic cleavages (for example, American Italians); rival nationalities, each seeking to control all or part of the territory of the state (classic examples would be Northern Ireland and Serbs and Croats in what was Bosnia); and finally 'nested' nationalities, meaning two or more territorially based communities within a single nation, such as Belgium, Spain, Britain. The last case, according to Miller, is the preferred one. The first thing to note is that, in Miller's writing, a 'single nation' actually stands for a common state and, as I have already argued and will be arguing throughout, equating the state with one dominant identity is either a nationalist idea or a not very democratic one but, in any case, it is an idea which is increasingly less relevant to the majority of states. Second, not all social divisions can be classified into categories. Some 'nested' nationalities have been 'rival' nationalities before their histories became 'interwoven' over the course of several centuries (for example, Scots within the United Kingdom), and the interwoven histories of the former Yugoslav nations led to rivalry. The rivalry does not exclude future co-operation, social divisions can be overcome, and ethnic cleavages can result in 'nested' nationalities.

There is a form of identity, also rooted in belonging, but a belonging to a polity: either as a place of residence, or because one identifies with some aspects of the society and its institutions. This latter, 'polity-based' identity[22] does not mean that one identifies with all aspects of it, its history and the interpretation or the majority of its members. It is an identity that enables political participation and advocates the compliance with its rules, co-operation, and commitment to its institutions – this would be the barest form of citizenship. Here, paradoxically, liberals, democrats and nationalists all concur in the suspicion that such a strictly political identity is too 'cold' actually to bind the community together in a more meaningful way. This is why minorities, even if subscribing to such an identity, are not fully trusted with the affairs of 'the nation' because the conflation of cultural identity with politics in the form of the nation state has made the subjective elements of belonging tantamount to political solidarity – as if the latter guaranteed political unity or political co-operation.

A multinational condition: devolution or evolution?

Most states consist of a citizenry that is not ethnically homogeneous, and they are therefore multinational, multicultural, multi-ethnic or a combination of those. The definitional distinction between these various forms of a state's character remains imprecise but let me unpick some of the meanings behind those differentiated and highly politically charged terms. There is a subtle difference between ethnic minority and national minority. Both denote an ethnic, thus a cultural (religious, linguistic), group of certain shared characteristics that in one or a number of ways (including some physical distinctions) differs from the majority in the state. Importantly, though, a 'national minority' is usually reserved for an established minority that claims minority rights in order to preserve their status (the language rights, other collective rights, territorial autonomy, and so on), while an 'ethnic minority' could also subsume migrants.[23] This is an important distinction in terms of policy-making. Migrants are people who are outside their country of citizenship for various reasons, economic and/or political; they could be refugees or temporary, legal or illegal, awaiting naturalisation or deportation. They could, with time, form settled communities and, in some cases, become established minorities, such as the Bangladeshi in Britain, Turkish *gastarbeiters* in Germany, Algerians in France and other similar examples.

'National minorities' are often remnants of shifting borders, in which case they are usually territorially concentrated, as is the case in Eastern and Central Europe and the post-colonial Middle East, Asia and Africa. They could be language groups who immigrated en masse to countries such as America and Canada (for example, the French-speaking Quebecois), or they may be an indigenous population whose land was overrun by settlers and they have been, often forcibly, incorporated into states run by settlers, such as in Australia or the United States. It is interesting to note that, in Eastern and Central Europe, where there are still many unresolved 'national' issues, a minority nearly always refers to an indigenous, historical or territorial culturally distinct group of a larger size, while migration is hardly on the agenda of political discussion.

Multinationality usually refers to a state where there is a constitutional recognition of the (co)existence of a number of national groups: federal states, such as Czechoslovakia or Yugoslavia were before their disintegration or Switzerland and Belgium are. Multi-ethnic is a state where there is a number of national minorities with varying degrees of political and cultural protection by the state; so, if Czechoslovakia was a multinational federation, the successor Slovakia, with between 14 and 18 per cent of its population in the minority, probably fits the multi-ethnic category. All states, whether multinational or multi-ethnic, are at the same time increasingly more multicultural in terms of the variety of culturally diverse groups they incorporate, so the other successor state of the former Czechosovakia, the Czech Republic, being some 97 per cent homogeneous, may not fit the multinational or multi-ethnic characteristics but is probably a multicultural society.

There are two important interrelated questions here. First, what are the traditional methods of constitutional accommodation in multinational states? and second, what are the options and expectations of minorities and states vis-à-vis one another? I shall deal with the first question first, while the remainder of the chapter probes the second question from a number of angles. One of the most traditional methods for the accommodation of diversity within the state, whether ethnic diversity or historically evolved diversity derived from the rejection of the centralised state, is decentralisation. The best known among the decentralisation strategies is the **federalisation of the state**. Federalism stands for the division of power and competencies between the central state and the territorial-administrative units. It has many forms, among which ethnicity can serve as the boundary of the unit as, for example, in Spain, India, Canada, Switzerland and Belgium, or it may not, as in Germany or the United States. In all cases, federalism is a form of governance that seeks either greater efficiency or greater accommodation of the historically evolved multinational condition (language, religion) while maintaining the integrity of the state externally and internally. The clues to a well-functioning federal arrangement are the adequate response to specificities of each unit and their political equality which, in an ethnic context, if federalism is to deliver the stability, is paramount. The formal communist multinational federations, the Soviet Union, Czechoslovakia and Yugoslavia, which are discussed in detail in the next chapter, are not good examples of the federal experience, not only because they disintegrated but also because communist federations were not good examples of governance, ethnic or otherwise. Nevertheless, given the experience of the continuous ethnic strife of some constitutionally recognised units within ethno-territorial democratic federations (for example, Basques in Spain or the Quebecois in Canada), the communal violence in India, and the general risk of disintegration in Belgium, one must recognise that, with the exception of Switzerland, federations do not quite live up to their own constitutional arrangements.[24] This is mostly because first, in very few cases, the relationship between ethno-federal units and the state is free of suspicion to either secede or overpower. Second, the federation by emphasis on identity in the administration of the state, can open avenues for more discord than reconciliation, particularly if the federal arrangement was meant to be an answer to problematic relationship among national groups in the first place.

Within the cluster of multinational accommodation strategies falls also the uniquely **British devolution** in the form of the Scottish

Parliament and the Welsh Assembly. At this stage, it is difficult to judge how successful this model of a slow but significant transfer of power from the centre to Scotland and Wales will be in terms of maintaining the unitary Britain. At the moment, the rise of the Scottish National Party, in conjunction with or because of the weakened all-national Labour Party, which enjoyed great support in Scotland, and increased decentralisation of funding and public policy within the European Union, look to strengthen the drive of Scotland for more and more independence from London. On the other hand, the simplicity of the union or separation option shows how embedded nationalist rhetoric is in political discourse and how inadequate that discourse is in addressing the new situations. The problems of Scotland have been hijacked by this agenda but, traditionally, identity in Scotland is very much formed around class: Scots hated Thatcher's neo-liberal policies and possibly were disappointed by New Labour's neo-liberalism too. At the same time, there is a great uncertainty about 'British' national identity, not because Scotland is seeking more independence but because people in Britain, as in many post-industrial countries, are dissociated from the state for many reasons which I cannot go into here.[25] One thing is for sure, the teaching of 'Britishness' in schools will not change much on that score. Will Britain disintegrate? Devolution may be an answer to established democracies' efforts to democratise further but it may also prove a strategy for a slow, albeit peaceful, disintegration of the state. On the other hand, the increased decentralisation, to the point of the redefinition of the role of the state, may be exactly where the unitary states are heading in the near and not-so-near future. As a sign of the times, British devolution may be the forerunner of more to follow while the British union will probably evolve even further.

In their majestic work on democratic transitions, Linz and Stepan have stressed the problems of stateness and nationhood in multinational settings and argued that federalism is only one solution.[26] Another strategy which could be implemented in a federal or non-federal setting is **consociationalism** which is a form of a 'power-sharing democracy'[27] between a number of societal groups which, as a coalition, share the executive power. As an answer to democracy in deeply divided societies, the consociational model was most famously analysed in the 1960s by Arend Lijphart in the Netherlands and later extended to the cases of Belgium, Switzerland and Austria.[28] The model was at various times adopted in different countries, for different kinds of divisions (religion in the Netherlands, language in Belgium, class in Austria), or elements of the model were employed in Malaysia (1955), Cyprus (1960), Lebanon (1943) and, most famously, Northern Ireland (1998). It must be said that, while the Netherlands and Switzerland are examples of stability, Belgium's consociationalism has moved towards federalism, and Lebanon and Cyprus are not exactly examples for the management of divisions.

Nevertheless, the principles of consociationalism are not only regularly employed in newly written constitutions (for example, Slovenia) but are very worthy of consideration. There are two main principles: (1) grand coalition representing all segments of society and (2) segmental autonomy; and two secondary principles; (3) proportionality and (4) minority veto. The first principle means that the grand coalition of main groups, whose elites agree on a 'deal', form joint executive power. In cases of geographically concentrated 'segments', the autonomy can take a form of federalism whereby the issues of interest are divided into common interests, such as the state, and others which would be segment specific; in ethnically divided societies, this would mean a substantial autonomy for ethnic communities. Proportionality as a basic principle of representation in divided societies is obvious but, in the consociational model, extends it to all levels of government, that is parliament, civil service, budgets, etc. The last principle – minority veto – is the ultimate provision for a minority's protection of its vital interests. I would like to pause here for a moment. There are differences between a unitary federal state with proportional representation, the unitary PR system that employs minority veto, such as in Slovenia where the Hungarian and Italian minority each has one reserved seat in parliament with full veto powers over their interests, the grand power-sharing coalition with the main minority in the government, such as was Slovakia in the period 1998–2006, and what can be called consociationalism. The last is a particular model of democracy, actually an agreement which is meant to hold because it is expected that segmental elites have substantial control over their electorates to maintain this deal.

So, what is wrong with this, at first sight, a very reasonable and appealing model?

1. The first problem is the assumption of the elite-driven compromise. Two interrelated points arise here: the first is from the point of view of democratic theory when democracy is actually reduced

to elite power; and second is the question of predetermination of segments. This is a serious point because societies are very dynamic and, while one predetermined minority may be demographically declining, the other, not recognised, may be rising. So, while Slovenia awards vetoes to relatively small Hungarian and Italian minorities (in total less than 1 per cent of the population), the larger numbers of Muslims from Bosnia and Serbs that emigrated to Slovenia during the Yugoslav conflict (an estimated 10 per cent of the population) are not party to this agreement.[29]

2. Where and when consociational agreements are needed to bridge a deep ethnic cleavage(s), it is usually where and when it is perhaps too late to implement the consociational model or too early to expect such a pragmatic solution to historical injustice felt by ethnic groups. Either the animosity is too great to come to an agreement or one of the 'segments' is too dominant (numerically, militarily, internationally, or a combination of those) to agree on a reduced position within the state (for example, Israel, Estonia, Sri Lanka). The political culture of compromise does not grow on the battlefields of ethnic politics. Hence, even if we accept its inherently 'divisive' pragmatism, consociationalism, has a limited applicability. There is the case of Northern Ireland as a shining example of a peace process in a deeply divided society. Not only is the province still struggling with its consociationalism but, crucially, Northern Ireland is not an independent state but a province of the United Kingdom and, therefore, this example is too specific to imitate. I have awarded a considerable space to this consociational model because, having been developed for ideologically divided societies (religion or class), I believe that it is its limitations that illustrate very well the difficulties in seeking power-sharing arrangements in ethnically divided societies. So, in our enthusiasm for peaceful resolution to ethnic conflicts, it is vital to consider the background from which these conflicts arise. [30]

Non-discrimination and 'group rights'

Leaving this comparativist field of political science behind and moving to the question of the options and expectations of minorities and states vis-à-vis one another, I must stress that identity-related conflicts are on the rise. Ethnic groups are seceding from larger states; minorities and majorities clash over language rights, regional autonomy and political representation; and even in stable democracies there is heightened awareness about issues of religious freedom, education, land claims and immigration policies.[31] It seems that the end of the Cold War has released cultural identities from the confines of the ideological division of the world only to sharpen the divisions between ethnic and national groups within states. This situation was further aggravated by the momentous events of 9/11, the subsequent terrorist threats, and the war in Iraq and Afghanistan. All these events have contributed to an often unreasonable, if not a hysterical, conflation of ethno-cultural difference with security which has deteriorated inter-ethnic relations throughout the world. The rise of newly independent democracies in post-communist Europe has also added to questions about the expectation of democracy by minorities and majorities, both of which are in the process of asserting their rights. Neither democratic theory nor experience of established states has satisfactory answers regarding the relationship between ethnic groups and the state, for all our traditional understanding of democracy is actually based on the rights of the individual in relation to the state. It is becoming increasingly clear that individual rights and the notions of citizenship do not satisfy the need for recognition and accommodation of cultures, and that the state is expected to provide more than the freedom to belong, more than the possibility to practise one's religion, more than to tolerate a different understanding of individuality and community, and much more than the right to practise and experience one's culture in private. Namely, the state is expected to create conditions conducive to the maintenance of minority cultures which stretches the premise of liberal democracy ever further.

Removing assimilation from the repertoire of the political unity-seeking options, there are broadly two other options. First, a 'non-discrimination' principle by which the state is neutral and whereby cultural diversity is not a matter of public policy but remains firmly in the private sphere. The second option is to draw ethno-cultural identity into the public sphere and make the protection and the promotion of 'group rights' matters of public policy.[32] Both models face innumerable problems. The 'non-discrimination' paradigm is a claim of most liberal-democratic states, except that there is no such thing as a neutral state; most states promote their official, thus dominant, culture but some do it to a greater degree than others which does not make the latter neutral. States are a result of either a historical contingency or national self-determination but none begins with identity *tabula rasa* and, in nearly all cases, the foundations of what will become the official culture of the state exist prior to the inclusion of minority cultures. All state symbols, official language(s), public holidays, history books, monuments, and all other attributes of national identity are rooted in this dominant culture (with possibly the notable exception of New Zealand where the indigenous Maori culture has been included in national symbols to a greater extent than elsewhere). In the case of ex-colonial powers, these symbols and the national story are not just not neutral, they can be offensive to many ethnic groups. The more democratic a 'non-discrimination' state is, the more allowances it will make and depending on the history of its peoples, it will have developed over the time certain official rulings by which certain cultures, usually religions, can be practised. For example, in the United Kingdom, the Sikh turban has been incorporated into the police and other uniforms. The problem here is twofold: the increased diversity demands ever greater number of exceptions and produces inconsistent and incomprehensible legislation that, while still leaving minorities dissatisfied, alienates the dominant population who feel that their own culture is being eroded.

On the other hand, the 'group rights' model, while not very welcome by states generally, is faced with a difficulty to specify groups and decide the extent of protection. Moreover, the protection of a group may conflict with liberal individual rights and often even against the law of the state. One could argue that this is a question of common sense and that people choose whether or not they live by the strict rules of their community, and that if they need protection from the way of life subscribed to by the traditions of their own community, the state is there to protect them under normal law. For example, there is a substantial difference between accepting the tradition of arranged marriages among more or less consenting adults still prevalent among many ethnic communities (Muslim, Hindu, Jews) and a practice of underage forced marriages which is, and should be, in contravention of human rights and against the law. In practice, we actually end up with a continuum between a minimalist 'non-discrimination' model, which is becoming less and less acceptable, and more robust versions that end up with 'groups rights' in which some ethnic groups have negotiated better terms than others. This is not a question of cynicism but a reasonable assessment of the current minority provisions among liberal democracies.

Multicultural Britain

The nation state does not give up on its homogenising pretensions so easily, and the public policy reflects that position. There are, however, states that cannot pretend to be homogeneous because their very origins as modern states are based on immigration. Canada is such a country. Will Kymlicka[33] uses this example to point to differences between the current 'citizenship' debates in the United Kingdom and Canada. In Britain there is an ongoing debate about the justification of naturalisation tests for new citizens – the language tests, citizenship oaths, etc. While the British effort at the re-evaluation of citizenship is commendable in its pragmatic and sensitive approach, there is a number of minor differences that add up to a considerable difference:

1. Britain has a colonial history and therefore many aspects of such a test can be perceived by participants as betrayals of their own histories;

2. In Canada, dual citizenship and therefore the acceptance of non-exclusive dual affiliation are allowed while, in Britain, citizenship is perceived as a kind of reward instead of a beginning of what may be hoped for as growing civic affiliation which is not exclusive of other identities;

3. During the 'waiting' period, the legal position of non-citizens in Canada is less threatening and more welcoming: they are allowed to work, they can receive unemployment benefits; and, with the exception of voting rights, there are no social, political and economic stigmas attached to migrants.

This is not to say that the acquisition of citizenship is particularly difficult in Britain; on the contrary, but it is to say that Britain shares the anxiety about the changing character of national citizenship with the majority of nation states. The anxiety is actually understandable because, while minorities are ever clearer and more strident about their own expectations, the majorities are losing the previously unquestioned security of cultural dominance in their own state.

Tariq Modood[34] sheds some light on the further predicament of 'Britishness', this time in terms of what appears to be a rather exaggerated issue of 'British Muslims'. The integration of 'British Muslims' into British society has become a political issue since the attacks on the World Trade Center on 11 September 2001 and the July bombings in London in 2005. Muslims have lived in Britain for decades. Their way of life has not changed that much but their position in the society has changed dramatically and, therefore, their culture is under magnified scrutiny and accused of self-segregation and intransigence. One of the problems, and only one, is that Muslims are considered a religious minority and, while the United Kingdom is very generous in its attempts to accommodate ethnic minorities, its liberal tradition considers religion a strictly private matter. Islam is, in that sense, an alien culture because it seeks to regulate both the private and public lives of its members and does not recognise the liberal distinction between the state and the community. While there is a considerable effort to achieve 'racial equality', Muslims do not quite fit because, in law, they are not considered an ethnic group and they are clearly not a 'race' for there are many Muslims who classify themselves as 'white'. As a heterogeneous group, they are disadvantaged in law when compared, for example, with Jews and Sikhs who have negotiated an ethnic label that protects their religious practices and generally raises less anxiety among the British public.

This case, and there are many others, points towards the complexity of the multiculturalism debate which is decreasing in popularity because the half-hearted efforts to implement it have not delivered the desired results – not in terms of equality and not in terms of societal cohesion. Multiculturalism cannot mean the right to assimilate to the dominant culture in the public sphere while keeping the difference safely tucked into the private sphere. It must mean the right to have the difference recognised publicly and supported in the public and in the private spheres.[35] In simple terms, it means that the toleration of minorities and peaceful coexistence are not enough to call it a meaningful multicultural society because it is just a minority-friendlier version of a neutral state.

Bikhu Parekh draws a relevant distinction between multicultural as a 'description of the fact' and multiculturalist as a 'normative response' to that fact.[36] Normative response then, over and above some institutional compromises that revise the traditional understanding of the state, politics and religion in the view of the changed composition of the citizenry, requires the dominant population to view minorities as a part of the nation's identity and future. When it comes to future, the acceptance of minorities as a part of the nation is not merely a question of morality and norms, it is a question of accepting that, without minorities, there is no future, not economically and not in terms of security. The issue of citizenship needs redeveloping in view of this reality and in view of the fact that – and this is difficult for majorities to accept – many minorities and migrants will never become 'nationals' in the traditional sense because they do not wish to, and the ties to their home countries are too strong. This is the faith, the challenge, but also the beauty of the contemporary nation state.

Multinational states, multi-ethnic polities and all forms of settings where *demos* and the nation do not overlap, democracy in any substantive form worth imitation depend largely on policies that 'grant inclusive and equal citizenship and that give all citizens a common "roof" of state-mandated and enforced rights'.[37] How difficult it is, how complex and slow in the implementation, and how intricate in terms of political imagination and lengthy in terms of societal embeddedness are other questions, but they are not questions of whether they are right and possible. We really must reject the idea that democracy should in any way depend on the ethnic composition of the state. When viewed from this perspective, our contemporary nation state bears less and less relation to its nineteenth-century ideal, and the challenges it faces find fewer and fewer answers in theorising about its origins.

Notes

1. I have borrowed this expression from Oren Yiftachel.
2. Migdal (2004), 'State Building and the Non-Nation-State', p. 22.
3. Ibid., p. 24.
4. Brubaker (1996), *Nationalism Reframed*, p. 5.
5. Özkirimli (2005), *Contemporary Debates on Nationalism*, pp. 1–2.
6. Brubaker, *Nationalism Reframed*, p. 5.
7. For a full discussion of forms and methods of homogenising states see Peleg (2007), *Democratizing the Hegemonic State: Political Transformation in the Age of Identity*.
8. Harris (2002), *Nationalism and Democratisation*, p. 33.
9. For example: Harris, *Nationalism and Democratisation*; Peleg, *Democratizing the Hegemonic State*; Snyder (2000), *From Voting to Violence*.
10. Migdal, 'State Building and the Non-Nation-State', pp. 29–33.
11. From the 1990 declaration of the leading democratic party, Verejnost' Proti Násiliu/ Public Against Violence, which was instrumental in bringing democracy to Slovakia.
12. Harris, *Nationalism and Democratisation*, p. 113.
13. Žižek (1997), 'Multiculturalism, or the Cultural Logic of Multinational Capitalism', p. 42.
14. Žižek, 'Multiculturalism, or the Cultural Logic of Multinational Capitalism', p. 42, for the distinction between the primary (primordial, immediate) identity and the secondary (nation state, citizenship) and the tension the reassertion of the former causes in today's world.
15. Brubaker and Cooper (2000), 'Beyond "identity"', p. 1. This article also provides an excellent review of literature about 'identity'.
16. Ibid., p. 34.
17. Kedourie (1960), *Nationalism*, p. 118.
18. Brubaker and Cooper, 'Beyond "identity"', p. 14.
19. See also Moore (2001), 'Normative justification for liberal nationalism: justice democracy and national identity', pp. 2–19.
20. Mason (1999), 'Political Community, Liberal-Nationalism, and the Ethics of Assimilation', p. 263. See also Moore, 'Normative justification for liberal nationalism: justice, democracy and national identity', pp. 2–19.
21. Miller (2000), *Citizenship and National Identity*, pp. 125–41. See also Miller (1995), *On Nationality*; and Tamir (1993), *Liberal Nationalism*.
22. Mason, 'Political Community, Liberal-Nationalism, and the Ethics of Assimilation', p. 272.
23. Sasse and Thielemann (2005), 'A Research Agenda for the Study of Migrants and Minorities in Europe', pp. 655–60; and Harris (2007) 'Moving Politics Beyond the State: The Hungarian Minority in Slovakia', p. 44 and note 2.
24. Peleg, *Democratizing the Hegemonic State: Political Transformation in the Age of Identity*, pp. 39–44.
25. The points made here are inspired by Michael Keating's paper 'Unionism, constitu-

tional change and independent Scotland', given at the conference 'Beyond the Nation?' in Belfast, 12–14 September 2007.

26. Linz and Stepan (1996), *Problems of Democratic Transition and Consolidation*, p. 429.
27. Lijphart (1995), 'Self-Detemination versus Pre-determination of Ethnic Minorities in Power-Sharing Systems', p. 275.
28. Lijphart (1968), *The Politics of Accommodation: Pluralism and Democracy in the Netherlands*, Berkeley: University of California Press. For a more complete bibliography of Lijphart's writing see Lijphart, 'Self-Detemination versus Pre-determination of Ethnic Minorities in Power-Sharing Systems'.
29. Harris, *Nationalism and Democratisation*, notes 40–6, pp. 180–1.
30. Peleg, *Democratizing the Hegemonic State: Political Transformation in the Age of Identity*, p. 38.
31. Kymlicka (1995), *The Rights of Minority Cultures*, p. 1.
32. Ibid., p. 9.
33. Kymlicka (2003), 'Immigration, Citizenship, Multiculturalism: Exploring the Links', pp. 195–208.
34. Modood (2003), 'Muslims and Politics of Difference', pp. 100–15.
35. Ibid., p. 105.
36. Parekh (2000), *Rethinking Multiculturalism*, pp. 6–8.
37. Linz and Stepan (1996), *Problems of Democratic Transition and Consolidation*, p. 33.

CHAPTER FOUR

The Fall and the Rise: Post-Communism and Nationalism

This chapter picks up the relationship between nationalism and democracy from Chapter 1 and argues that the early years of post-communism in Eastern and Central Europe showed us the ambiguity of this relationship in all its theoretical depth, historical compatibility and empirical evidence. I also argue that post-communism should have sharpened our understanding of nationalism as an '-ism' that can be very effective among societies experiencing a dramatic systemic change: collapsing ideological framework; failing states; repositioning of geographical boundaries and the consequent reconfiguration of inter-ethnic relations which necessitates a redefinition of collective identities; the total overhaul of socio-economic relations followed by a temporary redefinition of individual identities; fear of the future and haunting from the past.

It remains a mystery why the disintegration of Yugoslavia (which I will use as the case study of post-communist nationalism in this chapter) has not alerted politicians to the dangers of the possibilities of ethnic conflict connected to the dismantling of totalitarian regimes, and not prepared the international community for the disastrous consequences that followed the fall of Saddam's Iraq. We have seen the euphoria of falling partition walls and statues of dictators in the 1989 'revolutions' only to be shocked at the vehemence with which post-euphoric people, overwhelmed by new realities, attack their neighbours. Is the state of unpreparedness a consequence of not accepting that transitions to democracy, even if home grown (let alone foreign imposed), are full of pitfalls, and that the negotiation of the unknown is full of unexpected developments? Or, indeed, is it the undiminished belief – against all evidence – that the possibility of democracy unites people and that nationalism and democracy are not incompatible ideologies? The subject of this chapter is first to explain the salience of nationalism in the region after the fall of communist regimes and to highlight the most significant factors that contributed to its salience. Implicit in this chapter are the links we can make between post-communist and contemporary international developments with the fall of other authoritarian regimes. In the concluding section of the chapter, I shall argue that post-communist nationalism, just as post-communism itself, is a transitional period with its own dynamics which incorporate many features of the classical nationalism of the nineteenth century with some new features, specific to democratisation and the near simultaneous process of European integration. Examples throughout are drawn from the countries of the region but particularly from the disintegration of Yugoslavia and Czechoslovakia.[1] As we are witnessing the struggles to establish democracy in Iraq and Afghanistan, a study of sociopolitical and historical context within which these transitions take place seems more timely than ever. This is the reason why post-communist transition is included in this book about nationalism.

The end of communism in Eastern and Central Europe (1989–91) ushered in a period of intense national reawakening with dramatic consequences for nations and people. By post-communism I am referring to the state of affairs after the fall of the communist regimes in Eastern and Central Europe only. I shall therefore refrain from discussing the changes in existing communist countries, such as China,[2] North Korea and Cuba. The main features of the European- (Soviet-) style communist regimes were mainly: (a) supreme authority and the unchallenged hegemony of the Communist Party; (b) a high degree of centralisation and discipline within that organisation with no space given to intra-party debate; (c) state ownership of the means of production (with some exceptions made for agricultural, but not industrial, production in some countries, that is, Poland, Hungary and Yugoslavia).[3] Eastern and Central Europe (henceforth ECE) is not strictly a geographic area but tends to be synonymous with post-communist European states.[4]

The establishment of new successor states from the disintegrated communist federations of the Soviet Union, Yugoslavia and Czechoslovakia meant also that a deep re-examination of the relationship between all national groups in the region was necessary – and in some cases still continuing. This salience of identity at the centre of political life, which was at the same time focused on the transition from communism to democracy, led some political theorists such as Ghia Nodia (currently the Minister of Education and Science in the Georgian government) to controversial statements that 'democracy never exists without nationalism' and that, if Ernest Gellner says that 'nationalism engenders nations', then it is equally true that 'democratic transitions engender nations'.[5] This statement will be challenged on its basic assumption that democracy and nationalism are mutually supportive but first, I would like to reiterate that Gellner's main argument is not about nationalism as an emancipatory movement but about nationalism as a corollary of industrialisation.

It cannot be denied, though, that some twenty-eight new states were born out of the disintegration of the Soviet Union, Yugoslavia and Czechoslovakia, which gives a degree of credibility to Nodia's view and that, in my comparative study of the newly nationalising and democratising Slovakia and Slovenia, I have also argued the inherent link between nationalism and democracy. My argument, however, was and remains that nationalism became an integral part of post-communist transitions to democracy for many time- and place-specific reasons which will be discussed in this chapter. The mobilising and energising capacities of nationalism, however, while conducive to the initial transitory pressures of societies struggling to shake off the 'old' system, are also challenging to a sustained democratisation, particularly in multinational settings. Beissinger goes so far as to argue that, while a strong sense of national identity or, in his account, ethnic nationalism produced 'unambiguously successful democracies' in Estonia, Latvia and Lithuania, the 'absence of a strong national identity against Soviet rule' produced an authoritarian Belarus.[6] Whether the ethnic Russians in Estonia perceive their adopted country to be a successful democracy and whether the Hungarians in Slovakia feel that the strong sense of Slovak ethnic nationalism has brought democracy to Slovakia are questionable. On the other hand, we must concede that the 1989 'revolutions' had a 'nationalist' element in seeking to regain political sovereignty out of the Soviet sphere of influence and popular sovereignty out of an oppressive and undignified political system. At the same time, it is foolish to sideline the Yugoslav conflict as an exception rather than as an example of post-communist ethnic mobilisation. Thus, the task of this chapter is to explore the reasons for the intensification of nationalism in post-communist societies and the extent to which nationalism is an 'indispensable element' of democracy in general,[7] or is it merely a necessary and logical concomitant of post-communist transitions?

The principal argument here is that democratisation contributes to nationalist mobilisation but that its intensity in post-communist societies depended largely on the legacy of the previous regime and the events surrounding the end of it; in the newly independent states this includes the extrication from the communist federation. If the conclusion argues that nationalism became a logical concomitant of transition to democracy, it is not because democracy needs nationalism but because a weak democracy is too weak to legitimise the enormous task of the transition in new states – post-communist states were all new states, if not in terms of a newly acquired independence then in terms of newly gained political and international sovereignty.

From authoritarianism to nationalism

The toppling of the Berlin Wall and the subsequent fall of communist regimes led to enthusiastic comparisons of the '1989 revolutions' with the French Revolution (1789). If we take Fred Hallidays' definition of revolution as a 'major political and social transformation in the context of a contradictory modernity involving mass participation and the aspiration to establish a radically different society',[8] then there is some relevance in comparing 1789 to 1989 because both events were of historic proportions in the consequences they carried for societies, international politics, and political theory for that matter. Yet, the 1989 revolutions are associated rather with 'the end',[9] than with 'the beginning': the repeated 'endism' referred either to the now infamous 'end of history' or the 'return' to independence, a common European home or democracy. All these claims can be disputed historically and ideologically. Most post-communist states in their current form did not exist before they became communist, or if they did, with the exception of Czechoslovakia, they were not democratic and, moreover, the pluralist democracy and market economy they adopted were not new either. The 'revolutionary' character lay in the inauguration of a new social order and the removal of the Leninist system based on ideological uniformity, coercion and suppression, possibly for ever.

Political scientists in the early 1990s sought the comparison between post-communist transitions and other transitions to democracy from other authoritarian regimes (southern Europe and Latin America) in order to draw out common problems of democratisation processes.[10] While it is important to be aware of common issues facing all democratisation processes, for the understanding of the societies undergoing this process, including the anticipation of problems that may arise, it is more important to examine how the previous regime operated and which historical resources it tapped into.

The simultaneous transition to pluralist democracy and the market economy has specific implications for democracy and the society which go beyond the creation of a whole new social order, including the formation of a new middle class and a transition from a relatively socially equal society to a system of an increased social inequality.[11] The communist parties' political monopoly and complete penetration into the private sphere deprived the populations of the distinction between private and public and of the ability even to define their interests. There is a reason why I am emphasising the lack of political thinking and experience in post-communist societies because, as will become apparent, national identity was probably one interest that was easily identified and articulated among the many personal and collective identities and interests that needed definition and articulation. This is a fundamental difference between post-communist transitions and transitions in southern Europe and Latin America. The relevance of the 'national' issue was further compounded by the second crucial difference, namely the simultaneity of the transition with national liberation. This was unavoidable because democratisation could not be divorced from national liberation from Soviet influence, and national liberation, combined with democratisation, for reasons discussed below led to more national mobilisation.

The most distinguishing characteristic of post-communist transitions is the merging of popular and national sovereignty into one process which was not too dissimilar to other periods of national reawakenings, for example, in 1848 and 1918 in Europe and partially during all the decolonisation processes elsewhere. Hence, I would argue that the comparison with southern Europe and Latin America, while useful in sharpening certain common features of democratisation processes, is less meaningful for drawing out conclusions about these transitions.

Every time nations seek liberation the assumption is that the establishment of the nation state is the best and the only framework for the exercise of democracy. Therefore, the linkage between democracy, as the most desired form of government, and the nation state, as the best framework for it, had to bring national self-determination and post-communist transition together. In the successor states of the multinational federations, democratisation, in addition to the reconfiguration of state's boundaries and state's identity, also entailed the carving out of a new international position and, most significantly, the decisions about who 'the people' who constitute the new state are, and what should the role of the state be in their lives. The previous chapters have already spelled out how the interpretation and the meaning of national community affect politics and democracy in the state, which is not to say that there is a causal relationship between ethnic homogeneity and democracy. Empirically, it would appear that transition processes fared better in ethnically more homogeneous societies but the fluidity of these transitions also means that even this well-established assumption that it is easier to achieve democratic consensus in less ethnically diverse societies, can be refuted. Ethnic diversity makes the decision-making process perhaps more difficult but, for example, Romania, Slovakia and Estonia, with major ethnic cleavages, eventually produced relatively stable democracies. Similarly, while fighting a separatist war with Chechnya, Russia has not descended into the ethnic conflicts that, given the huge ethnic diversity, could have been expected while, on the other hand, relatively homogeneous Poland tends to experience nationalist mobilisation periodically. Other examples from both inside and outside the ECE, such as Turkey and Spain which manage the ethnic division better than Egypt and Lebanon, show that ethnic homogeneity matters in democracy but seldom directly.[12]

Thus, on the issue of comparison with transitions from other authoritarian regimes, I would like to suggest that the strong ethnic division of societies and the changing status of ethnic groups, combined with the history of the Ottoman and Austro-Hungarian Empires, the character of the previous totalitarian regimes, and

103

the intense involvement of the international community (whether in the form of the EU in the ECE, or the 'coalition of the willing' in Iraq) make the comparison with current Middle Eastern transitions more knowledge-inducing than the comparison with southern Europe and Latin America. I am not in a position to embark on such a comparison here but it is certainly an area of research that should be undertaken.

The argument of the book and of this chapter is that it is the politicisation of ethnicity, rather than the fact of ethnicity, that affects democracy. Very soon after the collapse of communist regimes it became obvious that the simultaneous transition in political, social and economic spheres would trigger a fourth process involving a major 'national' revival. Not only because the end of the Soviet external empire meant the restoration of national sovereignty and, in a number of cases, the establishment of new nation states – often as the culmination of historically arrested national development as in the cases of Slovakia, Croatia, Armenia and Slovenia – but because the national revival required the renegotiation of inter-ethnic relations in the new conditions of political pluralism and the altered status between new majorities and new minorities. We were observing, and still are in the current conflict in Georgia,[13] a truly unprecedented nature of post-communist transitions where the reconfiguration of geopolitical space and the new institutions instigated inter-ethnic dynamics far beyond those which theories of nationalism or democracy could have prepared us for.

In connection with the rise of nationalism and identity-related conflicts in post-communist transitions, there is a number of idiosyncratic factors but also some universal ones which could be applicable to other regions in the world. The newly expanded political arena, in the form of new political parties, free elections and the freedom of the media, requires competition for resources and voters' constituencies. Nationalism appeared to be an important asset in those circumstances on two related levels. First, the collapse of the existing state power and the weakness of the new institutions left an emptiness in the political heart of societies seeking to make sense of the new situation; one identity, now furnished with a new popular sovereignty that remained fairly fixed and coherent and, moreover, was uncontaminated by the 'foreign' imposition, was the national identity and therefore could easily fill the political vacuum. Second, the injustices of the past which could be aired as never before, combined with the insecurities of the present, turned 'the nation' into a refuge, and ethnic identity became an effective tool for new and old elites to mobilise voters' support. Such mobilisation is an obstacle to democracy because it is inherently divisive and exploitative of the turmoil from which it arises.

There cannot be much doubt that democratisation creates turmoil, unsettles societies, offers possibilities for some and jeopardises others and, by implication, creates conditions conducive to ethnic mobilisation.[14] I am stressing the societal conditions in the early stages of democratisation following the breakdown of existing ideological, institutional and identificational frameworks because elites can intensify the ethnic mobilisation by exploiting these conditions for their own political gain. Their influence should not be overstated, though: it is the conditions and the political and historical context of the society that allow for democratisation to be overwhelmed by nationalist rhetoric. On the other hand, democratisation requires a huge effort on the part of the population and its elites; it requires legitimacy to push through reforms, sometimes at high financial costs; it requires solidarity and faith in the future, energy and popular support. Nationalism, with its connection to popular sovereignty, can legitimise actions that otherwise could falter; it offers a vision where the future looks uncertain and creates a sense of collective endeavour. Thus, post-communist nationalism was a challenge to democratisation but also the energiser of democratisation. This duality of nationalism has a historical legacy in ECE. As I have already discussed in Chapter 1, in the nineteenth century when Slovaks, Croats, Poles, Czechs, Serbs and Slovenes tried to liberate themselves from the autocratic empires, their only identity was ethnic but the nationalism that drove their revolutionary struggle would not have been called illiberal ethnic nationalism because nationalism was associated with liberation rather than with exclusion. In post-communism a similar situation appeared to emerge: strong ethnic overtones combined with democratisation not only because of historical antecedents but because, at the time when democratisation required compromise, pragmatism and inclusion and when states were disintegrating, civic affiliations were unavailable and too weak to appeal to.

The important lessons from the collapse of communism should be that, in conditions of historically complex ethnic relationships, (1) institutional breakdown is likely to be followed by a societal disintegration along ethnic lines because (2), when civic affiliations cease to function as rallying calls for unity, ethnic affiliations will replace them at the centre of the political stage. Hence, while the salience of nationalism in post-communist transitions can be explained, its contribution to democratisation remains limited – and that applies in nearly all contemporary democratisation processes.

Too many pasts to reckon with

Nowhere could the poetic question 'is not the pastness of the past the more profound, the more legendary, the more immediately it falls before the present?'[15] be more pertinently asked than in connection with post-communism. The past in post-communist societies was many pasts and all conspired in affecting its character: the pre-communist past, communism itself and the immediate end of it. Thus far I have established the reasons for the presence of nationalism in post-communist transitions. But, post-communism does not last forever, and ECE countries are no longer post-communist; some are consolidated democracies and the new members of the EU, and the rest are struggling democracies at various levels of consolidation and regression; some are more nationalist than others but all seek European integration and none seeks to return to communism. And yet, it is nearly impossible to think about post-communism without thinking about the catastrophe of the Yugoslav conflict and the depths of human tragedy that nationalism can lead to. So, how do we explain the intensification of nationalism in post-communism more concretely than in the first section of this chapter? And what is the value of this forthcoming exercise when communism is unlikely ever to return? The answer to the second question has been partially answered already. Moreover, while there are ethnic conflicts in the world and while there are minorities struggling with oppressive states, all insight into the conditions in which these conflicts have arisen in recent European history are relevant to the contemporary debates about nationalism. The rest of this chapter is concerned with the first question – why?

Post-communism may have been a unique historical experiment but the politics of nationalism are universal. Therefore lessons should be learned and comparisons can be made in our endless effort to construct stable political communities. In my previous work on post-communism, I have argued that from the national pasts of post-communist countries derive a number of mutually aggravating factors which shaped the role of nationalism in those societies. I identified: historical animosity, communist nationality policies, communist ideology, elite competition and the altered relationships between majorities and minorities as analytically most important.[16] Here, with the benefit of a number of years of reflection, I shall offer a revised version, still arguing that post-communist nationalism arose from a number of simultaneous processes triggered by democratisation in a setting where each factor and process by itself would not have been sufficient but that the combination of a number of them was.

Historical developments

I shall not discuss the 'ancient hatreds' thesis which was commonly employed by western analysts, journalists and observers in the early years of post-communism as a way of explaining the rising tensions, mostly with reference to Yugoslavia. Not only is such a view, that presents a large part of Europe as a simmering cauldron of anachronistic hatreds an oversimplification (often historically erroneous),[17] it does not contribute to a greater knowledge of the conditions from which post-communist nationalism arose.

The most important consideration is the relationship between the state and the nation which has been discussed at length in the previous chapters and hence needs only a quick reiteration here. The nation state's role in people's understanding of politics is as the main and indispensable provider of economic and physical security. Post-communist nationalism flared up, without exception, when and where the old states collapsed and new ones were not able to provide either security adequately. While most ECE countries were very quick in adapting to the reduced role of the state in a contemporary politically integrating Europe, the initial stage of post-communism confirmed the significance of the state and its inherent link to nationalism. Here I would like to stress the remaining relevance of John Breuilly's theory of nationalism as politics.

The legitimacy of the state depends on much more than its performance because all aspects of government, how the state is governed and by whom were exacerbated by an extra dimension – who constitutes the state? While politicians and the populations are seeking reassurance, both rely on the nation, the former for loyalty and the latter for supposed privileges. All this was happening in conditions where the new rules of the game were not established yet, where journalists were not trained sufficiently in ethics, where the population confused freedom of speech with the incitement of hatred and where old elites who were used to the monopolisation of power were still operating, usually under the new national label. The extent to which history can be manipulated has been amply demonstrated by the extreme case of the Serbia–Kosovo conflict in which Serbian nationalist elites used events from 600 years ago to legitimise the oppression of ethnic Albanians in Kosovo.[18]

There are two further points to add to the link between state and nationalism that are relevant in the present context. First is the matter of 'sequence'[19] – what comes first, the state or nationalism? When, under the impact of the French Revolution and industrialisation, nationhood became the basis for political organisation and group identification, Eastern Europe was divided and ruled by the Romanov, Ottoman and Habsburg Empires. While some Western European states were already in existence, the statehood aspirations of Eastern Europeans, if existent at all, were crushed time after time. The implication of this is twofold: the emergence of nation states in Eastern and Central Europe was, and remains, a belated process associated with conflicts between national groups which are further exacerbated by the changing status of previously dominant nationalities in the new states. The consequences of the latter are very significant for minority relations in post-communist states whereby demands of the minority, perceived as historically hostile to the newly dominant nationality, are often treated with suspicion. Consequently, the minority issue, which should be a part of normal democratic politics within a multi-ethnic state, assumes an unnatural role associated with issues of the state's integrity and security[20] which increases the overall perception of mistrust among national groups. This has long been the case, for example, of the Hungarian minorities in Slovakia and Romania.

The second point also relates to the belated nation-building process. The nation-building elites of non-ruling nationalities, who were fighting imperial rule for representative rights, presented these rights in 'national' terms for the lack of any other political tradition (for example, liberal). Hence social progress in ECE is also traditionally associated with 'national' struggle. The Czech historian Miroslav Hroch (see also Chapter 2) argues that post-communist nationalism should be seen as analogous to nineteenth-century national movements.[21] According to him, the similarity lies mostly in the rapid change in the ruling elite and the formation of the nation state simultaneously with the new capitalist order; thus, with the added democratisation process. Another similarity to the nineteenth century, concerns the emphasis on language as an expression of independence for example; following the independence of Croatia, the Croat language was divorced from Serbo-Croat as was used (written in Cyrillic) in the former Yugoslavia; Moldavia, too, reclaimed the Latin alphabet; the Baltic states have made their languages preconditions for attaining citizenship, and the Slovak language is strictly guarded by a Language Law.

The histories of Eastern European societies are full of national frustrations and situations where, particularly in the twentieth century, the frequent wars and changes of regimes, accompanied by major shifts in borders and populations, made human destinies significantly affected by their collective identity. As an illustration, let me provide a brief litany of human misery connected to ethnicity in ECE. The Versailles treaty (1919) 'rewarded' the victors of World War I. The new successor states that replaced the dynastic empires were actually smaller versions of the empires they seceded from. The new states incorporated 'beneficiaries' of the new order (Czechs, Slovaks, Croats, Serbs, Slovenes, Bosnians and so on) and other apprehensive minorities of the 'disadvantaged' (such as the Hungarians and Germans). Hungary lost two-thirds of its territory to the new Czechoslovakia, Yugoslavia and Romania; this led to an attempt for a territorial recovery during World War II and the annexation of the subcarpathian region of Czechoslovakia. Stalin's and Hitler's rule meant that there was another major geopolitical shift, accompanied by the brutal methods of genocide and expulsions. Post-1945 Czechoslovakia lost subcarpathia to the Soviet Union (80,000 people); 140 000 Jews perished in the concentration camps; and three million Germans and Hungarians were expelled from Czechoslovakia in the period 1945–8. Poland lost nearly all of its Jewish population, and approximately three million people were involved in repatriations between the Soviet Union and Germany. This permanent sense of ethnic insecurity is only a short step from the radicalisation of politics along national lines. Where ethnicity matters – and we have established that in ECE it does – history matters, too, for they are uncomfortably connected. There is a difference, however, between a historical perspective on the mobilising potential of nationalism and the simplicity of historical animosities view because the latter can be minimised as much as it can be exploited – the success of some states in the region in curbing ethnic disharmony and consolidating their democracies to the point of becoming members of the European Union supports this suggestion.

The irony of communist nationality policies

The disintegrations of the Soviet Union, Yugoslavia and Czechoslovakia are undisputed cases of heightened national sentiments during the communist period and expressed in separatist tendencies in the period shortly after. If the national banner replaced the banner of 'brotherhood and unity', the questions then must be why and what were the theoretical assumptions, institutional arrangements and practices which regulated national policies in multi-ethnic communist states and the extent to which they contributed to the subsequent disintegration of these states? The first thing to convey is the irony of it all because the communist nationality policies were designed for precisely the opposite reason: to withstand national cleavages. Yet, communism dedicated to internationalism seems to have inadvertently fostered policies which made an independent nation the obvious option after communism.

This is truly a case of a self-fulfilling prophecy because everything that failed to fall within the framework of the party diktat was seen as divisive and therefore nationalistic. So, for example, when Tito removed the Croat reformist leadership (1971) which sought to loosen the command system in politics and in the economy, he justified the action by accusing them of divisive nationalism. The same applied to communist show trials in Czechoslovakia (known as the 'Slánsky Trial', 1952) in which a number of high- and middle-ranking communists (including the Party Secretary, Rudolf Slánsky, and the Foreign Secretary, Vladimír Clementis) were executed and many arrested (among them Gustáv Husák who, after his rehabilitation, became the president of the post-1968, post-Soviet-invasion Czechoslovakia) on a charge of 'bourgeois nationalism'[22] which was considered treason in the Stalinist Czechoslovakia.

The communist federations, first the Soviet Union and then, with some modifications, Yugoslavia and, after 1968, Czechoslovakia, were built on the principle of ethno-national territorial autonomy. Federalism is associated with deeper democracy and decentralisation but the communist federal arrangements sought exactly the opposite: a more unitary and a more controlling one-party state. Arguably, without democracy, federalism is unsustainable in the long term and, as communism demonstrated, can be a basis for national mobilisation. The fundamental principle of communist federalism was the 'linkage'[23] of ethnicity, territory and administration; it is obvious that the only attribute missing in this nearly sovereign territory is the most important one – political autonomy.

Ethnicity became institutionalised on a group level by the various forms of territorial administration (from districts to semi-autonomous regions, to republics, depending on the size of the population and other less transparent reasons) and on an individual level by the clear distinction between state affiliation, thus citizenship, and nationality (for example, citizenship – Czechoslovak or Yugoslav; nationality – Slovak, Czech, Magyar, Croat, and so on). This distinction is crucial because, paradoxically, having to mention your ethnicity in every document – and there were many documents to fill under communist bureaucracy – and being permanently reminded of your ethnic background made ethnicity a legitimate form of identity while officially its importance was denied in the name of the socialist 'proletariat of the world unite' rhetoric. In long term, nations under communism were given the chance to enhance their national consciousnesses through education and through the development of indigenous elites. The denial was at the level of political expression, and thus this schizophrenic attitude to nationalism kept national identities alive and growing parallel with the shrinking of communist identities.

Indigenous elites were fundamental to the maintenance of the centralised communist state which relied on them to contain national grievances, particularly in highly decentralised Yugoslavia where, when the rule weakened, these national elites were ready to take control. The cases of Slovenia and Croatia, which directly affected the break-up of Yugoslavia, demonstrate that the communist Yugoslav system did not prevent their elites from growing in confidence and influence, and independence from the centre. The existence of these federal units with their own federal administrations also explains the speed and relative ease with which, for example, Czechoslovakia fractured. It is nevertheless essential to remember that behind federalism hid a totalitarian state with different levels of authoritarianism that employed various methods, including the manipulation of the nationality question, in order to maintain its grip.

Post-communist elites in defence of the nation

Thus far, the discussion has focused on the past but, as I suggested before, the transition project itself was a major stimulus to the increase of nationalism during post-communism. Rogers Brubaker tells us that 'far from solving the region's national question the most recent nationalising reconfiguration of political space has only reframed the national question, recast it in a new form'.[24] Hence, I am shifting my argument that nationalism, while not unavoidable, was nevertheless the likeliest concomitant of post-communist transitions because the democratisation process itself contributed to homogenising policies, particularly in the newly nationalising states.[25] The elites of these new states conceived of them as nation states of and for particular ethno-cultural nations but, in reality, they are 'incomplete'[26] in the sense that many of their populations belong to other ethno-cultural groups, or nations, often across borders.

This situation prompts national elites to an excessive promotion of the nation in an attempt either to compensate for the incompleteness of the new nation state or to rectify the past by settling old scores in a new setting. Usually, it takes the form of politics seeking linguistic, economic, cultural, demographic and political benefits for their national group – all of which stand for ethnic politics. Ethnic politics and democratic politics tend to pull in opposite directions: the former appeals to collective identity and descent, the latter to individual choices and political participation. Ideally, there shouldn't be any tension, for collective identity does not exclude individual choice and political participation has little to do with descent. By the elites who tended to dominate post-communist politics I mean political decision-makers; in other words, who rules, who decides and who gets what in terms of resources, both human and material, on behalf of a group, in this case an ethnic group.[27] Post-communist elites were more than channels for negotiating state authority and people's interests, they were the true shapers of societal consciousness in these transitions because, significantly, in post-communist transitions, the radical change of the system failed to bring a radical change in elite structure.[28] Many of those 'recycled' elites used nationalist rhetoric to bridge the credibility gap between themselves and the population. The collectivist, black-and-white, populist and enemy-identifying rhetoric came easily to post-communists; politicians were well trained in this style, and populations were responsive after decades of having heard little else.

Democracy needs a popular base and politicians need voters. The existence of ethnic diversity means that ethnic identity is an easy way to determine one's constituency for those elites who choose to play the 'ethnic card'. Except that nothing is so simple in post-communism. By itself, the increased political competition would not have been a sufficient reason for the identification of political interest along ethnic lines. The added dimension was that, once the opposition to the communist regime ceased to be a mobilising factor, the other political interests were not so clear. One would be well advised not to explain all post-communist nationalism by the ideological vacuum, but the lack of identification with political parties is an important consideration because, unlike in the West, the left–right spectrum made little sense in societies emerging from a perceived classlessness. Hence, economic and all other interests were often articulated through national rhetoric rather than in individual terms.

Two considerations arise from the significant role of elites in post-communist societies. When democratic values and norms are thin on the ground, the newly opened political arena encourages political elites competing for influence and struggling with challenges of democratisation to politicise ethnicity; and they are often not scrupulous in the methods they use. In the forthcoming case study I argue that Milošević's greatest crime was that, instead of using his powerful position to calm the rising nationalist tensions in the rapidly disintegrating Yugoslavia, he in fact chose to exacerbate them in order to shore up his position. Having said that, elite-driven nationalist mobilisation also depends on the resonance their claims find in the population which is also not innocent in the whole process of mounting tensions. What we have observed in nearly all post-communist states were the heightened nationalist appeals wherever ethnic differences could be effectively used to secure the popular base. This dynamic leads to the last major factor contributing to the intensification of nationalism in post-communism, that of the increased number of ethnic actors, thus more elites appealing to and on behalf of a more divided audience.

New states create new minorities

The complex interplay of democratisation and post-communist nationalism culminated in the disintegration of multinational states which opened the way to more nationalist mobilisation by restructuring a number of national questions. Simply put, new states create new minorities.[29] I am suggesting that the disintegration of larger states unsettles the inter-ethnic relations within and beyond the new successor states. The intensification of nationalism in the new nationalising states intensifies the insecurity among minorities and brings in the involvement of the minorities' homelands whose elites invariably, when given the opportunity, exploit the position of their ethnic kin across the border for purposes of political competition. The experience shows that nationalising elites in new states hardly ever seek to reassure minorities about their new position prior to the implementation of policies that are threatening, as they hardly ever consult the ethnic reconfiguration in the immediate region with the neighbouring states. In reference to the post-communist exacerbation of nationalism, Rogers Brubaker developed the theory of 'triadic nexus' which is the dynamic between at least three nationalisms: that of nationalising states, minorities, and their 'external' homelands.[30]

The break-up of Czechoslovakia seemed baffling because there appeared to be no support for independence and no violence whatsoever; at the same time it is reasonable to assume that the continuation of the federation also lacked popular support. If the split of Czechoslovakia is viewed, plausibly, as the culmination of the disintegration of the Austro-Hungarian Empire, which started before World War I and was interrupted by the Cold War division, then a similar explanation could be sought for the disintegration of Yugoslavia – at a stretch though. But, where does this historical account leave the disintegration of the Soviet Union? A more convincing answer lies in the extreme conditions of post-communism, as has been maintained throughout. This, however, leaves other questions unanswered. Why was the peaceful Czecho-Slovak split followed by very difficult, albeit a non-violent, relationship between Slovaks and the Hungarian minority who were a minority in Czechoslovakia, too? Why was the conflict between seceding Slovenia and Serbia less violent than between seceding Croatia and Serbia?

The Slovak–Hungarian relationship[31] is well exemplified by the 'triadic nexus' theory because, not only are there some three million Hungarians spread over a number of ECE countries, mainly Slovakia and Romania (approximately 600,000 and two million respectively) as a result of the disintegration of the Austro-Hungarian empire after World War I, but the position of those minorities has always been a part of domestic politics in their external homeland – Hungary. The issue at hand operates on two levels. The minority is accused of a lack of loyalty to their (new) state of residence and citizenship, which may or not may not be true, but, in any case, it is not a straightforward relationship. This awkward relationship is further exacerbated by the involvement of the external homeland which leads to a further deterioration of the relationship between the majority and minority in the state of residence. The nationalising policies of Slovakia, for example, included a Language Law (1995, adapted in 1999) which required the safeguarding of the purity of the Slovak language used in all spheres, and in theory jeopardised a whole range of job opportunities for Hungarians. This was an example of a nationalising project designed for a domestic political situation, which in its short-sightedness, uses state power against a national minority with a strong affiliation to a neighbouring state accused of historical injustice committed against the dominant nation. On the other hand, while adopting a political agenda vis-à-vis the nationalising state, minority nationalism has an interest in presenting that state as threatening in order to increase the credibility of their mobilisation.[32] It is not difficult to see how potentially dangerous this dynamic can be, and let us not forget that the onset of World War II was also accompanied by examples of homeland politics, resulting in the 'revision' of the Hungarian borders into eastern Czechoslovakia (Ruthenia) and the annexation of Bohemia by Nazi Germany which claimed that it was protecting its ethnic kin in the Sudetenland. A fitting example with tragic consequences is the case of the former Yugoslavia, which is included at the end of this chapter.

The 'triadic nexus' thesis is empirically compelling and yet, it no longer applies to the Slovak–Hungarian relationship which, while not beyond improvement, is well beyond the 'triadic' dynamic described above. The intensification of democratisation in the region, for and through European integration, brought a fourth actor – the European Union – into the equation. The evidence shows that the change of institutions, the scrutiny of minority policies and another level of arbitration – removed from the immediacy of regional squabbles – have had positive affects on inter-ethnic relations in the region. While Europeanisation brings in a whole set of new questions about the relationship between the nation and the state,[33] I would argue that, on the whole, regional solutions are the best way forward for seeking ethnic harmony which, indirectly, is another lesson to learn from post-communist transitions.

Post-communism and the collapse of Yugoslavia

The break-up of the Yugoslav federation was followed by the eruption of violent conflict between ethnically based former republics (and statelets) and escalated further into murderous ethnic conflict. The total number of casualties in the War of Yugoslav Succession (1991–5 and 1998–9), as this conflict between Serbs, Croats, and Bosnian Muslims, and between Serbs and Kosovar Albanians is aptly referred to,[34] is around 240,000, two-thirds of them civilians; it produced four million refugees, coined the term 'ethnic cleansing', and thousands of women were raped.[35]

It is usually assumed that the main culprit behind the collapse of the Socialist Federal Republic of Yugoslavia (SFRY) and the vicious war that followed was Serbian nationalism, unscrupulously manipulated by Slobodan Milošević. He died during his trial at the International Criminal Tribunal for the Former Yugoslavia in The Hague (Netherlands) before he could be convicted for crimes against humanity. At present, Serbia is a struggling democracy, seeking integration into the European Union, and trying desperately to hold on to Kosovo, which has de facto seceded (for the case of Kosovo see Chapter 7), while the international community remains involved in Bosnia to secure its fragile multi-ethnic constitution. The puzzle that was Yugoslavia is still not completely resolved and its legacy is likely to affect the inter-ethnic relations in the Balkan region for a long time to come. One executor of Milošević's political ambitions, the leader of the Bosnian Serbs, Dr Radovan Karadžić, has been delivered to The Hague (2008) but his military counterpart, General Ratko Mladić, is still at large. The gallery of culprits, it is argued in the huge academic and journalistic output produced by the Yugoslav tragedy,[36] should be further extended by a number of other actors. In the first place, the gallery could include the late Croat president, Franjo Tudjman, a self-confessed adherent of the Croat nationalist cause who, if not inciting Belgrade's mobilisation of their ethnic kin in Croatia, certainly did nothing to assuage it. Arguably, there are further culprits, even if this is stretching the blame too far: the hesitant European Union, the British and the French governments for supporting the Serbian leadership for too long, Germany for the unilateral recognition of Croatia and

Slovenia,[37] thus setting off the domino effect of the collapse, and the United Nations for recognising Bosnia–Herzegovina but not allowing them to defend themselves, which may have prolonged the war.[38] Between reasonable and downright conspiratorial, the range and combination of arguments can be endless and not very helpful. Part of the problem is the conflation of a number of questions which, however interrelated, need to be separated. The questions are: 'why did Yugoslavia collapse?', 'why did the disintegration of this particular communist multinational state degenerate into ethnic war?' and 'why was there such unspeakable violence among friends and neighbours?'

I am including the case of Yugoslavia as an example of post-communist nationalism in order to answer the first question and offer a suggestion of an answer to the second question. I will not tackle the third question because the dynamics of the actual conflict are beyond this case study.[39] My argument is that the answer to the disintegration of Yugoslavia is connected to post-communist nationalism, superimposed on the particular legacies of the Yugoslav communist system, which was already in the throws of a significant ethnic mobilisation before the actual disintegration, including the position of Milošević at the centre of the collapsing state. I divide this necessarily brief case study into two uneven sections: the external and the internal factors.[40] The former concerns the impact of the end of the Cold War on Yugoslavia and the latter follows the intensification of nationalism in post-communism, as discussed in this chapter, but emphasises the ethnic principle of the federation and the conditions under which ethnicity could rise over any other form of solidarity.

External factors

There is a number of issues connected to the impact of the end of the Cold War on Yugoslavia.

1. The former Yugoslavia enjoyed a privileged status in the West as the most favoured communist state for its more liberal system and anti-Soviet stance. This included much financial support but also a perception among the Yugoslav people that they may have found the 'third way' between west and east. There was a difference between the Warsaw Pact countries and Tito's regime: the system of worker self-management, a lower degree of coercion, the significant degree of liberalisation, foreign travel, limited private ownership, the possibility of study abroad, the availability of Western goods and media broadcasts and so on, with Croatia and Slovenia leading the push towards greater pluralisation. But Yugoslavia was not a democracy. The Yugoslav communists never won a free election in any part of Yugoslavia nor did the regularly proclaimed sovereignty of the republics ever stop the

Communist Party from using the threat of force whenever its position was threatened as for example, against the liberal insurgency in Croatia (1971) and against demands for more autonomy in Kosovo (1981). Despite offering its population more rights than the systems in other Eastern and Central European countries, the Yugoslav political system was nevertheless an authoritarian system because a semblance of democracy does not stand for democracy, which cannot develop under one-party rule.

2. At the end of the Cold War, Yugoslavia became just another post-communist state in the midst of the most dramatic systemic change. The withdrawal of Western support plunged the already slowly disintegrating federation, suffering from increased political and economic crisis since the mid-1970s, into even greater chaos.

3. The communist leadership struggled to retain power as everywhere else. In other post-communist states, however, communism was defeated before nationalist forces entered the political struggle. In contrast, in Yugoslavia, communist leaderships hijacked the nationalist cause while still in power and, in Serbia, used it as the strategy to retain hold of the federation which, inevitably, exacerbated the nationalist tensions among republics and autonomous provinces.[41] This is a fundamental difference. Whether democ-ratisation before the crisis of the regime could have saved Yugoslavia is debatable but the crisis of the regime, amid the intensely growing fear and resentment, certainly added to the ensuing conflict.

All Eastern and Central European nationalisms sought inspiration in their nineteenth-century struggles – romantic, somewhat mythical notions of national struggle against historical enemies. While Croatia sought to re-establish its Central European credentials and, once and for all, make a clean break from Serbia, Serbia sought to re-establish its historically presumed dominance in the southern Balkans. The war of succession is often the last resort in political opposition to perceived threats. The reassertion of Serbian nationalism could lead only to competing claims of historical justice. The threat to Croatia, which historically relied on Serbian support, first against the Hungarian overlord and then against the Soviet Union, changed direction and now came from Serbia; Serbia on the other hand, perceived the loss of its dominance as yet another proof of its long-cherished resent-ment against Croatia and the West for undermining its historical place. Let's keep the word 'resentment' in mind for the remainder of this case study. Resentment feeds ethnic nationalism. It is imbued with indignation of his-torical injustice, driven by a vindication of it, distorted by the selectiveness of historical memory and devoid of goodwill in the fear of repeated humiliation.

Internal factors

I   Nationalism and communism in Yugoslavia

Ethnicity was the basis of the Yugoslav federation. The 'Kingdom of Serbs, Croats and Slovenes' emerged out of the ruins of the Austro-Hungarian and Ottoman Empires at the end of World War I, and embodied a nineteenth-century intellectual vision of the southern Slavs' unity against oppressive empires, championed by the largest of them – Serbia. The illusion among Serbs of deserved dominance was a constant source of resentment within the state which, under the centralising pressures of Serbia, became a dictatorship in 1929, and was renamed the Kingdom of Yugoslavia (incorporating the Kingdom of Montenegro). The communists' accession to power under the leadership of Josip Broz Tito (1892–1980) followed a period during the war in which more Yugoslavs were killed by one another than by occupying forces owing to the many competing affiliations among Yugoslavs to either Nazi Germany and national aspirations or partisan resistance. The organising bodies of the Communist Party were established along national lines in the post-1945 Yugoslavia, without actually settling national issues which were to plague this federation from beginning to end.

Yugoslavia was an ethnically based federation with decentralised political and party organisations but with central economic planning.[42] More than any other communist state, Yugoslavia tried to implement the 'dictatorship of proletariat' by a complex system of self-management which, nevertheless, could never reconcile the problem of one-party rule and a democracy it purported to represent. The continuing economic reforms and the ever-growing power of republican elites in the face of the ever-decreasing power of the federal treasury led to severe economic problems. Yugoslavia became a federation of eight competing economies which together produced more than they earned, imported the raw materials for their industries without exploiting their own resources, and borrowed heavily to the point where the central state had no control of the extent of it. After the final stage of reforms (1971–6, including the new constitutional arrangements), the state lost all control over monetary policy: the uncontrolled inflation was exacerbated by the foreign debt (US$ 20 billion in 1980) at the time of the worldwide economic downturn. The foreign borrowing, which was much increased during the last two years of Tito's life,[43] was used to quell ethnic unrest in disadvantaged regions and, by 1989, inflation had risen to 3,000 per cent and the Yugoslav political and economic system was in fatal crisis.

The dichotomy between rhetoric and the reality, similar to that in other communist regimes, caused the accumulation of economic and political problems beyond the state's capability to sustain it. Tito, the supporting pillar of this economically ailing and disintegrating mass of inter-republican infighting, was dead and communism lost all credibility for further reform. Years of devolution of power to the republics created resentment towards Belgrade which, in fear of loosing its position, pushed for more centralisation. The nationality policy of the Yugoslav federation had an unintended effect: nations turned to their own policies without regard for the federation, and the process could no longer be reversed.

After Tito's death, the looming threat of disintegration led to the establishment of an annually rotating 'president of presidency' in which each ethno-federal unit was represented by one elected representative. In 1990 Milošević, having reduced Vojvodina, Montenegro and Kosovo to mere satellites, held four out of eight votes in the presidency and could thus block any decision. This was not the reason why Yugoslavia ceased to function but a symptom of what it had become. There were many reasons for the 'national' character of each unit's leadership. The real decision-making emanated from the regions rather than from the centre, whereby all conflicts deriving from the incredible diversity of the periphery were translated into 'nationally relevant conflicts of interests',[44] for lack of any other category in which they could be expressed in an ideologically uniform communist system. The Communist Party continued to be organised along national or ethnic lines. Each of the eight party organisations held its own congress, scheduled before the all-Yugoslav League of Communists of Yugoslavia (LCY) congresses, thus indicating that the national organisations did more than merely approve the policies. At the end, in 1990 the LCS (the League of Communists of Slovenia) seceded from the LCY (immediately followed by the Croats), renamed itself the Party of Democratic Renewal, and abrogated all obligations, including financial ones, to the LCY. By then the LCY was in an advanced state of decay, accelerated by the fusion of the Serbian communists with the local 'Socialist Alliance' and the subsequent election of Slobodan Milošević as their leader.

Belgrade and Zagreb had less and less in common, each claiming defensive nationalism, the former preaching a strong Yugoslavia (or rather strong Serbia), the latter rejecting its eternal role of a minor partner. Not for the first time in modern history, the answer to the political and economic crisis became nationalism. This spelled an inevitable disintegration of the state in which all differences, whether they were cultural, economic, structural, political or ideological, were linked to ethnic/territorial frameworks which were initially designed to prevent the ethnic cleavages. As indicated above, communist nationality policies failed and nowhere as bitterly as in Yugoslavia. Secession from a multinational federation is often the only way to make a clear political stand about the intended direction of political developments. We have observed similar developments in Czechoslovakia and the Soviet Union.

2. Ethno-national mobilisation

The story thus far has been that, externally, despite its special status, Yugoslavia found itself in the throws of post-communism. While communism was better for Yugoslavs than for others, the communist legacy left the state on the brink of a conflict that even Milošević could not have anticipated – after all, he sought a strong Serbia, not the internationally, morally and territorially diminished Serbia which he achieved. All multinational communist federations were overwhelmed by a nationalist resurgence but, in Yugoslavia, the situation was worse. Having institutionalised a federation along ethno-national lines with strong autonomist legislation, but short of political autonomy, the country was facing the collapse of communism economically devastated and ethnically divided. Classical theories of nationalism tell us that there is a certain trajectory of national movements and that the rising awareness, particularly in combination with the divergent levels of development, which can be translated into national conflicts, will lead to demands for political independence.[45]

Just as in Czechoslovakia and the Soviet Union, Yugoslav communists considered nationalism an enemy and linked the Communist Party to the integrity of the state. When the party lost credibility, the state it represented lost the last bits of legitimacy it could still muster. In the republican multiparty elections in 1990, which preceded the all-Yugoslav elections, all opposition forces to the party presented themselves as democratising national movements.[46] To add to the already rather impossible situation, the post-communist nationalism, as already explained, tended towards strong ethnic overtones generally but, in Yugoslavia, ethnicity was already established as the line of division. All ills of post-communist ethno-national mobilisation were present in Yugoslavia to a greater degree than anywhere else, including unscrupulous elites competing for influence and exploiting ethnic divisions with no regard for the consequences. Moreover, each republic contained large mobilised minorities which, feeling threatened by the prospects of being left on the wrong side of the border, sought protection from their ethnic kin. The convergence of human anxieties and conditions that could be related to one's ethnic identity reached unprecedented levels. It would have taken heroic and honourable political leadership in all republics to calm the situation, not ethnic entrepreneurs such as Milošević and Tudjman and the slowly emerging leaders of minorities.

I have mentioned 'resentment'[47] as a strong factor in ethnic mobilisation before but the term could have been invented for post-communist Yugoslavia. The list of various resentments felt among the Yugoslav people, once the gloves were off, was endless especially among the Serbs and Croats who had a history of rivalry and some bitter memories from World War II. These were augmented by the new opportunities and recent events: Croats felt that Croat Serbs were dominating the upper ranks of the party and police force; Serbs resented Croats for not accepting their leadership; Serbs and Croats resented Bosnian Muslims for their numerical domination of the Bosnia they would have preferred to control themselves and for the cosmopolitan sophistication of Sarajevo; and, of course, Serbs resented Kosovar Albanians for wanting to dominate the mythical home of Serbian nationhood. Slovenia, on the other hand, stood fairly remote from such inflammation of emotions but quietly and determinedly pursued democratisation and, if necessary, secession.

The Kosovo uprising in 1981 opened the floodgates of Serbian discontent with their position within the federation. In 1986, the Serbian Academy of Sciences and Arts, under the leadership of Dobrica Ćosić, produced a *Memorandum*[48] which catalogued the injustice of the 'win the war, but loose the peace' position of Serbs within the federation. It was full of indignation that touched every Serbian soul but, more importantly, it claimed that Serbs have 'never been as endangered as they are today' and that they were dying at the hands of Albanians in Kosovo. This memorandum was a watershed because of its timing when the Yugoslav system was failing and there were power struggles at the top and among republics. While debate about the *Memorandum* raged throughout Yugoslavia, nearly all communists rejected it – except Milošević, the leader of the Serbian Communist Party. The dynamics and the relationships within the party machinery are not as important as the fact that the nationalist course was being hijacked by the communists while they were still in power and in command of official rhetoric. The language of nationalism, previously unacceptable to the regime, became the political discourse in Yugoslavia after 1986.

By 1991, it was clear that Yugoslavia would not survive. The political disintegration was slow, though; in early 1991, Slovenia and Croatia proposed some form of confederal arrangement but this was rejected by Serbia and Montenegro. A similar 'confederate' proposal preceded the disintegration of Czechoslovakia. One must wonder how seriously these last gasps of commitment to a common state should be taken but the point I am trying to convey is that the dissolution of Yugoslavia was a long and painful political process before it became a war. In the spring of 1991 the political chaos continued and Serbian bellicosity grew in parallel to the political machinations in the Federal Assembly (*Skupština*). Slovenia and Croatia declared their independence on 25 June 1991. This was followed by the brisk military response by the Belgrade-dominated Yugoslav People's Army (JNA). Meanwhile, Croat Serbian militias attacked Croat villages and the war between Serbia and Croatia de facto began. In January 1992 Macedonia declared independence and finally, amid rising ethnic tensions, Bosnia–Herzegovina, left with no choice, also declared independence. The Yugoslav War of Succession began in earnest.[49]

My concern in this case study has been to convey the collapse of the Yugoslav multinational communist federation and identify ethno-nationalism as the rising force of post-communist politics. Yugoslavia represents an extreme case of this phenomenon which was followed by a vicious ethnic war. Why? Because ethno-nationalism of epidemic proportions was rising on the back of two mutually reinforcing factors: the fallout from the end of the Cold War which discredited the failing communist system even further and changed perceptions about the role of Serbia within republics which no longer needed its protection and, in fact, viewed it as the new enemy; the ethno-territorial principle which, over the decades, entrenched ethnicity as a legitimate form of identification, intensified by the failure of Yugoslav communism.

The collapse of Yugoslavia and its aftermath comprise the most appropriate study of ethnic nationalism rooted in a reproduction of historical imagery and the entrenchment of ethnic identities. Milošević was not the cause of the Yugoslav tragedy but he was responsible for making ethnic nationalism a credible policy which tipped a conflict between constituent republics over the precipice into ethnic conflict (not states but ethnic groups became the units of solution). Milošević was guilty because he did not use his considerable power and talent for manipulation to diffuse these tensions but chose to exacerbate them in an attempt to increase his own power through Serbian domination of the federation. Was the collapse inevitable? Probably, but the war was not.

Lessons from post-communism

Post-communism was happening faster than it could be analysed. Now that we have had a few years to reflect on those bewildering developments, and when many post-communist states can be considered relatively stable democracies and members of the European Union, it is perhaps the time to draw some conclusions that could be meaningful for other parts of the world. The argument advanced in this chapter is that democratisation contributed to the increased national mobilisation in post-communism and that the intensity of nationalist mobilisation depended on the accumulation and combination of historical and communist legacies. As nationalisms go, the post-communist version is a complex phenomenon of modern politics and anachronistic sentiments, a combination of ethnic and civic nationalism, with a surprising adaptability to external stimuli whether in the form of European integration or less positive mobilisation from beyond the boundaries. The main lesson to be derived from post-communism is that authoritarian regimes do not fall and become democratic without a significant danger of ethnic mobilisation. Democratic institutions can be designed, erected and established but their sustainability is a fairly prolonged and difficult process during which ethnic mobilisation lurks behind each disappointment and each failure. The democratisation process thus depends very much on the ethnic constellation within the state and on inter-ethnic relations in the immediate neighbourhood.

The conclusion to this chapter thus forms three themes. The first theme concerns the relationship between democracy and nationalism. Post-communist transitions did not merely establish a new legitimate system. In many cases the very boundaries of political community were challenged and the answer to this challenge was not the continuation of democratic effort to regain the legitimacy of those states but their disintegration. In modern times, a sovereign political unit is a prerequisite for a modern democracy. So, contrary to Nodia's argument from the beginning of this chapter, democratic transitions do not engender nations, post-communist transitions engendered new sovereign states and that is a considerable difference – in theory and practice. The building of a nation is a different process from the building of a democratic state which usually incorporates a number of national groups; in post-communism these fundamentally different processes were happening simultaneously, hence the overenthusiastic equation of nationalism and democracy. Finally, legitimacy is central to democracy, and the legitimacy of the state is central to nationalism but, in post-communism, democracy is too weak to legitimise all processes necessary to consolidate the regime and state power – this is where nationalism fills all the gaps. So, nationalism is not indispensable in democratic transitions. It was, however, a logical concomitant of post-communist transitions. Here, I have not changed my opinion from my original work on post-communist nationalism.

The second theme relates to the theories of nationalism. The combination of politics, democratisation, ethnic mobilisation and the creation of new states in early post-communism is, indeed, as Hroch argued, in some aspects analogous to nineteenth-century nationalism. In this respect, a number of classical theories could be applied to post-communist nationalism, namely: the ethno-symbolist use of historical markers in elite mobilisation; Hobsbawm's invention of traditions; and possibly, most appropriately, the strong politically founded Breuilly theory of nationalism. Overall, as in nearly all nationalisms, the post-communist version was also too multifactorial to be grasped by one theory. The civic/ethnic dichotomy looks weak and somewhat meaningless in a democracy and in ethnicity-driven post-communist transition because demands of all national groups were simultaneously civic and ethnic. Importantly, though, these historically unprecedented democratisation processes involved a whole new aspect: European integration as the final objective. The national rhetoric in the newly independent states thus took on an unusually international guise in its appeals to the nation which was to relinquish its new independence as soon as it fulfilled the expectations of the European Union and was internationally recognised as democratic enough. Classical theories of nationalism have little, if anything, to say about this form of integrationist nationalism.

The third theme, and probably the most relevant for contemporary politics, is the relationship between majorities and minorities. Ethnic groups may be relatively stable categories but the relationships between them are dynamic and respond to the opportunities and constraints of institutional and constitutional processes within the state which, in turn, respond to changes in domestic and international developments. The majority–minority relationship as the most symbolic inter-ethnic relationship depends on many variables: the policies of the residence state; the political, historical and socio-economic position of the minority; the political environment in the 'external' homeland; and the regional international relations. All of those factors were in flux in post-communist states. The important implication from it, though, is that for all its state-centric appeals, nationalism is affected by politics from beyond the state's boundaries as from much as within it. Equally, ethnic mobilisation reaches, and is reached across, the boundaries of states. Hence, the following chapters turn to the international aspects of contemporary nationalism.

Notes

1. This chapter draws on my previous work (2002), *Nationalism and Democratisation: Politics of Slovakia and Slovenia,* but is revised and updated by years of reflection on the subject of postcommunism.

2. For Chinese nationalism is Chen, Cheng (2007), *The Prospects for Liberal Nationalism in Post-Leninist States*.
3. Adapted from Linz and Stepan (1996) in *Problems of Democratic Transition and Consolidation*, p. 44.
4. For a more in-depth discussion see Hyde-Pryce (1996), *The International Politics of East/Central Europe*.
5. Nodia (1994), 'Nationalism and Democracy' pp. 4 and 9 respectively; Gellner (1994 [1983]), *Nations and Nationalism*, p. 55.
6. Beissinger (2008), 'A New Look at Ethnicity and Democratization', p. 95.
7. Fukuyama (1994), 'Comments on Nationalism and Democracy', p. 28.
8. Halliday (1999), *Revolution and World Politics*, p. 21.
9. In this instance I am not referring to the article by Fukuyama 'The End of History?', *National Interest Summer*, 1989, pp. 3–18, which seems to have appropriated the term 'the end'.
10. For the review of this 'transitology literature', see Harris, *Nationalism and Democratisation*, chapter 1; for the theory of democratisation see Linz and Stepan *Problems of Democratic Transition and Consolidation*.
11. Offe (1991), 'Capitalism by Democratic Design?'.
12. Beissinger, 'A New Look at Ethnicity and Democratization', p. 87.
13. In August 2008, the conflict between Georgia and its separatist regions of Abkhazia and South Ossetia led to the military involvement of Russia in the name of protecting the Ossetian allies and to the international condemnation of Russia, if not international crises following the Russian recognition of Abkhazian and Ossetian independence. The struggle is not only the usual question of who controls the territory but serves also as a proxy for the international conflict between Russia and the West about the reassertion of Russian influence in the region.
14. Elster, Offe and Preuss (1998), *Institutional Design in Post-communist Societies*, p. 254, point out pithily that 'democracy is good for ethnic mobilisation, but not so vice versa'. For a similar argument see Snyder (2000), *From Voting to Violence: Democratisation and Nationalist Conflict*.
15. Cited in Judt (2007), *Postwar: A History of Europe since 1945*, before the contents page.
16. Harris, *Nationalism and Democratisation*, chapter 1.
17. See, for example, Katherine Verdery (1993), 'Nationalism and National Sentiments in Post-Socialist Romania', *Slavic Review* 52: 2, 179–203, p. 179; Jack Snyder (1993), 'Nationalism and the Crisis of the Post-Soviet State', *Survival* 35: 1, 5–27, p. 5; Ivo Banac (1992), 'The Fearful Asymmetry of War: The Causes and Consequences of Yugoslavia's Demise', *Daedalus* 121, 141–73, p. 142.
18. It is important to add that Serbia is a special case and that, as much as the disintegration of former Yugoslavia fits the post-communist correlation, the conflict between Serbia and Kosovo does not. The conduct of Serbia under Milošević's regime was that of an oppressive state trying to maintain the regime and, as such, should not be compared with developments in other post-communist states.
19. Leibich, Andre (1995), 'Nations, States, Minorities: Why is Eastern Europe different?', *Dissent*, summer, 307–13, p. 313.
20. Kymlicka (2004), 'Justice and Security in the Accommodation of Minority Nationalism: Comparing East and West', p. 5.
21. Hroch (1993), 'From National Movement to the Fully-Formed Nation'; and by the same author (1985), *The Social Preconditions of National Revival in Europe*, Cambridge: Cambridge University Press.
22. Judt, *Postwar*, pp. 185–6.
23. For a comprehensive treatment of the national questions and Marxist theory see Connor (1984), *The National Question in Marxist–Leninist Theory and Strategy*.
24. Brubaker (1996), *Nationalism Reframed*, p. 4.
25. The term 'nationalising' here refers strictly to post-communist states. For the discussion about nationalising policies elsewhere, see Taras Kuzio (2001) 'Nationalising states or

nation-building? a critical review of the theoretical literature and empirical evidence',
Nations and Nationalism 7: 2, pp. 135–54.

26. Brubaker, *Nationalism Reframed*, p. 9.
27. Harris, *Nationalism and Democratisation*, pp. 29–30.
28. Iván Szelényi and Szonja Szelényi (1995), 'Circulation or Reproduction of Elites During the Postcommunist Transformation of Eastern Europe' in *Theory and Practice* 24: 5, pp. 615–38.
29. Donald Horowitz, cited in Beissinger, 'A New Look at Ethnicity and Democratization', p. 92, refers to this dynamic as 'the logic of infinite regress'.
30. Brubaker , *Nationalism Reframed*, p. 4.
31. For a detailed study of the Hungarian minority in Slovakia see Harris (2007), 'Moving Politics Beyond the State: The Hungarian Minority in Slovakia'.
32. Brubaker, *Nationalism Reframed*, p. 115.
33. Harris (2004), ' Europeanization of Slovakia'; and Keating (2004), 'European Integration and the Nationalities Question'.
34. Ramet (2004), 'Explaining Yugoslav meltdown I . . .' *Nationalities Papers* 2: 4, 2004, p. 731.
35. Mann (2005), *The Dark Side of Democracy*, p. 356.
36. For the most comprehensive review of the academic output see Ramet (2005), *Thinking about Yugoslavia*.
37. Silber and Little (1996), *The Death of Yugoslavia*.
38. Ramet (1994), 'The Yugoslav Crisis and the West: Avoiding "Vietnam" and Blundering into "Abyssinia"'.
39. See Mann, *The Dark Side of Democracy*, pp. 382–428.
40. This framework follows Ramet (2004), 'Explaining Yugoslav meltdown I . . .' *Nationalities Papers* 2: 4, 2004, pp. 731–2.
41. Republics: Slovenia, Croatia, Bosnia and Herzegovina, Serbia, Montenegro, Macedonia; autonomous provinces: Vojvodina and Kosovo.
42. For a detailed account of political and economic developments in Yugoslavia during 1946–91 see Harris, *Nationalism and Democratisation: Politics of Slovakia and Slovenia*, chapter 5.
43. Tito died 4 May 1980.
44. This expression is borrowed from Miroslav Hroch (1993) 'From National Movement to the Fully-Formed Nation', and was discussed in chapter 2.
45. Hroch 'From National Movements to the Fully-Formed Nation'; and Nairn (1975), 'The Modern Janus'.
46. Linz and Stepan (1992), 'Political Identities and Electoral Sequences' in *Daedalus* 121: 2, pp. 123–39, explain, taking Spain, the Soviet Union and Yugoslavia as examples, that if all-union elections are held first (Spain), there are strong incentives for political activists to create all-union parties, and all-union agendas which can make or break the multinational polity. In the case of Yugoslavia I would say that the republican elections were only a contributory factor to the final stage of the disintegration that was in an advanced stage anyway. The Czecho-Slovak split does not fit this model because the all-state elections brought victory to parties with a strong 'national' emphasis which then proceeded to press constitutional issues until the final break-up.
47. See also Greenfeld (1992), *Nationalism,* pp. 15–17. In the present context, see Roger D. Peterson (2000), *Understanding Ethnic Violence*; and Ramet, 'Explaining Yugoslav meltdown I . . .' p. 752.
48. Harris, *Nationalism and Democratisation*, p. 156; Silber and A. Little, *The Death of Yugoslavia*, pp. 31–5.
49. Ramet (2002), *Balkan Babel*, chapter 3.

CHAPTER FIVE

Ethnic Violence

In the title of his book, *Identity and Violence*, Amartya Sen captures the most significant forces at play in contemporary international politics. Each is an illusion. Identity offers an illusion of the uniqueness of, and therefore a destiny for, a particular group, and violence is an illusion in that its force can and will achieve a desired destiny. As we are confronted by ongoing and recurrent violence taking place in Iraq, Sudan, Israel, Palestine, Somalia, the Basque Country, Sri Lanka, Indonesia, Tibet, Kashmir, Congo, and so on and on, all in the name of freedom and justice, we must at times wonder about the feebleness of those cherished values and the cruelty with which humans are willing to pursue them. The aims, the retributions, the reasoning, the intensity and strategies change but the story of identity-inspired violence remains a bewildering one whereby universal principles of freedom, choice and justice are betrayed by beliefs in a uniqueness and righteousness of a particular identity. To Sen, the reason lies in the 'solitarist' view which 'miniaturizes' human beings by ignoring their other than ethnic identities, such as gender, hobbies, intellectual and political beliefs, and profession, and thus diminishes the number of ways in which people relate to one another.[1] While it is true that ethnic violence is rooted in the 'illusion of unique and choiceless identity',[2] and therefore the emphasis on the plurality of human identities offers hope, hope does not even begin to tackle the issue because the problem is not people's misunderstanding of the manifold of identities but the institutionalisation of that one particular ethnic identity in the form of the nation state.

It is clear from previous chapters that, in the world of nation states, nationalism, if it is not a political process by itself, then it is a part of political processes, including democratisation. The reason is that nationalism is at the heart of all processes by which we define modernity: national self-determination, that is, the carving out of territory for the nation state which is a sovereign entity peopled by citizens who are equal before the law and in charge of their political destiny. The indivisible trinity, 'democracy, citizenship and national self-determination',[3] is nationalism's claim to the empowerment of people, hence nationalism positions itself within the realm of human dignity and political legitimacy. As is abundantly clear, this universality of aims and claims has a 'dark side' because the definition of sovereign people is not in their universality but in their cultural particularity. The exercise of sovereignty needs boundaries; both the territorial state and 'the people' need to be demarcated, and, hence, ethnicity completes the fundamental question about boundaries – whose territory and whose state? More to the point, the assumption that there is something 'natural' about the division of humanity into vertical cultural groupings equipped with citizenship and the protection of their state has become a mutually dependent dynamic: people define the state and the state defines the people. Hence, the politicisation of ethnicity is part and parcel of modern politics. The argument in this chapter centres on violence deriving from struggles of ethnic groups for the control of the state or for the territory they wish to control. I shall discuss the interplay between ethnic mobilisation, territory and state power, using the Israeli–Arab conflict as the main case study.

At the heart of the politics of nationalism is the conflation of cultural and political in the form of the nation state; while humanity remains divided into national groups, based on some putative reference to ethnic homogeneity, the ethnicity-driven competition for power and control of resources is never too far away. No matter how many well-intended strategies exist out there to ameliorate the preferential treatment of the dominant ethnos, the politicisation of ethnicity more often than not leads to exclusion, marginalisation and human misery. I have already suggested that the distinction between civic (inclusive) and ethnic (exclusive) nationalism is only an attempt to deal with this evident fact because civic and ethnic nationalisms are in the business of maintaining or seeking the 'autonomy, unity and identity'[4] of their people. The distinction is actually in the extent to which state power accepts the limits of the cultural homogeneity of their citizenry (civic, more realistic; ethnic, less so) or the intensity with which state policies pursue the preference for, and demands on behalf of, the core ethnic group (in theory: civic, less intensively; ethnic, more so). The operative matters here are the state's policies of exclusion or the lack of multi-ethnic accommodation; the characterisation of nationalism one way or the other is merely a label. The label is academically well established, however, and therefore a political strategy of the appropriation of state power by one ethnic group leading to ethnic conflict and violence is here referred to as ethno-nationalism.

This chapter is concerned with the dynamics of ethnic conflict which largely account for the bad track record of nationalism because that is where its insidiousness is the most tangible. When referring to conflict, we are invariably looking at the power politics between ethnic groups over and within certain territory. Conflict, however, has varying degrees, from mild hostilities and political rhetoric to outbursts of violence and even attempts to eliminate a group of people, but all conflicts have the intention to maximise the power of one ethnic group over another or over a number of them. Ethnically motivated violence is on the increase, in parallel with the intensification of globalisation and overall cosmopolitanism of international institutions. The truth is that the 1990s, which began with the hope of a new (meaning peaceful, democratising, international) world order, has also exposed 'severe pathologies in the sacred ideologies of nationhood'.[5] Conflicts in post-communist Europe, the violence of the Yugoslav conflict, the communal violence in India and the Rwandan genocide, and the cataclysmic events of 11 September 2001 have been followed by a global 'war on terror' which also has a strong cultural core. How does ethnic violence happen? As a political phenomenon, ethnic violence is possibly the least suitable subject for sober political analysis and critical assessment but, in undertaking this challenge, there are two crucial factors that need elaborating, first: ethnicity and territory.

Lands of 'hope and glory': ethnicity and territory

Modernisation, democratisation and globalisation do not appear to have lessened ethnic consciousness; on the contrary, the last tends to be invigorated by processes that should, in theory, eliminate it. There are some rather obvious reasons. Modernisation equals heightened levels of communication and transport; democratisation requires a degree of bureaucracy and alerts people to their political and socio-economic positions and how to challenge them; globalisation affects the lives, hopes and dreams of all but, at this stage in history, delivers only to a few. The result is an overall confrontation with the political significance of ethnic identity – one's own and that of others. While assumed to be a 'normal' condition in our world, nationhood is highly problematic. First, being a political nation is actually an exception rather than a rule, as the surprisingly low number of officially recognised states in the world (under 200) illustrates. Second, nationalism's real success is in the advancement of the idea that the ultimate recognition of the nation is having a state which stands for a degree of control over the destiny of the nation. But, there are no qualifying clauses in the nationalist programme about the possibility of the state becoming dysfunctional or authoritarian; there is no warning that secession may not deliver prosperity, let alone democracy; and there are no manuals for national leaders about what is expected of them. The simplicity of the national self-determination doctrine in the face of historical evidence, the complexity of the implementation, including violence, remain astounding.

Equally surprising is the selectivity with which the international community accepts the struggle of one group as legitimate and others as not. The independence struggle of Kosovo was rightful, therefore their ethno-nationalism was legitimate, but the ethno-nationalisms of Abkhazia and South Ossetia are deeply suspect. There is no logic here. What we are observing is, first, the difference in the geopolitical position and situation which will be discussed in Chapter 7, and second, the ambiguity between national self-determination and ethno-national mobilisation. The suffering of Kosovo because of Serbian ethnic expansionism should not presuppose that Kosovo's ethnic nationalism is different from any other. This, and many other examples, can be explained only by the general emotiveness, tinged with value judgements and stereotyping, with which we approach all things ethnic, our own and those of others. Even in its most democratic efforts, nationalism is embellished by romanticising the heroism of the victors; it seeks support on the basis of 'brotherhood'; it sings praises to national unity while, deep down, it is really the unity of its own people.

The ethno-national bond is exclusive; it is based on perceptions about and against 'the other' which seem always to be better formulated than perceptions about 'us'. I have spent years looking into the relationship between democracy, nationalism and, lately, European integration in post-communist societies, and do not want to demonise nationalism because, as a political reality, it needs to be understood rather than rejected. But, understanding nationalism requires a concession to its close link with ethno-national mobilisation and the emotionality that it triggers.

This is not the place to delve into how the emotiveness of ethnicity happens and what are the psychological effects of our first memories which contain recognition of: the place and its words; the first awe and fear of becoming a person; observations of the people around you; the fear of not being understood or recognised; the story that comes with you and can never be taken away but can be belittled and thwarted; and other experiences, which are all, somehow, subconsciously connected to 'home'. As Walker Connor reminds us, the near universal recognition of phrases and imagery associated with ethnicity and, by implication, with nationalism – blood, family, brothers, sister, motherland and forefathers – suggests a closeness and a bond that are in their invocation apolitical, virtuous and therefore honourable. The politicisation of these emotions, therefore, can and does illicit popular support,[6] and the consequences are nearly always less honourable.

Another of those universal images connected with identity is the 'homeland'. Unlike other less easily described emotions connected with one's ethnicity, the home land is a concrete place and, as such, not only the subject of much poetry but also the space of struggle and political contestation. The concreteness of the homeland as the territory of and for a people who give it a name makes the emotional attachment to it more intense (also, in cases of people who do not reside on its territory, as I argue in the section on diasporas in the next chapter) and the struggle for control of it more legitimate. One does not need to repeat many examples of a homeland's inspiration to poets, but let me remind the reader of a speech Slobodan Milošević made to Serbs who, in fear of the increasingly unhappy Kosovar Albanians, were emigrating in large numbers in April 1987:

This is your land! These are your houses. Your meadows and gardens. Your memories. You shouldn't abandon your land just because it is difficult to live, . . . It has never been part of the Serbian character to give up in the face of obstacles, to demobilise when it is time to fight. . . . You should stay here for the sake of your ancestors and descendants . . .[7]

The date here is important because this is long before Yugoslavia was considered to be 'disintegrating' and, therefore, obvious signs of ethnic mobilisation, mainly by Serbian politicians, went unnoticed. Every tool in the trade of ethnic mobilisation is used in this short fragment: homeland, the invocation of the ownership of the land, the continuity of history, the reminder of national heroism, and the appeal to arms. Kosovo is a homeland and has been for centuries to Serbs and Albanians but this is not how ethnic mobilisation happens so it should not be surprising that Serb–Albanian violence, not assuaged by appeals to the true nature of their shared homeland but incited by the exaltation of its uniqueness to Serbs only, would eventually follow.

Homeland psychology is not bothered by cumbersome details that may detract from the appeal it is making, and hence the success of such rhetoric – it hits the target that the audience is waiting for anyway. In the case of the homeland, the appeal is that, in the first place, it belongs to people whose name it carries; what happens to others who may not have another homeland or who even think of it as their own is a secondary consideration, if a consideration of ethno-national movements at all. Let me be clear, there are differences among the politics of nation states, the efforts to create an overarching national identity for which purpose the homeland is then also used, and the ethno-national 'call to arms' to secure a greater autonomy for the homeland or full independence. Ethnic violence is usually about control of the territory. There is no ETA violence without Euskadi, there is no Kashmir conflict without Kashmir; there is no Israeli–Arab conflict without the territorial dispute between them; there is no potential for conflict anywhere without disputed territory, as there is no peace without territorial settlements. Homelands are spaces where national narratives are made, to which past struggles and dreams of the future belong. All homelands are 'lands of hope and glory' but also spaces where the nightmares of ethnic violence take place. In more political terms, ethnic identity is associated with a specific territory (a homeland) and, while increasingly activated in farther away places, ethno-national mobilisation is inherently attached to identity which is as specific as the territory to which it pertains.[8]

133

Territorial disputes are lengthy, bloody and notoriously difficult to resolve and, while territories of states have to be shared, these disputes are here to stay. While discussing ethnic violence, I feel compelled to mention another type of violence associated with an identity, but not territory, which has become particularly relevant in the first decade of the twenty-first century – international Islamic terrorism. When it comes to terrorism, the difficulty, the incomprehension and the inability to deal with it are augmented by our understanding of the world as divided into territories and struggles for their political control, but a much lesser understanding of violence that does not appear to entail these elements. The violence perpetrated by Islamic terrorist organisations, in places that do not seem to relate to particular homelands (such as New York, Madrid, London), are much more difficult to comprehend and nearly impossible to resolve through any treaty or agreement because they do not relate to states, and the grievances that inspire this violence comprise a kind of abstract 'long-distance' hatred, rooted in economic and moral confrontations between different ways of life and huge global chasms between peace and equity, but made plausible by the demonising of the entire Western world. Noteworthy in terrorist rhetoric is, however, the emotiveness of a symbolic bond of 'brotherhood', injured pride, suffering of 'the people', the fear of encroachment and the hatred of others so, all in all, the recognisable rhetoric of ethnic violence but not attached to a particular territory. The panic fuelling the 'war on terror' is not only the fear of large-scale violence against civilians but also fear of the style of these cellular organisations which operate 'outside the existing frameworks of sovereignty, territoriality and nationalism and thus pose a threat to the world organised into nation-states'.[9]

Dominant ethnos: the case of Israel

Israel emerged as an independent state in May 1948 out of a fierce conflict between the indigenous Palestinian Arab population and the Jews of Palestine (*Yishuv*). The declaration of independence, on 14 May 1948, marks the beginning of the Jewish dream of statehood in 'a land without people for people without a land' as the Zionists who believed in the return of Jewish people to their ancient homeland used to say.[10] The date also marks the beginning of what Palestinians refer to as *nakba* (catastrophe). The land was won, against mighty Arab armies (Egypt, Jordan, Syria, Iraq, Saudi Arabia and

Lebanon) by Jews who, indeed, had no homeland to call their own, only a history of persecution in countries they lived in. The problem was, however, that the newly established homeland intended for all Jews in the world was *not* without people – it was also home to Palestinian Arabs. The latter, some 700,000 people, fled or were forced to leave, hundreds of their towns and villages were destroyed and only the smaller proportion (160,000) remained and became Israeli citizens. Following the 1967 victory in yet another attack by neighbouring Arab states, Israel has extended its control beyond the original (and internationally recognised official) 'green line' borders over the entire historical Palestine and thus is illegally occupying Palestinian territories. Today, there are 950 Jewish settlements while the number of Palestinian localities has remained unchanged since 1948 despite the five-fold increase in the population.[11] There have been many empty efforts, and some serious ones, to resolve the conflict, such as the Oslo agreements (1993), but there has been no resolution. The violence between Israeli Jews and Palestinian Arabs continues and has probably intensified since the failure of the Camp David talks which sparked off the second intifada (uprising, 2000) and the rise of the Islamic movement, Hamas, to power. The result has been a security fence between Israel and the West Bank to keep out terrorists; this means more army checkpoints, more loss of valuable arable land, more hardship and anger, and less faith in peace.

This sketchy account of the Israeli-Palestinian conflict is not intended to cover the historical roots of this conflict, nor the various interpretations of it of which there are many and nearly always mutually incomprehensible, nor a chronology of events of the last sixty years.[12] The fact is that there is a whole generation of Palestinians who have known nothing but occupation and repression, and that even Palestinians in Gaza, 'free' from Israeli occupation since 2005, live a cruel and miserable existence full of political chaos because years of conflict have left them divided and brutalised. Israel, once admired for its heroism in the face of adversity, is in some parts of the world becoming a byword for a 'rogue' state, its population is not safe, and its society is traumatised by violence – perpetrated against Palestinian Arabs and vice versa. Many nations have been born in blood and frequently in sin.[13] It is a historical tragedy that, not only was Israel born that way but its founding ideology – Zionism[14] – also was born that way, in the pogroms of Eastern Europe, and further confirmed by the Holocaust; when Palestine becomes independent, for it eventually will, its beginnings have already been marked by too much blood and too many sins against its own people and against Israeli Jews.

Israel's intransigent policy of territorial expansion has undermined any trust among Palestinians for the planned two-state solution. Even worse for the peace process is that secular nationalism seeking national self-determination for Palestine, which was the original demand of Arafat's

Palestinian Liberation Organisation (PLO), is in decline and is being super-seded by loyalty to Islam.[15] The latter involves the already victimised people in a wider regional conflict and in terrorist tactics, and makes promises that are unlikely to be fulfilled. The beginnings of the Israeli-Palestinian conflict have to be sought in two competing nationalisms, both claiming the right to the territory: the Jews on the basis of their millennia-long bond with the land from which they were exiled and for which they fought; and the Palestinian Arabs, on the basis of being the indigenous population having the right to national self-determination.

A number of Israeli academics have tried to move the boundaries of studies of nationalism and tried to analyse the political system in Israel (and similar cases). The Israeli state appears to combine protracted ethnic con-flict, sustained terrorist activities against its population, and the military occupation of Palestinian territories with a form of democratic politics, including a degree of minority protection, while the dominant Jewish popu-lation exercises a hegemonic control over the state. It is always a mistake to select one state as exceptional and therefore beyond comparative politics but, if there were such a state, Israel constitutes a truly exceptional amalga-mation of all the ills of modernity: from its emergence from the genocide of the Holocaust to the presently entrenched and violent conflict between two peoples seeking control over a territory. Between is a nationalising state, settlers and refugees, diaspora politics, a mistrusted minority divided from its ethnic kin by army checkpoints, security walls, militarisation, terrorism, and the international community also divided on how to resolve this conflict. In the analysis of the Israeli political system and its 'flawed' democracy, there are many inconsistencies, such as the tight link between the military and the government and between religion and the state but, for present purposes, the most significant is the role of ethnicity and its relation to democracy. Israel counts as a democratic state mostly due to high levels of political and societal openness and the robustness of its civil society, and the acceptance as such by the international community.

In his commendable effort to capture the tension between democracy and nationalism, Sammy Smooha coined the term 'ethnic democracy',[16] sug-gesting that the model constitutes a democratic state that is ruled and owned by one ethnic nation. While other groups are allowed political and parliamentary struggle, the state perceives them as a threat and imposes a degree of control over them. The term was intended to broaden democratic theory by a distinct type of democracy, alongside the republican model (France), multicultural democracy (Belgium or Switzerland), and consocia-tional democracy (Netherlands), and could be compared with other states, namely post-communist states, such as Serbia, Slovakia and the Baltic states. Not only is 'ethnic democracy' an oxymoron, the model fails to convince because it is static and does not actually capture the explosiveness and dynamics of the majority–minority relations in regimes with such a narrow understanding of democracy.

All states engage in homogenising tendencies to a lesser or greater degree. Ilan Peleg argues that states such as Israel and Sri Lanka are actively engaged in policies of exclusion, control and domination towards a minority. He refers to such regimes as hegemonic, meaning a state that 'energetically promotes the interests of a single ethnopolitical group in a multinational setting' and, where this regime is designed to sustain the continuation of ethnic hegemony, as Ethnic Constitutional Order.[17] The hegemonic state, he reckons, is a result of a deep-seated fear of the hegemonic group towards the minority. He touches on a particularly relevant point in the escalation of nationalist rhetoric into ethnic violence: the fear and experiences of the past projected into the future, or a strong sense of victimhood to be rectified and prevented forever. All states where these perceptions constitute the main theme in the national narrative show a problematic relationship with the nationally significant minority. Examples are too many but the obvious ones are: Serbia versus Kosovo, Israel and the Arab minority, Turks and Kurds, Tamils and Sinhalese in Sri Lanka, Hutu and Tutsi, and so on.

Since the democratisation of post-communist countries and the international community's involvement in the initiation of 'regime changes', the literature abounds with terms designated for 'hybrid' regimes, meaning various 'diminished subtypes' of democracies (Schedler), or 'illiberal democracies' (Zakaria) and 'pariah regimes' (Pridham) on the continuum between authoritarianism and consolidated advanced democracy.[18] The question is how far can the concept of democracy be stretched before the negative adjectives do not suffice and the regime should be called something else? In his critical analyses of the inter-ethnic relations in Israel and other similar cases, Oren Yiftachel contributed immensely to this debate by bringing in the concept of 'ethnocracy' as a regime 'designed for, and by, a dominant ethnic majority which has appropriated the state apparatus to advance its control over a contested territory and power apparatus'.[19]

Ethnocracy is not a democracy that has not matured; it is not going through a stage towards improvement (while this is inevitable given the internationalisation of human and minority rights); and it is not suffering from misconceptions about the role of ethnicity in democracy as was, and partially remains, the case in a number of post-communist countries. It is a regime that utilises ethnicity to structure society into a major ethnic cleavage in which the dominance of one and the oppression of the other are not the results of a homogenising shallow democracy but the structural reality with the clear aim of territorial control. The key characteristics of such a regime, based on Yiftachel's typology, are:

- Ethnic definition of citizenship, thus power and resource allocation with only partial rights and, by implication, capabilities extended to the minority; ethnically defined *demos* favours co-ethnics from a diaspora over minority citizens.
- The dominant *ethnos* appropriates the state and its apparatus and shapes a political system which – importantly, a mutually reinforcing dynamic – is also shaped by its own exclusionary policies into a sense of perpetual tension.
- The rigid form of long-term ethnic stratification (often aided by religion) in political and economic spheres deeply polarise society.
- The ethnocratic system has a built-in destabilising dynamic whereby the growing resistance of the marginalised minority tends to perpetuate the ethnocratic efforts only to generate more resistance. [20]

The specificity of the ethnocratic regime is twofold. Ethnicity is no longer merely an 'identity' – if it ever is! – but is directly linked to political power, public policy and economic opportunities. The importance of this concept in the present chapter is that ethnocratic regimes, while dynamic in terms of the majority–minority relation, are inherently susceptible to ethnic violence. This is because the imposition of ethnic control over the mixed territory (and beyond, as is the case in Israel), which is assumed rightfully to belong to the dominant ethnos, produces a significantly marginalised and mobilised minority, and fuzzy boundaries of both the state and the *demos*, the definition of which is the source of constant tension. Second, the regime is commonly represented as a democracy, both externally and internally.

The paradox of 'ethnocracy' is that it contains many, and some well-developed, democratic features, such as periodic elections, free media and the freedom of association, and an independent judiciary which often protects some human rights legislation against the government.[21] On the other hand, there are other objective criteria as how to assess democracy,[22] such as inclusive citizenship for all people living in the territory of the state and the rule of law, with individuals and minorities protected from the 'tyranny of the majority' (including independent armed forces). For a regime to call itself democratic, there should be little, if any, scope for disregard of those criteria. Because there are no final democracies, only more or less established ones nearer or further away from the elusive ideal, all democracies must engage in continuous democratisation. In ethnocracy, though, where the erected political and societal structures have become mutually reinforcing and self-legitimising, the democratisation would require a fundamental alteration of the assumptions that underlie it. So, taking the examples of other states that, at some point, showed tendencies towards an ethnocratic system, such as pre-1999 Northern Ireland, pre-1974 Cyprus, pre-EU accession Estonia, pre-1998 Slovakia, the prefix 'pre' signifies the fundamental reorganisation of political life and the incorporation of the minority into power structures in order to democratise the system.

The suggestions here are that the legitimacy of the ethnic element in national self-determination and, hence, the tolerance of a degree of homogenisation perpetrated by nation states, have blurred our understanding of popular control and political equality in the exercise of democracy, and that the solution is more likely to come from the international discourses on human rights and multiculturalism rather than from politics of nation states (I shall return to this theme in the final chapter).

Dynamics of ethnic violence

In his seminal work on ethnic conflict and its possible culmination, ethnic cleansing, Michael Mann offers a shocking statistic: the twentieth-century toll through ethnic cleansing is over seventy million.[23] Mann argues that ethnic cleansing is not primitive, tribal and alien to civilised societies; on the contrary, it is its modernity that needs to be emphasised. There is a number of interrelated factors that have been emerging throughout this text but they need spelling out.

As has been stressed many times already, modernity is structured by ethnic and nationalist principles, and its institutions and citizenship are tied to ethnic and national forms of exclusion. There were many reasons for the disintegration of Yugoslavia (see the previous chapter) but the tragedy of the subsequent violence has to be sought in the ethnicicised constitution. A part of the colonisation of the territory by the dominant nationality (and not necessarily in terms of numerical preponderance) is also the establishment of 'settler democracies', such as South Africa and Australia which was accompanied by widespread violence against the native populations. With a few exceptions, the establishment of political and territorial control of the dominant ethno-nation, promoted in the twentieth century by the lofty principle of national self-determination, continues to be accompanied by ethnic violence.

The resistance to the domination and the subsequent stratification of society into its own socio-economic patterns is often violent. I am mentioning the socio-economic aspect here because, while the economy follows its own dynamics and is subject to many theories beyond my expertise, the denial of economic opportunities to

minorities and native populations in settlers' societies also constitutes a 'darker side of democracy'. Class is not often mentioned
in the writing on ethno-nationalism, not even by experts such as
Horowitz (1985) and Connor (1993) who stress the emotiveness
of ethnicity as its main mobilising potential. While it may be true
that the ethnic bond has a supreme capacity to invoke passion, it is
hardly the case that emotiveness by itself would give rise to hostile
feelings towards other ethnic groups. The sense of solidarity that
ethno-national mobilisation requires is usually strengthened by a
sense of indignation at the position of one's ethnic group. That
sense of indignation can derive from many sources, such as the
threat to physical security or the neglect of full democratic rights,
but also from the overall socio-economic position within the
society. In that sense, as Mann argues, ethno-nationalism 'is the
strongest where it can capture other senses of exploitation'.[24]

Conflict happens, and often becomes murderous, when there is a
claim of political sovereignty to the territory by two rival groups,
one of which is the power holder, and where rivalry is laid on
top of other ideological and religious differences (Kashmir, Israel,
Yugoslavia, Chechnya). The usual scenario is: the military dominance of one group is compensated for by the rival group's reliance on the civilian population (guerrilla warfare) or on help from
outside (African conflicts, Kashmir, Palestine, Northern Ireland).
The latter increasingly falls under the label of terrorism. [25] Among
the many difficulties in combating terrorism, particularly terrorism
aimed at the independence of an ethnic group who perceive themselves to be in a subordinate position,[26] thus already highly mobilised, is that strategies employed to stop terror, instead of reducing
conditions that instigated it, lead to further alienation of the group
and that in turn to more radicalisation.

The intensity of the violence depends on a number of mutually
interrelated internal factors: motives, elite constellation, popular
support, paramilitaries, etc. The creation of ethnic tension can be
intentional for the political purpose of mobilisation, but murder
and genocide are rarely planned in their full horror (with some
exceptions, perhaps Hitler, but even there the extent of the murder
was partially a result of party politics and failed military cam-
paigns). Ethnically motivated conflict creates its own expanding
elites who, for political or ideological reasons, may be more radical
than the original elites responsible for the initiation of the conflict.
The radicalisation of the existing conflict easily spirals into more

violence, precisely because ethnic leaders engage in factional struggle and seek alliances, mobilise the population to further their agenda, enlist paramilitary groups, and increasingly use organised crime to finance their operations. While ethno-national mobilisation has an overall agenda and appears to follow nationalism's ethos of homogeneity, it is increasingly obvious that ethnic struggle is as much subject to intra-group rivalry as any other political struggle is. [27] For example, while the plight of the Palestinians has an overarching agenda, within this agenda, the two main factions, El Fatah and Hamas and their respective supporters pursue different 'narrower' agendas – the problem is that, at the other end, there is the population whose interests can get lost in the fluidity of the dynamics that evolve during ethnic conflicts.

Are there solutions?

Just as there are no 'murderous' nations, there are no 'virtuous' nations. People, so it seems, will commit ethnic violence under certain circumstances.

1. They will commit such violence if they are told that 'the other' will harm them or has an intention to do so on the basis of a historical narrative which is always given to stereotyping. For example, the disintegration of Czechoslovakia was peaceful because there was no historical precedence of violence between Czechs and Slovaks. The disintegration of Yugoslavia descended into violence because the mobilisation was partly founded on a violent history between all main ethnic groups (Serbs, Croats and Muslims).

2. The initial violence tends to radicalise groups and produce more violence. This is the case of the Israeli-Palestinian conflict.

3. When an ethnic group is committed to certain goals regardless of human cost, believing in the righteousness of their cause beyond any doubts, the peer pressure then begins to demand absolute commitment, and thus more violence.

4. When state policies, no matter how obscene and how dehumanising for victims and perpetrators, are executed by the regime, modern bureaucracy shows more concern for efficiency than for the consequences of the actions. This extreme form of violence against a people was exemplified by the Holocaust and described famously as the 'banality of evil' by Hannah Arendt (*Eichmann in Jerusalem: A Report on the Banality of Evil*, 1963). In all cases,

the institutionalisation of crime against an ethnic group allows for the worst of humanity to emerge but it would be a mistake to class all conflicts as 'identity' conflicts and neglect the political power which remains decisive to ethnic violence.

Ethnic conflict is on the increase rather than on the decrease. Peace treaties fail. But, we know from the history of the north (America and Europe) that ethnic violence is also a passing phenomenon. More recognition of reasons, more accumulation of knowledge, more critical assessment of previous conflicts and their roots, more sensitivity to local conditions in the implementation of peace, and more equal wealth distribution may lead to solutions, as they did in the northern part of the globe.

I end where I began. The answer we are looking for is not that ethno-national bonding has dangerous implications – we know that. At some point, and it is hopelessly late already, we must be able to decide what other kind of solidarity can be forged that offers an identity meaningful enough to fulfil the sense of uniqueness without the exclusion of others. While we are conflating ethnicity and politics, politically motivated, identity-driven violence remains the dark side, not only of democracy but of humanity because, as Sen rightly remarks, 'the connection between cultural bigotry and political tyranny is very close'.[28]

Notes

1. Sen (2006), *Identity and Violence*, p. xii. See also Erika Harris (2007), 'Identity and violence in international politics', *Filozofia*, 62:6, pp. 560–2.
2. Sen, *Identity and Violence*, p. xv.
3. Wimmer (2002), *Nationalist Exclusion and Ethnic Conflict*, p. 2.
4. Smith (1991), *National Identity*, p. 74.
5. Appadurai (2006), *Fear of Small Numbers*, p. 1.
6. Connor (1993), 'Beyond reason: the nature of the ethnonational bond', p. 384.
7. Connor (2001), 'Homelands in a World of States', pp. 54–9; Harris (2002), *Nationalism and Democratisation*, p. 156.
8. Yiftachel (2001), 'The Homeland and Nationalism', p. 360.
9. Appadurai, *Fear of Small Numbers*, pp. 127–30.
10. Ian Black, 'Six days of war, 40 years of failure' in *The Guardian*, 5 June 2007, p. 21.
11. Yiftachel and Ghanem (2004), 'Towards a theory of ethnocratic regimes', p. 182.
12. Shlomo Ben-Ami (2006), *Scars of War, Wounds of Peace: The Israeli–Arab Tragedy*; Benny Morris (2008), *1948: A History of the First Arab–Israeli War*; Edward Said (1994), *The Politics of Dispossession: The Struggle for Palestinian Self-Determination 1969–94*; Walter Laqueur and Barry Rubin (eds) (2001), *The Israel–Arab Reader: A Documentary History of the Middle East Conflict*; Mehran Kamrava (2005), *The Modern Middle East*, chapters 4 and 7.
13. Shlomo Ben-Ami (2008), 'A War to Start all Wars', p. 1.

14. Shlomo Avineri (1981), *The Making of Modern Zionism: Intellectual Origins of the Jewish State*, New York: Basic Books; Gideon Shimoni (1997), *The Zionist Ideology*, Waltham, MA: Brandeis University Press.
15. Shlomo Ben-Ami, 'A War to Start all Wars', p. 4.
16. Smooha (2002), 'Types of democracy and modes of conflict management in ethnically divided societies', pp. 423–31.
17. Peleg (2007), *Democratizing a Hegemonic State*, p. 3.
18. Diamond (2002), 'Elections without Democracy: Thinking about Hybrid Regimes'; Schedler (1998), 'What is Democratic Consolidation'; Zakaria, (2003), *The Future of Freedom: Illiberal Democracy at Home and Abroad*; Pridham, (2001), 'Uneasy Democratisations – Pariah Regimes, Political Conditionality and Reborn Transitions in Central and Eastern Europe', pp. 65–94.
19. Yiftachel and Ghanem (2004), 'Towards a theory of ethnocratic regimes', pp. 179–97.
20. Ibid. p. 181.
21. Ibid. p. 188.
22. See Roald Dahl (1982), *Dilemmas of Pluralist Democracy*, New Haven: Yale University Press.
23. Mann (2004), *The Dark Side of Democracy: Explaining Ethnic Cleansing*, p. 2.
24. Ibid. p. 5.
25. Ibid. p. 6.
26. Ignatieff (2005), *The Lesser Evil*, p. 83.
27. Caspersen (2008), 'Intragroup divisions in ethnic conflicts: from popular grievances to power struggles', pp. 239–65.
28. Sen, *Identity and Violence*, p. 105.

CHAPTER SIX

Imagining 'the Nation' Beyond the State

In the last two chapters I have intimated a number of times that ethnic mobilisation crosses state boundaries. In shall chapter I will argue that ethnic kin has become an important category in the studies of nationalism and in international relations. The ethno-national group as a political actor is not new; this is where the territorialised nation state enters the political world. Ethnic identity as a political actor operating within, beyond and between states is also not new but the scale and the political consequences for our understanding of the impact of ethnicity and its interplay with the nationalisms of nation states are relatively new and increasingly more compelling aspects of identity politics. This chapter is concerned mainly with diasporas and other forms of transnationalism which pertain to ethnic identities but they are a sure sign that the geopolitical space of the nation state is no longer a sacred territory of and for its nationals. The implications are that the tightly connected trinity of the nation, its territory, and the state are disturbed and so are the classical meanings of citizenship and political communities because the boundaries of who is 'in' and who is 'out' are very blurred.

Diaspora: a fractured identity

To be a host is also to be a guest. This is the defining purpose, the justification of Diaspora.[1]

Diaspora (from the Greek *diasperien* meaning to scatter/split seed) in its original use in Greek translations of Hebrew scriptures identified Jewish communities in Hellenic Alexandria. The connotation is clear: people dislocated from their homeland, or more precisely, 'a people of common origins who reside, more or less on a permanent basis, outside the borders of their ethnic or religious homeland – whether that homeland is real or symbolic, independent or under foreign control'.[2] It is also clear that, with the rising number of people around the world who are living elsewhere than where they may think of as their homeland, whether willingly or for other reasons, any debate about the role of identity in our 'nomadic' world[3] of immigration and increased refugee crises would be incomplete without the inclusion of this phenomenon.

As with all collective identities and their external manifestations (for identity always makes more sense to the bearer than to the observer), the diaspora is a difficult category of people to theorise about. First, diasporic identity is a construct that amalgamates a number of supposed identities which are a construct in themselves. Second, diasporas are rooted in longing – hence, the aim of activity is the maintenance of melancholy not of contentment. Third, for a student of diasporas there are more questions than answers. Is everybody who does not live in their original homeland a members of a diaspora? How long does a person need to be away to justify a diasporic identity? Is it self-definitional or is it a label given by others? Is it an identity or a state of being? Is, for example, a Jew living in Israel in diaspora if he or she feels more affinity towards a country of origin than towards Israel? Finally, what is the difference between a minority, a diaspora, and migrants? There are many other questions, all suggesting a hazy category of a collective identity that lumps together political and historical processes and economic globalisation, and therefore methodologically possibly too confused to be of serious analytical consequence. Despite this, diasporas are emerging as the most fascinating and increasingly more relevant identity-related category participating in international politics.

Diasporic identity is a hybrid in the sense that there are other identities accompanying it. The inherent amalgamation and intersection of cultural, physical and temporal boundaries reflect rather well the fractured and complex condition of our world when we are asked to re-examine what we assumed were the well-established concepts of the nation, citizenship and the nation state. On the other hand, diasporas also offer some respite from the insecurities of homogenising globalisation by their stubborn ethnic connotation. We are in the realm of 'trans-nationalism' but, while the increased movement of ideas and goods across the globe – globalisation – may be responsible for the increased number of diasporas, the latter, unlike other movements, refers specifically to the combination of human experience and territorial dislocation, that is, the move from the 'home nation state' to the 'host nation state'. Diaspora is also an 'imagined community', but a word imagined is hardly ever more appropriate because 'imagining' in diasporic identity not only crosses the boundaries but creates a new identity, with a whole new dimension of being in diaspora.

Such a person is not merely someone who left their state for a while and may or may not return, this is a person who joined a new society, a new polity and whose life and identity have been touched by this experience (for how could it be otherwise) but who remains closely tied to memory, image and geography, and at times even to the economy and politics of the state of presumed origins. This person is a member of a new imagined community with overlapping boundaries of membership whose daily experience of life is in one place but whose belonging is a composite of who they are and the imagination of who they were or would have been; this is a human condition which enables them to join the imaginary community of all diasporic peoples, but particularly their own diaspora. So, for example: part of Jewish identity is actually being in perpetual diaspora with a sense of attachment to the land of Israel, even before the modern state of Israel had been established and even if most Jews in the world have never set eyes on the land of Israel. In Britain (not elsewhere to my knowledge), at weddings and other major events in Jewish life, there is always a celebratory toast to 'the Queen and the land of Israel' which demonstrates the hybridity of Jewish identity rather well. Equally, a necessary part of the Caribbean imagery is the African past – thus an identity attached to the present homeland but combined with the identity of a far-away place and time, not necessarily seen or experienced. West Indians living in diaspora then tend to maintain their Caribbean culture with all its dimensions but, necessarily, will add a new dimension that reflects their relationship with the host country.

William Safran[4] argued that Jewish diaspora is the 'ideal type' but there are many other dispersions of peoples, such as Armenian,

Turkish, Palestinian, Greek, Irish, Cuban, Chinese and North African diasporas, to name but a few of the more numerous ones. He also sketched a six-point characterisation of diasporic identity:

1. they or their ancestors were dispersed;
2. they retain a collective memory, vision, and myth about their homeland's physical location, history and achievements;
3. they believe they are not and perhaps cannot be accepted fully by their host country and therefore feel partly alienated;
4. they regard their homeland as their true ideal home where they or their descendants should return when conditions are appropriate;
5. they believe that they should collectively be committed to the maintenance and restoration of their homeland and its safety and prosperity;
6. they continue to relate personally or vicariously to that homeland in one way or another, and their ethno-communal consciousness and solidarity are importantly defined by the existence of such a relationship.

This is a fairly exhaustive list of characteristics which does not mean, however, that all are present in all diasporic groups. While return when 'conditions are appropriate' may be the primary element of the Palestinian diaspora, not many Irish Americans dream of return, just as many Jews would not consider living in Israel, but probably most Irish Americans and Jews consider the safety and prosperity of their respective 'homelands' to be paramount. Interestingly, it is the Hungarian diaspora in Eastern and Central Europe that fits all these characteristics more accurately but hardly ever appears in the ever more prominent writing on diaspora in scholarly literature because its identity is usually dealt with under the rubric of minorities. The Hungarian minority will be discussed below in more detail.

For the present purposes, it is most important to reiterate that: (1) the defining characteristics of diaspora are the collective consciousness and solidarity based on the experience of displacement and loss whereby 'not belonging' is a constitutive element of identity in itself; (2) diasporas do not seek a nation state – they have one somewhere, whether real or mythical; (3) if the homeland remains the subject of the ongoing prejudice or injustice, the sense of diasporic experience is intensified (for example, Palestinians,

Jews, Chechens, Kosovans, Irish until recently); (4) diasporic identity is not temporary; inevitably it involves a degree of accommodation of the host country. The black diaspora in post colonial Britain is seeking a different way of being 'British', and the same applies for British Muslims. The construction of identity here is of homeland and host land merged into one that is not transitional. In fact, there is a concerted effort on the part of these groups to entrench this identity but live and function in a new world as an accepted person. The distinction between diaspora and temporary residence in a host country is well illustrated by the example of migrant workers from Eastern and Central Europe within the European Union. There is a considerable Polish, Ukrainian and Latvian diaspora in Britain who arrived after World War II. These people could not go back to their countries because some ceased to exist and became the Soviet Union (Latvia and Ukraine) or, in many cases, they did not want to return for a number of reasons which are not relevant here. They have established robust networks in the form of clubs, meetings and bulletins, church services, delicatessens and so on. Interestingly, the migrant workers who arrived in Britain after 2004 and who expect to return to their homelands rarely participate in the life of these 'settled' diasporas because they do not see their situation in terms of permanence or future but as a transitional stage in their life. It is most likely that, apart from food and language, the new eastern Europeans have little in common with the post-1945 co-ethnic diaspora and more with other migrants with whom they share the experience of living and working in Britain today.

In terms of a greater understanding of contemporary nationalism, diasporas and related transnational networks, which link people in host societies across states' boundaries to their homelands and in the process produce something of overlapping affiliations, beg important questions about the role of ethnicity in our time: are we observing an emergence of a less national order or the return to atavistic primordial identities? I shall return to the first part of the question in the next chapter and to the second part of this question in the final concluding chapter.

It is difficult to deny that there are two major forces operating simultaneously in our world: on the one hand, increasing globalisation and regional integration facilitate more intense transnational linkages contributing to a greater sense of cosmopolitanism and inclusiveness; on the other hand, there is also rising ethno-nationalism. This dynamic is not as paradoxical as it appears; everything that has been said before suggests that diasporas, transnationalism, and ethno-nationalism are 'intertwined solidarities and practices'.[5] Many minorities, previously subordinated and denied recognition in their states, are, precisely because of opportunities offered by globalisation, becoming self-conscious diasporic transnational communities aided by new informal global networks of trade and communication that escape the constraints of national borders. Seteney Shami[6] illustrates these developments in the case of Circassians and Chechens of the north Caucasus. Without repeating the details of this case, the point is that these Caucasus people have been, over the centuries, separated by migration within the Ottoman Empire to modern-day Turkey, Syria and Jordan, and within the Soviet Union (with its complex web of republics, administrative districts and autonomous regions). The dissolution of the Soviet Union shifted political and geographic boundaries and led to a number of conflicts, among them Russian–Chechen and the Abkhasian–Georgian war. The events in the Caucasus mobilised and united Circassians and Chechens living in Jordan who began to provide financial aid and political support for the struggle in the homelands that, nevertheless, do not exist as a separate entity. There is a limit to what a diaspora can do when there is no home state as such, and no prospect for its emergence, but organisations such as The World Circassian Association have certainly reinvigorated ethnic identity among the diaspora, and there is no telling how this will affect the position of this minority within the Russian political space. For the moment, though, from some tiny airport in some far-away place on the Georgian border, flights are leaving for Dubai and Istanbul carrying people and merchandise. New networks have been established among a people separated by their recent histories and geographies but brought together by the change in local politics and global economic opportunities and especially by ethnic ties. It is ethnicity that produces diaspora and reinvigorates the ethnicity-based relationship between themselves and the homeland, thus intensifying the ethnic element in an otherwise global phenomenon.

Homeland politics and diaspora

There are statistics that claim that the risk of renewed conflict after five years of post-conflict peace is six times higher in societies with the largest diaspora in America.[7] Presumably this is through providing financial aid to rebel organisations and possibly providing recruits and arms for armed struggle. Examples are many: the support of the Irish diaspora for the Irish Republican Army during the Irish conflict; the continuous support for Israeli government policies in the occupied territories by some members of the Jewish diaspora worldwide; the support in terms of money and fighters for the insurgency in Iraq and Afghanistan from abroad; and so on. These are tangible and extreme examples of the role of diasporas in international politics but there are other more subtle ways in which diasporas operate as international actors. It must be argued that, at a time of increased migration and rising numbers of refugees and general internationalisation of minority issues, diasporas are no longer merely a fascinating subcategory of ethnic and anthropological studies but also a challenger for both the international relations theory and practice and our conventional understanding of national identities and notions of citizenship.

The leading Hungarian political party FIDESZ made its main policy goal (1998 governing programme) the creation of an 'organic relationship of the Hungarian communities with the motherland', thus unifying the Hungarian nation 'without border revisions'. FIDESZ tried not merely to expand its voters' base by declaring itself a party of the preservation of Hungarian national identity but also responded to the rising political profile of ethnic kin in the neighbouring states who 'at times are more loyal than a large proportion of the Hungarians within the border', and who 'constitute an additional resource for the entire Hungarian nation'.[8] This mutually reinforcing relationship between the Hungarian state and its diaspora eventually led to a legally dubious Status Law passed unilaterally by the Hungarian parliament (2001) and extending special benefits and subsidies (access to the Hungarian labour market and other social and cultural benefits) to three million ethnic Hungarians living in Slovakia, Romania, Ukraine, Croatia and Serbia on the presentation of ethnic identity cards. Leaving aside the issue of non-consultation with the neighbouring states about their citizens, the controversy surrounding the logistics of identity cards as an extension of the Hungarian state distributed on the territory of other sovereign states and the criticism by the European Union which eventually led to the acceptable revision of this law, the most important aspect to emphasise here is the extension of a partial citizenship to ethnic kin beyond the state. Hence, the elevation of the ethnic principle to the detriment of good neighbourly relations, which were severely tested over the centuries in the region already, has implications in terms of political theory and illustrates the direct influence of diaspora in political competition in Hungary and beyond.[9]

This is just one example of diaspora politics that, however disruptive, must not be viewed as leading to a potentially violent conflict. Hungary is not the only post-communist state with some form of kin-state legislation. Slovakia, Romania and Poland have also included links to their ethnic kin abroad in their constitutions. The controversy of the Hungarian Status Law when compared to, for example, a similar Slovak legislation, is in its assertive extra-territorial implications: the *Slovak Law* (culture and education only) is implemented exclusively by the Slovak governmental authorities in Slovakia to any persons from any country who can prove Slovak ethnic background. As Slovakia has no significant ethnic communities in the neighbouring countries, the law has few political and legal implications. This, however, is not the point I am making here.

The point I wish to emphasise is that, not only does diaspora seek links to homeland but homeland, particularly in times of insecurity and domestic political turmoil, seeks diaspora. Another example is the ethnic Russians in the Crimea, many of whom, in addition to their Ukrainian citizenship, carry a Russian passport which, in the light of the present tension between Ukraine and Moscow, could be problematic because, in the unlikely scenario of escalation, Russia has the right to defend its citizens.[10] The extension of partial citizenship rights to diaspora contradicts all our assumptions about a territorially bounded nation, coterminous with the geopolitical space of the state which extends rights and duties to its citizens.

A similar 'concern' for diaspora under different conditions can, however, lead to violence as it did in the former Yugoslavia. The complexities of the Yugoslav conflict are better understood if we add the diaspora dimension to the already fairly explosive mixture of post-communist turbulence and secessionist fragmentation: the role of Serbian state-sponsored irredentist activities of their ethnic kin in neighbouring republics, in tune with the overall Serbian effort to recover all Serb-inhabited territories for the greater Serbia. Similarly, if the Israeli prime minister, Ariel Sharon, says that 'the future of Israel is not just a matter for Israelis who live there' because 'Israel belongs to the entire Jewish people',[11] he is trying to legitimise Israeli foreign policy through a direct appeal to Jews everywhere and a suggestion that Israel is larger and stronger than just its Jewish citizens.

Not all homeland–diaspora–homeland relationships are equally effective when it comes to seeking support or influencing homeland policies. The effectiveness of this relationship is not determined by the strength of ethnic identity even if it is ethnicity that is the primary motivation. People may feel very strongly about their identity but that does not mean that they will, or can, support the homeland or that the homeland will appeal for their help. Shain and Barth argue that, for diaspora to exert influence there should be a motive, opportunity and means.[12] For example, while there exists a considerable Ukrainian diaspora in the West, during the Soviet era there was a minimal relationship between the communist Ukraine and its diaspora who were not perceived as an asset to the communist regime; and, communist Ukraine was not the homeland that fitted the diaspora's memory of home nor was it a regime they wanted to support. Similar arguments could be made about today's Tibet. No matter how much the Tibetan diaspora may wish to influence its homeland, while the latter remains under Chinese control, its efforts are limited to, at most, raising awareness about Tibet in the outside world with the aim of exerting some pressure on the Chinese government.

Opportunity and means depend largely on the nature of the host land and the receptiveness of the homeland. The host land needs to be democratic enough to enable diaspora to flourish and organise, while it is usually a degree of weakness or stress that makes the homeland seek diaspora's influence in its domestic affairs. The latter explains the increased interest in diaspora in newly formed states and in states that fear for their political and/or economic survival or are engaged in conflicts – in short, weak states. The motivations of the diaspora and the homeland do not run in parallel, though.

For the diaspora, the motivation is usually based on identity and self-image. In some cases, such as the Armenian diaspora's pursuit of the recognition of the genocide committed by the Turks (1915), it is a question of a great trauma suffered by people who formed the original diaspora and their need to have their suffering recognised by the world. For the homeland, the motivation is much more pragmatic and concerns mostly some form of advancement of national interest, in terms of domestic political competition, lobbying or increased international influence. As a rule, members of a diaspora do not vote, with the exception of those with dual nationality, but they tend to support certain political parties, usually nationalistically inclined parties, thus participating indirectly in the domestic politics of their homelands. Internationally, the actions of a thus-invited diaspora to participate in domestic politics can be counterproductive. When, after many years of lobbying, the Armenian diaspora finally succeeded in having the Armenian genocide recognised by the United States Congress (2007), this led to very strained relations between Turkey which has always denied the genocide, and the United States. The final success of the Armenian diaspora cames at a time when Turkey is one of the most important allies in the 'war on terror'[13] and when an Armenian state may be better served by better relationships with Turkey, possibly even at the cost of drawing a line under the historical injustice, than by the relationship with the much-involved diaspora whose *raison d'être* is actually in the past.

Ethnic kin across the border: the Hungarian minority in Central Europe

I am returning to Central Europe, namely the Hungarian minorities in order to unravel the concept of 'transnationalism' which is closely related to diaspora and, in certain geographical spaces, synonymous with it. Central European geopolitical space has been historically marked by both political integration and fragmentation and the turbulent changes of political regimes. This led to frequent repositioning of borders, and that to a changing status of ethnic groups vis-à-vis their states. The repositioning of borders due to the breakdown of old empires and establishment of new post-World War II states, left the previously dominant Hungarian nationality reduced in status and number as some three million ethnic Hungarians found themselves outside Hungary. There was further repositioning of borders during World War II when more fragmentation and annexation took place, only to be followed by further geopolitical shifts, repatriations and expulsions. Finally, more fragmentation followed the demise of communism and the dissolution of the communist multinational states. The Yugoslav conflict may have concluded the history of fragmentation in the region with more ethnic communities, such as Serbs finding themselves on the 'wrong' side of the border. The repositioning of borders has created a patchwork of diasporas, old, newer and very new, and their interrelations should be the subject of more research, but this is not the brief here.

European integration and transnationalism

The Central European region is once more becoming a new geopolitical space, this time under the latest political integration – the European Union. If there ever was a region in the world where ethnicity remains the only constant in the turbulence of failing regimes, changed fortunes of national groups and the names of the countries, then Central Europe must be the prime example. At the same time, though, Central Europe is also an example of the continuing efforts to improve inter-ethnic relations.

European integration disturbed the traditional relationships between the state, the nation, sovereignty and democracy. It is creating a multifaceted political entity with diffused sovereignty; it split state competencies into various levels of governance; and even seeks to exercise an influence over democratic processes from beyond the state boundaries.[14] The operative word here is 'multifaceted'. The assumptions are that identities and interests of national groups will also adjust and, where appropriate, assume multiple affiliations between the place of residence and 'kin' territory, and that this will (and, in some cases, it already does) involve institutional arrangements and policies that cross state boundaries, and that these 'trans-national territories emerge as a significant framework for economic, social and political change'.[15] This would lead to the politics of 'transnationalism' – that is, a form of affiliation that is less defined by the relationship of the individual to state citizenship and more by solidarity based on other factors, for example, region or ethnic kin.[16] Just as diasporas do transnationalism defies the conventional meaning of the state and does not fit easily into the classical nationalist doctrine because, while there is certainly an attempt at self-rule over such ethnically defined territory, it is not the same as the exclusive territorial control of the state. One ought to be aware that this is subtly different from substate regionalism, for example, Scotland or Wales with their devolved Scottish Parliament and the Welsh Assembly. In Central Europe, substate region usually denotes an ethno-region which is a territory on two sides of a state border based on ethnic kinship. We are observing an overlap between what a home state calls a diaspora living in the neighbouring state and a minority with an ethnic kin in the neighbouring state, when viewed from the host state's perspective. This ethnic community is thus politically significant for both home and host state. Under the present conditions of European integration, there is an increased transnational activity among co-ethnics across the border.

New institutional contours require a degree of speculation. Theoretically, the impact of this 'trans-national integration' can, at this stage, provide only some tentative suggestions.

1. European integration diminishes the role of the nation as the dominant

owner of the state which should make the position of all minority groups more secure in all spheres, cultural, economic and political.

2. European integration changes the traditional meaning of borders which brings diaspora and homeland closer together. This is of huge importance. Historically, borders in Central Europe have been subject to a constant renegotiation, always producing contradictory and overlapping ethnic zones and leading to increased ethnic and social divisions, exclusion and political conflict. When this is no longer the case, the borders become significant by their absence and, at this stage, it is difficult to ascertain what consequences this may have on the majority–minority relationships and how this may affect the sense of loss in diasporic communities who are no longer cut off from their homeland and live in similar economic and political conditions to those in it. This is probably best expressed in the words of a Slovak MEP for the Hungarian Coalition (SMK), Edit Bauer: 'No borders as such! It is an historic moment of unforeseen circumstances'.[17]

3. New political arrangements increase trans-border co-operation which we are assuming will reinvigorate kinship identity and produces ethno-regions. This is only as assumption, however, and, in the absence of sufficient empirical evidence, should remain so. It is clear, however, that there is a blurring of boundaries between national, international and regional and that this fluidity of spaces within which politics are conducted will lead logically to a fluidity of affiliations with varied consequences.

My own research confirms that there is an ethno-region emerging among the Hungarian minority in the southern Slovak–Hungarian border region. I am not suggesting that the region is ethnically homogeneous – on the Slovak side the population is mixed even if overwhelmingly Hungarian. It is important to note that the Hungarian minority is well represented by the Party of the Hungarian Coalition (SMK) which has been one of the most stable and dominant political parties in the Slovak government (1998–2006) even if, currently, it is in opposition. Owing to the combination of the historical significance of Hungary and the political weight of the Hungarian minority at the centre of Slovak politics, the national question in Slovakia is exemplified by this inter-ethnic relationship more than any other.

Ethnic Hungarians in Slovakia are perceived by their homeland as a part of their diaspora and, as has been suggested earlier, they are also perceived as an extension of the Hungarian nation and, thus, a subject of the Hungarian national consciousness, particularly its preoccupation with the post-World War I settlements by which these minorities were 'lost' to Hungary. Slovakia, too, sees them as an extension of Hungary which, in Slovak national consciousness, is synonymous with the national and political oppression within the Austro-Hungarian Empire, the annexation of its territories during World War II, and, in some extreme nationalist circles, accused of continuing irredentist aspirations. Hence, the relationship remains strained and is easily aggravated by the smallest political incident committed by either side. More serious complaints of the Hungarian minority concern firstly, the Slovak Constitution (1992) which refers to 'the Slovak nation', thus implicitly excluding Hungarians from 'ownership' of the state, as well as other demands concerning the constitutional guarantees, the boundaries of administrative districts and the legally and emotionally complex issue of the revocation of the Beneš Decrees. These refer to the post-World War II Czechoslovak President Beneš whose decrees legally justified the confiscation of Hungarian properties in Slovakia and the expulsions of some three million Sudeten Germans from the Czech lands. The Hungarian and the Czech minorities were accused of being 'collectively guilty' of collaboration with Nazi Germany. None of these decrees has actually been revoked and there are no restitutions for the confiscated Hungarian properties available under the current Slovak and Czech legislations. This is a sensitive and regrettable situation. While decrees can probably not be revoked, because that would bring into question other post-World War II settlements, the label of 'collective guilt' can and should be constitutionally removed because it weighs heavily on the majority–minority relationship and inhibits open dialogue about the events of World War II.

Cracks in the unity of the diaspora are also appearing, however: the more liberal and left-wing members of the diaspora are dissatisfied with the Hungarian Coalition as their only representative in Slovakia and accuse the party of being too conservative and of maintaining the ethnic tension rather than resolving the poor economy of the border region.[18] With reference to the already mentioned Status Law, interestingly, most representatives of the Hungarian minority I interviewed considered the law a form of political manipulation, orchestrated by the Hungarian right for the purpose of bolstering its waning pre-election campaign on the Hungarian side, and aided by the most nationalistic wing of the Hungarian Coalition on the Slovakian side. It would seem that, on both sides of the border, national(ist) elites use this minority for their own political purposes.

So, what has been gleaned from the empirical investigation I conducted among the Hungarian diaspora in the Slovak–Hungarian southern region? The focus of this ethnographic survey was to capture perceptions about politics and about sense of belonging among the minority one year after accession into the European Union, and test my assumptions about 'trans-nationalism'.[19] For the present purpose, the following is perhaps of interest.

1. In the Central European context, diaspora is often synonymous with an historical minority (autochthonous) whose state affiliation has changed because of the repositioning of borders following the establishment of new states whether after the collapse of the Austro-Hungarian and Ottoman Empires or that of the communist states. This is very different from Western

Europe where diasporas usually refer to immigration. Both types of diaspora face specific problems and require specific legislative arrangements for solutions. The geographic concentration of diaspora, and the existence of ethnic parties, contrary to Western Europe, puts diaspora into the centre of political life in the host state which perceives them as a minority. Depending on the historical relationship between the home and host state, this minority is then often scrutinised for its irredentist tendencies and generally carries a burden of the interstate relationship. This double-edged status of these ethnic communities means that their politics follow a minority route while their relationship with the home state and the construction of their identity tend to be those of the diaspora.

2. The identity of the Hungarian diaspora in Slovakia is overwhelmingly ethnic: some 84 per cent of respondents view themselves primarily as a 'Hungarian living in Slovakia'. This is further confirmed by the 80 per cent response to 'European, but ethnically Hungarian' identity. Interestingly, while the Slovak state is viewed strictly as a place of residence (75 per cent), the political affiliation appears to be European (80 per cent). When, however, compared with results concerning political interests, Europe is in third place after locality (the majority of respondents) and the national level (Bratislava). The external homeland, that is Budapest, takes precedence in terms of political interests only in places geographically nearest to the Hungarian border. The further away from the border, or nearer Bratislava (where the locality is actually the capital), Budapest ceases to be important.

I would conclude that we are probably observing a very slow regionalisation of the Hungarian diaspora within the European Union context. To make a more meaningful statement about 'transnationalism', one would have to conduct a similar survey among a number of different diasporas in a number of different border regions. In the absence of such a comparative study, a degree of caution is required when claiming the emergence of an ethnoregion in the southern 'Hungarian belt' between Slovakia and Hungary. On the other hand, my research confirmed that the Hungarian diaspora's cultural and political life takes place in their region and that state affiliation is marginalised in favour of ethnic affiliation. This could be for historical reasons but, most probably it is rather a reflection of the actual life which, is and has been for centuries, lived mostly among co-ethnics in overwhelmingly Hungarian regions where even Slovaks tend to speak Hungarian.

3. The most important finding concerns the relationship between 'transnationalism' and the long-term influence on the relationship between the host state (Slovakia) and homeland (Hungary). Some 90 per cent of respondents believed it to be positive. If transnationalism is also about stability in ethnically complex regions, then open borders and less state-centric politics of the nation state appear to be more conducive to regional stability. The

Slovak–Hungarian relationship, as it were 'on the ground', is much better than at political and interstate levels where tensions are often exaggerated for various political reasons but, in the conflict-ridden border regions, transnationalism is probably a way towards a more peaceful coexistence.

Defying the conventions of the nation state

Theoretically, diasporas defy many conventions of democratic theory, international relations and nationalism. The assumptions underlying our political understanding of the world can be summed up as follows:

1. Nationalism assumes that the world is, and should be, divided into nation states that embody distinct nations.

2. International relations theory takes the sovereign state exercising territorial jurisdiction to be the principal political unit of the international system.

3. The people, the political nation to whom the geopolitical space of the state is allocated, are its citizens. Citizens are accorded a whole set of rights and duties and, when democratically conceived, they are collectively entitled to self-government in pursuit of their personal projects and collective will;[20] importantly, this political equality is also the privilege of full members only.

Everything that has been said about diasporas suggests that these assumptions do not fully apply. Diasporas can, and increasingly do, actively influence a homeland's (ancestral or kin-state) foreign policies. This contradicts the state-centrically preoccupied foundations of international relations theory because diasporas reside outside the state but claim a stake within. The tightly connected trinity of the nation, its territory, and the state is disturbed, as are the arguments about citizenship, civic nations and political community because the boundaries of who is 'in' and who is 'out' are very blurred. We are entering a murky area of the de-territorialised nation, where civic equality is subordinated to ethnic solidarity reaching beyond the state's boundaries. As a word of caution, it is perhaps worth considering whether the use of nationalist rhetoric to appeal to diasporic communities may undermine their chances for full participation in the civic community of their residence? This question applies more to migrant communities who may benefit more from such participation and commitment to their new host country than a nostalgic hankering after a homeland to which they may never return. The more settled historical diaporas, such as the Hungarian diaspora, shows that they have found a modus vivendi in the host states and seem successfully to combine civic participation with diasporic identity. In the latter case, it is the states that find their duality more difficult to accept. I have also argued that the issue of dual affiliation is less problematic in more de-territorialised regions, such as the European Union.

Diasporas are a triumph of ethnicity and homeland territory but they are also a sign that the geopolitical space of the nation state is no longer a sacred territory of and for its nationals. The point of this chapter has been to describe a phenomenon of collective identity, operating within and beyond the nation state, which is not easily explained by any theory of nationalism but is nevertheless a phenomenon inspired by ethno-national identity.[21] The preceding discussion about diasporas and trans-nationalism endorses my argument, advanced throughout and emphasised in the concluding two chapters, that binary concepts of ethnic or civic identity and primordial or modernist approaches to nationalism no longer satisfactorily answer complex questions relating to various forms of ethno-political affiliations in our world, and that new theoretical imagination beyond the theories of nationalism is more urgent than ever.

Notes

1. Steiner (2008), *My Unwritten Books*, p. 116.
2. Shain and Barth (2003), 'Diaspora in International Relations Theory', p. 352.
3. Bauman (1992), 'Soil, blood and identity', p. 693
4. Safran, (1991), 'Diasporas in Modern Societies: Myths of Homeland and Return', pp. 83–99.
5. Shami (2000), 'The little nation' p. 103.
6. Ibid. pp. 103–26.
7. Shain and Barth, 'Diaspora in International Relations Theory', p. 449.
8. Waterbury (2006), 'Internal Exclusion, External inclusion: Diaspora Politics and Part-building Strategies in Post-Communist Hungary', pp. 497 and 496.
9. Harris (2007), 'Moving Politics Beyond the State: The Hungarian Minority in Slovakia', pp. 43–62.
10. Steven Eke, 'Alarm bells in Ukraine', accessed 28 August 2008 at http://news.bbc.co.uk/2/hi/europe/7594576.stm.
11. Shain and Barth, 'Diaspora in International Relations Theory', p. 455.
12. Ibid., p. 462.
13. David Barchard, 'Turkey recalls ambassador after US vote on Armenian genocide', *The Independent*, Friday, 12 October 2007, p. 30.
14. Lord and Harris (2006), in their defence of democracy beyond the state, argue that

159

there is a mutual interdependence between democracy beyond the state in the new Europe and democracy within the state.

15. For the impact of European integration on national groups and regions see mainly M. Keating (2004 and 1998).
16. Harris, 'Moving Politics Beyond the State: The Hungarian Minority in Slovakia', p. 48.
17. Interview with the author, June 2005.
18. This is informed by interviews conducted with mayors and other Hungarian representatives in the region in June 2005. For details of this research: Harris, 'Moving Politics Beyond the State: The Hungarian Minority in Slovakia', pp. 43–62.
19. Ibid.
20. Marin (2005), 'Transnational Politics and the Democratic Nation-State: Challenges and Prudential Considerations', p. 2.
21. Waterbury (2006), 'Ideology, Organization, Opposition: How Domestic Political Strategy Shapes Hungary's Ethnic Activism', pp. 65–86, refers to official and unofficial policies by a state using diaspora for domestic political goals as 'ethnic activism'. I find this term very suitable for all forms of nationalism which operates beyond and between states whether on behalf of a state or an ethno-national group.

Part III

Assessing theories of nationalism

CHAPTER SEVEN

The Nation in International Relations

Of course, it will be better. It is always better to have your own country.[1]

This first of the two concluding chapters begins to draw together the debates and themes discussed before. It combines an overview of the key concepts in studies of nationalism in the light of new issues that have entered the studies of nations and nationalism and, it is argued here, will dominate it in the future. The aim is to locate the issue of nationalism and the role of identity within the realm of international relations. In terms of nationalism, there are fascinating aspects to the post-Cold War era which are in direct tension with assumptions about nationalism:

1. The nation state remains the legitimate unit of international relations but the ever-increasing political and economic integration and the role of international organisations as co-arbiters of interstate conflicts have altered the meaning of sovereignty by entering into areas which previously fell strictly within a state's competencies. This should suggest that the role of nationalism in legitimating the state should be, if not diminishing, then seeking redefinition. Yet, the majority of conflicts in the world today are challenging the boundary of the nation state and seeking national self-determination for ever smaller ethnic territories while soliciting, if not using, the support of the international community (the case of Kosovo, discussed below, is an example par excellence).

2. The post-Cold War 'victory' of democracy as the world's dominating ideology has dismantled the ideologically constructed, two-pillar, Cold War structure of international politics, and the conventional thesis argues that this collapse accounts for the rise of cultural identity at the centre of global politics (alongside the global economy, terrorism and ecology – just to remind ourselves that cultural identity is not at the pinnacle of human concerns). This is demonstrated by the continuing fragmentation of states and, simultaneously, apparently by the new civilisational division between the 'West and the rest' (Roger Scruton) that goes under the 'clash of civilisations' thesis. The post-Cold War order seems to be defined by the 'end' and the 'clash'.[2] Both theses, while offering an explanation of the major historical change, are rooted in the old dualism of the Cold War and thus replace the old ideological monoliths with new ones. If we have experienced a major systemic change, the consequences and solutions to new situations need new conceptual tools because the well-used ones have ceased to function, and assumptions based on them contort the new reality into old patterns. What were some of these tools? The concepts relevant to the present discussion were associated mostly with assumptions about the nation state and its behaviour within and without: a sovereign state, endorsed by a comprehensive national identity of its citizenry within, and externally, allied to powers of the time, in a rather predictable pattern. It is possibly the time to review all of those assumptions.

3. Membership of international organisations, particularly the North Atlantic Treaty Organization (NATO) and the European Union, has become the official indicator of the democratic credentials of a state and, hence, the incorporation into these sovereignty redefining institutions has become a matter of national interest and moreover, for some new states, a matter of national prestige. As only a sovereign state can enter into international agreements and organisations, national self-determination – the beacon of national achievement – often becomes intertwined with the relinquishment of national sovereignty in the name of international integration. This revisionist national rhetoric was particularly visible in post-communist Europe. As far back as 1987, Slovene intellectuals argued that only 'a sovereign nation can give up a part of its sovereignty in a sovereign way and transfer it to a transnational community'.[3] Vladimír Mečiar, the architect of Slovak independence, on the very first day (1 January 1993) told the newly independent nation that

'the establishment of the state means that all its citizens can directly participate in European and world integration'.[4]

4. Globalisation assumes a cohesive world arena with global agendas. The technological advances in communications and transport have indeed reduced the geographical distances between people; global markets have made the world appear smaller; and political integration is blurring the distinction between the international and the national even more. This flattening of various boundaries, however, is accompanied by a fear of homogenisation that leads to new cultural, social and symbolic boundaries which are being erected across the physical boundaries of the states.

5. Some scholars of international relations suggest that the number of identity-related conflicts in the post-Cold War amounts to a 'new world disorder'.[5] Putting aside the seriousness of global terrorism, aimed not at the liberation of a people but at the destruction of democracy and at inflicting humiliation on the Western world, the Cold War era was not peaceful and not devoid of nationalist conflicts (for example, decolonisation following World War II, and the Middle East) anymore than it was devoid of large-scale conflicts such as Korea and Vietnam. The greater predictability about the direction from which threats were likely to come during the Cold War should not be confused with absence of threats. The Cold War was a dangerous and oppressive world order in which many people were liberated from foreign rule and many lived under oppressive regimes. Nationalism is present as ever, and fragmentation seems to be on the increase but so is political integration into the European Union and an increased awareness of human rights. Ethnic conflicts say something about our time but they say even more about the necessity to imagine a human community beyond the political frameworks of the nation state.

My concern in this chapter is mainly with how the post-Cold War era shapes, and is shaped, by nationalism. While tracing various forms of identities and identity-related conflicts emerging in our globalising world, I will explore the international dimension of the national self-determination doctrine. Before concluding my arguments about the position of the nation state in the global world, I will bring in the concept of Constructivism as the only theory of international relations which attempts to respond to the new post-Cold War lines of divisions and conflicts, and conceptualises identity as an important actor in international relations.

National self-determination and the international order

In yet another of the many definitions that try to capture its appeal and politics, nationalism could be viewed as the answer to the universal principle of self-determination for a people in a world characterised by cultural diversity. Nationalism, then, in one of its more positive forms, legitimises the existing international system of states that claim to represent the interests of separate, individually legitimate peoples.[6]

Since the horrors of World War II and the establishment of the United Nations, the principle of national self-determination is enshrined in the Article 1.2 of the United Nations Charter which declares as one of its purposes and principles to 'develop friendly relations among nations based on respect for the principle of equal rights and self-determination of peoples'. Article 1.1 commits the UN to 'maintain peace and security, and to that end: to take effective collective measures for the prevention and removal of threats to peace'.[7] But, the national self-determination doctrine is not a peaceful doctrine because the secession it seeks may threaten peace and the sovereignty of states which are the internationally recognised units of the system on which peace and security should rest. It is clear that the national self-determination doctrine is a universal principle but its applicability cannot be assumed to be universal. So, what are the consequences of this doctrine for international relations?

The national self-determination doctrine has a strong moral dimension but poses many legal and institutional challenges. The first point to emphasise is that there is no definition of 'the people' in international law, and it is probably safe to assume that, at the beginning of the Cold War, the United Nations took peoples to mean ethnic groups. Michael Freeman argues that the right to self-determination was interpreted to be limited to the decolonisation from European colonial rule, and the right not to be subjected to racist domination (as in South Africa) or occupation (as in Palestine).[8] The collapse of the Soviet Union and Yugoslavia (less controversially, Czechoslovakia) was followed by a frenzy of independence declarations by a number of ethno-national groups. This not only took the international community by surprise but showed how little clarity there is about what constitutes the just self-determination claim and how threatening these claims are for regional stability. With hindsight, the independence of the Czech

Republic, Slovakia, the Baltic states, and even a number of post-Soviet republics turned out to be relatively problem-free. On the other hand, the recognition of Slovenia and Croatia, followed by Bosnia–Herzegovina, began a major conflict in the Balkans. Some of these self-determination claims are still not resolved and remain internationally volatile. The independent status of Kosovo is still not accepted by Serbia nor by the majority of UN members. Thirteen years after the US sponsored Dayton peace agreements which ended the war, the stability of Bosnia, is in danger of collapse.[9] There is evidence that the Bosnian Serb enclave, Republika Srpska, is seeking secession, exploiting the weaknesses of the new Bosnian constitution and also particularly the international community's weariness with Bosnia in the face of other conflicts, such as Iraq and Afghanistan, and the European Union's lack of a coherent strategy in upholding its commitment to Bosnia. The conflict between Georgia and its separatist regions of South Ossetia and Abkhazia has been augmented by the provocative unilateral recognition by Russia of their independence claims, thus disregarding Georgian territorial integrity endorsed by her Western allies. This is not the first case of power politics being played out between important international actors at the cost of smaller self-determining ethno-national groups. The international community does not offer much clarity regarding secession; sometimes it supports secession without considering the long-term regional consequences and sometimes it prefers established states and treats nearly all self-determination claims with suspicion and caution, often exacerbating the conflict. An example could be the recognition of Bosnia–Herzegovina which then, in fear of wider conflict, was followed by an arms embargo, thus confirming the Serbian position as the regional power and leaving Bosnia defenceless in the face of a Serbian onslaught.[10] The initial prevarication and the continued negotiation with the Serbian leadership in an attempt to save the Yugoslav state did not comprise the 'finest' hour of the international community's efforts for peace and security.[11]

Putting cynical power politics aside for the moment, there is a good reason for caution towards national self-determination claims. Historical evidence shows that not many secessions follow the peaceful Czechoslovak or Baltic models (and even there the majority–minority relationships deteriorated and threatened to destabilise the new states) and that most independence declarations provoke conflicts and refugee crises, some with very long-term consequences. The tension between two principles of the nation-state system, territorial integrity of sovereign states and liberal-democratic principles of national self-determination, are not easy to reconcile.

The national self-determination dilemma   Freeman puts forward a number of theories of national self-determination in order to discuss the values and policies they imply.[12] Classical *liberal* theory rests on the rights of individuals and would have to show that, to protect an individuals' human rights, self-determination is neces-sary. The problem is that, given the state's general tendency to override the interests of minorities, the claim to self-determination could be made by many ethno-national groups, in which case the solution should be sought in concessions by states and not in secession. Obviously, this theory is easier to recommend than to implement, as all I have said in the previous chapters illustrates. Let me state most emphatically again that nationalism is not about individuals but about ethno-national groupings, as well as about politics and access to state power by those groupings.

The *democratic* theory of national self-determination rests on the right to democratic government and, in principle, is the same as liberal theory but with less emphasis on the individual and more on the national group. Hence, the *communitarian* theory, which sees the nation as the community of a kind; self-determination then seeks political power 'for the group over the group' in order to protect the group's national identity which is assumed to be best safeguarded by independent statehood. This theory awards great importance to nations, their identities and the value thereof to indi-vidual wellbeing. David Miller (1995) is among notable scholars who link self-determination with social justice and believe that nations bound together by their long history and shared obliga-tions are suited to representative governments. The problems con-nected with conflating nations with states (as Miller tends to do) have been discussed throughout, but mainly in Chapter 3, and do not need repeating here. Freeman continues with *'realist'* (meaning practical) theories which seek to balance the territorial integrity of states with the 'aspirations of aggrieved nations' through arbitra-tion by some form of international authority which would settle self-determination claims. This is a plausible and attractive theory, with one major obstacle: the territorial integrity of states is where the weight of the problem lies and the solution may be too difficult to come by. It has taken twenty-five years of negotiation and commitment from the British and Irish governments to resolve the Northern Ireland question in conditions of relative democracy and without the shifting of boundaries. Hence, while encouraging, the Irish example is not easily imitated.

Freeman moves then to the *cosmopolitan* theory. National self-determination is a universal principle and therefore the particularity of the group seeking it should not detract from the cosmopolitanism of human rights for all. There is a fundamental tension here between the cosmopolitan concept of the ethical community (less concerned with borders and states) and the national ethical community (seeking the recognition and jurisdiction over a clearly demarcated territory). The solution then lies in the recognition of the right to national self-determination, but only where it does not harm outside parties. Finally, Freeman combines the latter two theories in his final *cosmopolitan realism* approach. The principal assumption here is that cosmopolitan values are not contrary to nations and diversity because cosmopolitanism is fundamentally defined by a certain interpretation of the wellbeing of humanity and not by world government. Thus, while cosmopolitanism can 'endorse the right to national self-determination in some circumstances', it doesn't recognise it as the general right because cosmopolitanism does not endorse a world divided into nation states which is what the national self-determination doctrine presupposes.

We are not much further than where we started in the discussion about the national self-determination doctrine and its affects on international relations. The international system rests on sovereign states. While sovereignty implies that the existence of conflict between states is a characteristic of the international system (in theories of international relations referred to as *anarchy*), the other characteristic is that, for the system to exist and function, there should be peace. In the form of its defining self-determination principle that any self-differentiating people has the right, should it so desire, to self-rule,[13] nationalism is problematic for both peace and sovereignty. It remains difficult to juggle the justice of the self-determination principle with order and justice in a wider international arena, and sometimes the self-determination of one group must be set against the international order.

The international dimension of national self-determination The dilemma of the self-determination doctrine for international relations is a classical dilemma of nation formation. While not all self-determination struggles can be successful because they endanger international order, some are successful because of it. This is the other side of the national self-determination dilemma, as I have already intimated above.

Each systemic change brings an explosion of new states based on the principle of national self-determination. The end of the World War I and the consequent break-up of the Austro-Hungarian and Ottoman Empires were followed by the establishment of a number of new states in Europe, the Middle East and Asia (for example, Czechoslovakia, Yugoslavia, Iraq, Iran, Turkey). The outbreak of World War II was followed by new declarations of independence (Slovakia and Croatia under Hitler's tutelage) and more shifting of borders, mostly in an attempt to recover lost territories or gain new ones (Hungary annexed parts of Slovakia; Germany annexed Austria and occupied many other European countries; Italy ventured into Abyssinia; Japan annexed Manchuria and occupied Dutch and British colonies in Asia). After World War II, territories were being 'returned' and states reconstituted to within their original borders (Czechoslovakia and Yugoslavia), and new states declared independence (Israel and India), while the Baltic States were subsumed into the Soviet Union. The end of World War II also signalled the beginning of the end of colonisation which lasted well into the mid-1980s. The map of the world was redrawn, with a number of newly decolonised states appearing in Africa and Asia. The last major systemic change, the fall of the Berlin Wall, resulted in the disintegration of communist federations, the Soviet Union, Czechoslovakia and Yugoslavia, and some twenty-eight successor states emerged on their territories, the last being Kosovo (February 2008).

Can we really believe that being a nation state (or self-administering region) is a result of national movement only? The world order is national in its structure but the international system is a club and the admission of new members is an international affair. Let me take Slovakia, for example. The first appearance of Slovakia as a nation with a corresponding territory was within the newly established Czechoslovakia in 1918 as one of the successor states of the disintegrated Austro-Hungarian Empire. Why? Not because Slovaks were among those successful national groups whose national elites succeeded in their efforts. If they had been, Slovakia would have become an independent state, which may have been a dream of its rising nationalist elite but a dream neverthe-less. The establishment of Czechoslovakia was the result of many factors of which national struggle within the Austro-Hungarian Empire was the least influential. More influential than the national emancipation of Czechs and Slovaks was the endorsement of the Wilsonian national self-determination principle at the Versailles Peace Conference, where the Great Powers sought a solution to the post-empire Eastern and Central Europe. It was also a result of great diplomatic efforts by Czecholsovakia's founding president Tomaš Garigue Masaryk (and Slovak émigré organisations in the United States) who feared that the close proximity of Germany and the substantial three million German minority would endanger the sustainability of Czech independent existence. Slovakia, linguisti-cally the closest, could link the Czech lands to other Slavs. The result of these international agreements was a Czechoslovak nation of two dominant groups with a large number of minorities, only less multinational than the future Yugoslavia. This is not to belittle the Slovak or Czech nations but to point out that the formation of states is also subject to the international environment and its acqui-escence. Amid many recriminations about the degree of Slovak autonomy in the new Czechoslovakia, the Slovak delegation was not present at the declaration of the First Czechoslovak Republic (28 October 1918) and the Slovak population had no participation in what must be seen as the first step towards emancipation from Hungarian rule.[14]

The new post-1918 map of Europe made little sense in terms of the national self-determination doctrine, which was purportedly behind the establishment of these new states, because most of them were multinational and contained a number of nations with only fledgling national movements (Yugoslavia, Czechoslovakia), while the boundaries of the new Poland, with its long history of intense national struggle, were not settled until 1922. Many states in part owe their existence to the international constellation of powers at that time. The same applied to the successor states of the Ottoman Empire. To this day, nationalism in many of those territories is fuelled by resentment towards the international agreements among the 'superpowers'[15] of that time. It took the collapse of the Soviet Union and a new post-1989 world order for the rebirth of states whose growth was stunted by the superpower agreements in 1918 or 1945. Time after time, history shows that the attainment of nationhood depends on more than the strength of its national movement, the intensity of patriotic fervour or even its level of industrialisation; it depends on politics and on the constellation of power in the international system. I shall return to this point in the concluding chapter when I shall assess the shortcomings of approaches to nationalism when it comes to accounting for systemic changes and their affects on 'the people' who are both bearers and receivers of the drama of history.

Kosovo: a state in waiting?

The declaration of independence by Kosovo on 17 February 2008, its immediate recognition by the United States, but disagreements among European foreign ministers about how to proceed in the case of this new 'European protectorate', illustrate a number of confusions surrounding national self-determination about when and where the support of the international community, and even military intervention are justified. Kosovo's (its population is about two million, 88 per cent of whom are ethnic Albanians) unilateral declaration of independence followed a long process of the international community's efforts to find a solution to this last piece of the Balkan puzzle. Following the brutal suppression by Serb forces (1999) and attempts ethnically to cleanse the territory they regard as their historical and emotional homeland (to some, arguably made worse by the NATO intervention and the bombing of Serbia), Kosovo no longer accepts the Serbian state as its overlord. Serbia, and the 7 per cent Serbian minority concentrated in the north of the seceding province, refuse to grant Kosovo independence, however, and are emboldened in thier intransigence by the outspoken support of Russia and China which guarantee their case in the UN Security Council. The unfolding irony of Kosovo, protected and administered as it is by the international community's mechanisms in the form of the European Rule of Law Mission (EULEX) and the United Nations Mission in Kosovo (UNMIK), constitutes further 'balkanisation' of the already balkanised territories of the former Yugoslavia which were a result of a purely ethnic war waged by Serbia against the Kosovo Liberation Army (KLA), the latter now considered to be part of the 'democratic' solution in Kosovo. The General Assembly of the United Nations declared the independence of Kosovo illegal (9 October 2008),[16] but Martti Ahtisaari, the former Finnish president and winner of the Nobel Peace Prize for his mediation in Kosovo, argues that the 'Kosovo state in inevitable'. When challenged on the fact that the majority of states in the world have not recognised Kosovo, Ahtisaari explains that it is less important how many countries do not recognise Kosovo than the economic clout of countries which do recognise it (65 per cent of the wealth of the world) and that Serbia will have to relent if it wants to pursue European integration.[17] There is no doubt that he is right on all counts.

Serbs and Albanians shared the state for nearly a century and, while coexistence between Kosovar Serbs and Kosovar Albanians was never ideal, the relationship deteriorated after the constitutional changes in 1974 whereby Kosovo gained autonomy which many Serbs never accepted. Following Tito's death in 1980, tensions began to increase. Tito's death and the beginning of Yugoslavia's slow disintegration mentioned in one breath, lead to the misguided assumptions abroad and among many former Yugoslavs that he held the country together. In fact, Tito's reign created disastrous economic and political conditions which, after his death, opened the way for Milošević's rise to power[18] while the tensions in Kosovo had already exploded in 1981. The fear of mass migration of Serbs from Kosovo (and other provinces) and the intensified Serbian nationalism led Belgrade to invest heavily in the Serb areas to encourage the return of Serbs. The fear of the demographic rise of the Albanian population led to the introduction of family planning for Albanians, the sales of property to Albanians were annulled, and many Albanians were dismissed from administrative and teaching jobs. Finally, the autonomous status of the province was revoked. These are nationalist policies aimed at the slow and systematic nationalisation (if not colonisation) of a territory, populated by an ethnic majority, by a more powerful ethnic group seeking to dominate it.[19] I have discussed this type of ethnic domination hiding behind state power in Chapter 5.

The continuing violence in the province and the experience of the Bosnian war convinced the international community to try to seek a peaceful solution to Kosovo but this became increasingly less possible because the consensus on non-violence also broke down in Kosovo; by the time the Rambouillet talks in early 1999 broke down, the violence perpetrated against Kosovar Albanians by Serb forces could no longer be tolerated on moral and political grounds, and humanitarian intervention by NATO forces followed. There are two questions here: the first concerns the rights and wrongs of that intervention, the second, the contemporary status of Kosovo, and these should not be conflated. Whether this intervention in the territory of sovereign Serbia was legal under international law is a question well beyond the present brief. In seeking the answer, however, consideration must be given to the sheer outrageousness of the atrocities committed, indignation at the arrogance of the Serbian leadership, and the wider implications for regional peace and security. One must ask whether or not the intervention in Kosovo was, for once, driven by values rather than by cynicism, and whether sovereignty is so sacred that it is worth preserving in the face of such violation of human rights? Surely we know the answer to this. What happened next and the strategy employed by NATO, the ethics of aerial bombing, and the consequences on the ground are completely different questions, the answers to which are not positive.

My concern here is rather with the current situation, and I do not wish to argue the rights or wrongs of Kosovo independence. It is difficult to see how Kosovo can remain within the Serbian state unless serious concessions are made by the latter and considerable promises by the former as to the treatment of the Serbian minority. The point of this discussion is to empha-sise a number of very difficult problems that Kosovo has come to represent in contemporary international politics in relation to national self-determination. Has Serbia lost the right to govern Kosovo because of its aggression towards it? This line of argument would justify the secession of many territories around the world, some of which cannot rely on the inter-national community's commitment. Moreover, today's Serbia is not Milošević's Serbia; if regional security is at the heart of the Kosovo issue, then Serbia's attempts to democratise, however slow and half-hearted, should perhaps be considered. The speed with which the international community seeks a solu-tion to this conflict is baffling: the Israeli-Palestinian conflict has been con-tinuing for half a century, and Northern Ireland took nearly thirty years to resolve. The next question concerns the connection between national lib-eration movements and organised crime, and whether the mediation in inter-ethnic conflicts does not inadvertently end up taking part in support for one side against the other. There is enough evidence that various embar-goes imposed in the Balkans to prevent the escalation of conflict have suc-ceeded in boosting organised crime.[20] If, as is widely assumed, the KLA could be implicated in some of the criminal activities of the Albanian criminal gangs operating on a large scale in Europe in the drug trade, human trafficking and prostitution, should the international community allow it to be a part of its solution to police peace in the province?

Finally, is Kosovo a *sui generis* case, because of the wars in the 1990s or a dangerous precedent?[21] Many states in Europe which refuse to recognise Kosovo, such as Slovakia, Spain and Cyprus, have their own minority prob-lems and obviously fear so. It must strike one as ironic, though, that while thousands of people died in Bosnia in order first to preserve what was left of multi-ethnic Yugoslavia, and while we are constructing complicated con-stitutional arrangements to protect minorities around the world, the case of Kosovo does not follow this overall trend. There are many scenarios that suggest that the success of Kosovo in achieving its independent status will reinvigorate other dormant national movements or, at the very least, com-plicate the very fragile situation in Bosnia. This may or not may be the case because the European Union may, indeed, have established itself as a very powerful arbiter of inter-ethnic relations in Europe, and the Balkans will continue to muddle through. One thing is certain, however: the case of

Kosovo diminished the concept of sovereignty, which is a good and appropriate thing in our highly internationalised and interdependent world. On the other hand, it did not diminish the power of the national self-determination doctrine which, given its inherent interdependence with the sovereignty of the state, is even more confusing.

Identity in international relations: a constructivist approach

Two main streams in international theories are Realism and Liberalism moderated by various 'neo-' debates. The former puts the state at the centre of international relations, the latter takes the international system to be less state-centric, puts its faith in international institutions and acknowledges the role of non-state actors. In simplistic terms, with realism come concepts such as self-help, anarchy (the system of sovereign states with no central authority over them) and the security dilemma, all of which suggest the intention and the perceived necessity of states to maximise their position in the Darwinian system of sovereign states. With liberalism come co-operation, compromise, international institutions and other measures to try to curb the ills of the anarchical system. This is not the place to discuss the wealth of literature that analyses these theories of international relations. The point of this discussion is that 'the nation' and its identity do not appear to feature highly on the agenda that deals with 'real' national interest analysed by classical rationalist theories of international relations. A quick observation of international relations since the end of the Cold War brings culture and identity to one's attention in a 'dramatic comeback'.[22] The events of 11 September 2001 and the continued terrorist attacks, the insurgency in Iraq, the revival of the Taliban in Afghanistan, the ever sharper confrontation between the West and radical Islam, the barbarism of Darfur, the ongoing conflict in the Middle East and so on; there is no telling where the identity comeback will lead us. Simultaneously, the forces of globalisation and European integration, the unprecedented migration, ecological threats and the global human rights agenda suggest an emerging global order in which identity is in the ascendant, while the nation states' monopoly of political, physical and economic control over their territories is in decline. One does not have to be a student of nationalism to argue that, in all the theorising about international relations, there must be room for the nation and its identity just as there must be room for international relations in theorising about the nation. The former is the subject of the forthcoming paragraphs, the latter of the forthcoming chapter.

The end of the politically comprehensive and intellectually less taxing international relations of the Cold War brought new uncertainties and intellectual challenges to the assessment of international order. Identity remains a suspect and contested concept but, in a time when all else is being reassessed, identity can also be reassessed as a serious contender in the approaches to international relations. This is where 'constructivism' comes in as an approach to, rather than a theory of, international relations. Constructivism is centrally concerned with the meanings actors give to their actions and with the identities of these actors. Hence, the defining maxim of the constructivist approach is that 'Anarchy is what states make of it'.[23] As an approach, constructivism requires a case-specific analysis but with core assumptions, such as identity, ideology, perceptions and interests, in mind.

If nationalism is an action-orientated programme, then the action rationalises national interest to involve 'the nation' and its identity. It has been argued throughout that identity may draw on some primordial symbols and narratives but it is constructed and reconstructed through historical and political interaction. At the heart of the constructivist argument there is a similar observation that social reality, while situated in a particular context, is also reproduced and (re)constructed through actions. So, if the features of the post-Cold War order are different from the Cold War order, it stands to reason that features of state systems change throughout time and place. Constructivism, then, by incorporating identity and its links to nationhood and statehood in its theorising, may be in certain instances better equipped to deal with newly arising questions in contemporary international politics than other theories.

The main challenge to European integration, for example, is considered to be the perception that a political union of this unprecedented kind will conspire in the elimination of national identities and the loss of sovereignty of its member states. There is little logic in this argument. If national identity is inherent to nations, and so valuable that it needs protecting by a sovereign state, then how can it be at the same time so weak that it is threatened by a political process that does not seek to remove nations?

Or is it rather that national identity and sovereignty are so closely linked to the nation state that our cognitive powers do not extend beyond the state, and therefore the European Union must resemble a state if it is to have any political meaning? If, following the deep historical roots of state centricism in our minds and in international relations, the European Union is another state (for what else could it be?), therefore it can pose a threat to our nation state. This traditional zero-sum national framework does not reflect the reality of the diminished sovereignty of our less than national states and, more importantly, it does not offer many solutions to the problems that nation states are facing.

Similarly, if the Cold War was a realist dream of the minimalist bipolar power structure, then the end of it could be explained by the withdrawal of one power, and thus a tacit victory of the other, except that the structure collapsed under the pressure of the rather non-realist ideas of freedom and democracy. There is no realist explanation for the explosion of national emancipation in post-communist societies and the demise of the Soviet Union because both fell within identity-related politics before realist or even realistic considerations could be adopted.[24] Identity plays an important part in the creation of a state and, surely, there must be at least as much of a link between identity, national interest and national community as there is between states, national interest, and the structure of the international system (as in neo-realist perspective).

On the other hand, constructivism does not quite explain the efforts of newly independent states to integrate into the European Union and NATO, and thus relinquish some of their newly gained sovereignty in favour of becoming yet another unit within yet a different political structure. In terms of security and economic prosperity, realism offers a better avenue of exploration. Yet, the continuation of nationalist policies, for example in Serbia, after the total defeat of any fantasies it may have harboured to maintain the position of power in the region, cannot be explained by realism either. The subsequent international isolation of the country lost in the morass of national mobilisation tells us something about the power of perception, beliefs, ideas and identity generally. Constructivism explains better than other international relations theories how collective identities are mobilised and how they insinuate themselves into foreign policy-making. I would like to argue that nationalism, with its close connection to the state and its reliance on culture and identity rooted in perceptions and beliefs, fits the constructivist approach.

The constructivist approach is not without problems, though. First, identities are not static; they are partially constructed and reproduced by interaction and, therefore, there is always a danger that, once we satisfy the constructivist argument, identity becomes fixed at the cost of all other processes and identities. The second problem with constructivism is that it is a state-dependent approach, just as realism is, and thus takes the state to be the main unit of analysis; it replaces one stable unitary category with another, presumably equally stable – identity. Not only are identities not stable but I have established that they are too complex to be reduced to boundaries.[25] What happens if maintaining identity is a matter of national interest? How is Israel supposed to change its identity, assuming that it would lead to the resolution of the conflict, when the whole foundation of the state is the maintenance of the Jewish identity which is perceived to be in danger? Co-operation, and hence peace, are negotiable but is collective identity? What about interaction? If the interaction is good enough to change identities and interests, it is surely good enough to sustain them? Interaction doesn't only change identity. The collective insecurity and myths can be sustained by repeated hostile interaction. It is feasible to argue that the European Union's recognition of Kosovo will have confirmed the Serbian national narrative that the West is hostile and that their natural ally is Russia, and thereby increase Serbian intransigence on the issue of Kosovo's independence. It is also reasonable to understand the Israeli reluctance in the negotiations with Palestinians and vice versa because the interaction between them has only confirmed the initial mistrust.

Nevertheless, the value of this approach for present purposes is in the sophistication and conceptualisation of identity as an important actor in international relations. States have multiple identities, (sovereign, imperial power, a 'leader of the free world', expansionist, and so on).[26] These identities are grounded in a collective perception about a state's place in the world and thus define its interests. But, as with all identities, they exist in relation to others. Was there an identity prior to interaction with others? Probably not. The interpretation of that interaction creates reaction and the expectations of further action and so on. Eventually there is a pattern of ideas about each other and, if repeated long enough, can become relatively stable.[27] If 'the other' is threatening, the collective sense of security is a threat and a consequent response to a threat is defence or attack – the security dilemma, the mainstay of realism, is not a beginning of interaction but a process. Once institutionalised, it is difficult to change. To break this down-spiralling pattern, constructivists argue that there must be an offer that is so significant that the other state has to reconsider its position. Wendt uses the example of Gorbachev: the withdrawal from Afghanistan and Eastern Europe, the emphasis on commonalities, the admission of economic weakness, significant cuts in nuclear and conventional forces, and so on and so on. At the end, the whole basis for the mistrust of the Soviet Union was dismantled – the West had to reconsider not only the identity of the Soviet Union but also its own interest in maintaining the arms race.

A similar argument could be used for conflicts among ethnic groups. Only a serious offer, backed up by resistance to retaliation for long enough, international guarantees, and an inspired leadership can break the pattern of mistrust and hostilities. The constructivist approach has not been thought out for the purpose of ethnic conflict but, as a social theory, it can teach us something about the resolution of conflicts which, after all, arise from interaction among ethno-national groups in a cycle of mistrust and historically accumulated hostilities, not too dissimilar to interaction among states.

Transcending 'the nation' in the global world

There is a tension between some ethnic identities and national identities and between national identities and global processes. There are reasons for these tensions. Let me reiterate that the tension between ethnic and national identity arises on the back of perceptions about the nation state. National identities have been constructed and engraved in our political consciousness (to the point of unconscious acceptance of the social reality thus constructed) within the contours of the classical nation state.[28] But national identity is broader, it incorporates a number of other-than-ethnic aspects in order to blend linguistic differences, historical disagreements and varied 'ways of life' contained within a modern nation. My point is that national identity is, in most cases, a composite of the immediate, 'thick' ethnic identity and the somewhat 'thinner' identity underpinned by a sense of a common political existence within the state which, ideally, should rely on trust and motivation to sustain it. National and ethnic identities rest on commonality but national identity also implies a political centre, while ethnic identity can exist without one. The recognition of ethnic identity, however, if it is to survive must rest on some universal principles of tolerance, civil liberty, equal rights and other forms of political arrangements which should be reflected in national identity. The problem is that the nation state does not have a good historical record on reconciliation between cultural identities and tends to prefer one over the other.

There are many attempts among scholars to find a way out of this national conundrum of culture and political unity. This is where the distinction between civic and ethnic nationalism entered the studies of nationalism in a thus far not very successful effort to accommodate and resolve the troublesome issue of the over-whelmingly ethnic character of the nation state. Jürgen Habermas proposes a sophisticated and normatively very appealing notion of 'constitutional patriotism' which, in contrast to civic nationalism, removes the cultural element of the commitment to the common state and replaces it with commitment to procedures and principles outlined in constitutional terms. [29] Thus, 'culture, history and geography' all tend to point towards the ethnic origins of the nation state and produce minorities with all the ensuing consequences whereas, in Habermas's nation state, the points of references would be 'political, moral and juridical'. [30] This is not the place to discuss the pros and cons of constitutional patriotism, bar mentioning that national constitutions tend to be a result of historical processes and experiences of 'the nation', hence the built-in ethnic overtone of the territorial nation state and the lesser likelihood of constitutional patriotism.

All theories of nations, from Smith's *ethnie* to Habermas's constitution suffer from the inability to reflect the precarious position of the contemporary state even if the latter suffers less so: 'under the pressure from beyond and within, but with substantially reduced ability to influence either'. [31] The pressures from beyond the state come in the form of globalisation, here understood as rapidly expanding trade, investments, financial flows, travel and other forms of worldwide communication. [32] Connected to globalisation are other processes: the ever-increasing economic interdependence in which financial markets have fast exceeded state control, [33] social interaction, non-state actors' intervention into political and security spheres, overuse of global resources and pollution, the ever-increasing concerns for societal security and human rights, and the increased legitimacy of regional and other organisations as well as the increased polarisation of the world into poor and rich countries. In short, the boundary between national and international is blurred to the point where an assessment of one requires the assessment of the other. The pressures from within and below the state come from an ever-increasing diversity, the various forms of autonomy seeking self-rule and trans-border activities but with a reduced ability to homogenise the population while facing the general demise in citizens' commitment to participation and increased expectations for welfare, This is a 'new' nation state, a multicultural state, participating in international relations and seeking more and more global interdependence to fulfil the expectations placed upon it.

'New' nationalism for a new nation state? Why are we assuming that this 'new' nation state should be the subject of the same identity as the classical nation state? Going back a few paragraphs, national identity has always been a construct and a composite of many identities, a complex construction which is now under severe stress because the object of its commitment, the nation state, is under pressure, too. If there always was a tension between an ethnic identity and a national one, this tension has increased. Not only are the assumptions about the nation state in need of adaptation but national identities are, too.

So, what of nationalism, and are there other forms of identity emerging? I concur with Mary Kaldor[34] that the external influences on the nation state and the changes in its functions (even though I do not necessarily connect it to the decline in military function, as she does) have changed the character of nationalism, which stands to reason. We are experiencing the rise of ethnically stimulated violence, locally and internationally. This is a result of the lack of clarity about the international order which is in transition from the classical nineteenth-century nation state order to something as yet unknown. While the answer can be sought in cosmopolitanism and its near example of European integration, these need certain preconditions which are not present everywhere, while opposition to the unknown comes in the vehement defence of the existing ethnoterritorial understanding of the world.

'New' nationalisms mobilise on the basis of past experiences, invoking a world which does not exist in the present and probably has not existed for a long time, if ever. Nationalists believe in territorially based sovereignty and they want either to control the state or to create one they can control, in the name of the nation or of religion.[35] The strategy for mobilisation is the invocation of a mythical past but the methods and violence are modern – these are the characteristics of 'new' nationalism, the ancientness combined with all the benefits of modernity they so reject.

The rise of Islamic militancy among young men around the world is a result of a sense of displacement and insecurity in a world where they often find themselves living in sprawling urban slums resulting from high migration into the industrial centres in their own country or elsewhere in the West and where their dignity and resolve are tested every day. Criminal, nationalist and religious groupings prey on them at every turn in their new and disappointing life, offering a sense of belonging and a false dignity – but false dignity may appear very attractive in the absence of any other. The confrontations between the consumer paradise on display and the reality of poverty, between one's cultural principles and moral and cultural relativism, between the vision of the future and the opaqueness of possibilities, are too difficult to comprehend. Hence, there is the perception among some people that ethnic (and religious) identity must remain uncontaminated and therefore defended. This is by no means an excuse for violence but an acknowledgment that violence is the last refuge of the frightened and angry.

Another aspect of the new ethnic and religious violence is its international character. The features of new nationalisms are: the international mobilisation of ethnic kin; the recruitment and training of combatants on a transnational scale with the use of modern technology, television channels, the use of languages as it fits the relevant audience and complex international finance; the involvement of organised crime; the use of a civilian population in the manifestation of power; and rape as a tool of warfare. There is nothing parochial about the external presentation of these movements, not in organisation and not in strategies. The nation and ethnic identity have assumed a worldwide audience which is invited to hear the political aims but is not invited to argue or to disagree with them. A narrow and exclusivist identity is reasserting itself in a very post-modern way. We are a long way away from nationalisms of the past.

In juxtaposition to these movements is the increased relevance of cosmopolitanism in a contemporary world searching for 'peace among nations'. Following Immanuel Kant, cosmopolitan thought seeks to subordinate politics to morality; it stresses the contingency of borders and the dignity of a person. The modern-day Kantians, such as Habermas and Held,[36] are looking to update the moral Kantian principles and work out how they could be institutionalised on international levels. On offer is the form of legal cosmopolitanism concerned with human rights, either universally or within the European Union (Habermas), or a more political model of cosmopolitanism in the form of 'cosmopolitan democracy' (Held), as the best answer to the multi-layered governance characteristic of globalisation. In both cases, the fundamental question underlying the cosmopolitan endeavour is whether the territorial sovereign nation state can remain the only moral community 'when the opportunities for, and the incidence of, transnational harm continue to rise alongside increasing interdependence'.[37] It is also time to question the moral ambivalence attached to a moral landscape that is delimited by something as banal as a border[38] in the intensely internationalised world. My answer would be that the territorial nation state has emerged in different conditions in order to answer different questions, and that it is time to acknowledge its deficiencies in providing answers for our time.

This is not likely to happen for some time yet, however. Can we imagine the world – moreover, can we manage it – without the nation state? The European Union is pioneering a vision of the world in which democracy within the state is backed up by democracy beyond the state (not very successfully thus far) and in which supra-national institutions underwrite the legal, political, social and cultural rights of all European citizens.[39] This new, unprecedented political community, reason would dictate, should transcend the nationalism of its member states and move our imagination beyond the national. The early indications are not auspicious, which does not mean that the idea is failing but it does say a great deal about the tenacity of our faith in national states.

In our effort to theorise democracy in the new Europe and explore the reciprocity between the nation state and 'Europeanisation', Professor Lord and I have developed an argument for a mutual dependence between democracy within the state and democracy beyond it. In terms of identity, we argued that 'only democracy within the state can draw on the motivational force of cultural identity and hand its benefits as it were to the legitimation of laws and policies democratically agreed from beyond the state'.[40] This was our attempt to square the 'large ideological jump between the national and the global' with the more modest jump between the national and regional,[41] in a concession to the reality and tenacity of the nation state, which is not going to disappear for a long time. As I have argued throughout and in this chapter, however, it cannot continue in the classical nineteenth-century form either.

Notes

1. Mustafa Blakqorri, ethnic Albanian, quoted in *The Guardian*, 20 February 2007; Ian Traynor 'Hope and fear as Europe's poorest region awaits a birth of a new country', p. 23
2. Fukuyama (1989), 'The End of History?', *National Interest*; and Huntington (1993), 'The Clash of Civilizations?', respectively.
3. Hribar (1987) 'The Slovenes and European Transnationality', p. 33.
4. Cited in Leško (1998), 'Príbeh sebadiskvalifikácie favorita', p. 16.
5. Booth (1995), 'Human wrongs and international relations', p. 118.
6. Halliday (2005), 'Nationalism' p. 528.
7. Charter of the United Nations and Statute of the International Court of Justice, published by the Department of Public Information, United Nations, New York, 1994, p. 3.
8. Freeman (1999), 'The right to self-determination in international Politics: six theories in search of a policy', p. 356.
9. Paddy Ashdown and Richard Holbrooke 'A Bosnian powder keg', *The Guardian*, 22 October 2008, p. 28.
10. Ramet (1994), 'The Yugoslav Crisis and the West: Avoiding "Vietnam" and Blundering into "Abyssinia"'.
11. Simms (2002), *The Unfinest Hour: Britain and the Destruction of Bosnia*.
12. Freeman, 'The right to self-determination in international Politics: six theories in search of a policy', pp. 359–68.
13. Connor (1972), 'Nation-Building or Nation-Destroying', p. 331.
14. For a detailed bibliography on the history of Czechoslovakia see Harris (2002) *Nationalism and Democratisation*, note 6, p. 92.
15. O'Leary (1998), 'Ernest Gellner's diagnosis of nationalism: a critical overview, or, what is living and what is dead in Ernest Gellner's philosophy of nationalism?', p. 61.
16. 'Serbia overjoyed, Kosovo calm, after the UN Vote', Balkan Insight.com, at http://www.balkaninsight.com/en/main/analysis/13868, accessed 25 October 2008.
17. Julian, Borger 'Kosovo state is inevitable', *The Guardian*, 18 October 2008, p. 28. (Fifty-one out of 192 countries have recognised Kosovo as of the date of this article.)
18. Harris, *Nationalism and Democratisation*, chapter 5.
19. See Tim Judah (2000), *Kosovo: War and Revenge*, New Haven: Yale University Press; Noel Malcolm (1998), *Kosovo: A Short History*, London and New York: Macmillan and New York University Press; Miranda Vickers (1998), *Between Serb and Albanian: A History of Kosovo*, New York: Columbia University Press. For an excellent review of many books about Yugoslavia see Ramet (2005), *Thinking about Yugoslavia*; for the section on Kosovo, chapters 9 and 10.
20. Ramet (2005), *Thinking about Yugoslavia*, pp. 230–2, cites the research and evidence.
21. Ian, Traynor 'Spain exposes EU split as US leads recognition', *The Guardian*, 19 February 2008, p. 15.

22. Lapid and Kratochvil (1997), *The return of culture and identity in IR theory*, Introduction.
23. Wendt (1992), 'Anarchy Is What States Make of It: The Social Construction of Power Politics'.
24. Lapid and Kratochvil, *The return of culture and identity in IR theory*, p. 205.
25. Zehfuss (2001), 'Constructivism and Identity: A Dangerous Liaison', p. 333.
26. Ibid. p. 135.
27. Ibid. p. 142.
28. Lord and Harris (2006), *Democracy in the New Europe*, p. 185.
29. Habermas (1992), 'Citizenship and National Identity: Some Reflections on the Future of Europe', p. 7. For overview see Laborde (2002), ' From Constitutional to Civic Patriotism', pp. 592–5.
30. Laborde (2002), 'From Constitutional to Civic Patriotism', p. 593.
31. Lord and Harris, *Democracy in the New Europe*, p. 184.
32. Tønnesson (2004), 'Globalising national states', p. 179.
33. Since the global banking crises in 2008, some states have been forced to impose stricter controls on financial markets to prevent the collapse of their economies, but this is a different argument from the one I am making.
34. Kaldor (2004), 'Nationalism and Globalisation', pp. 161–77.
35. Ibid. pp. 167–70.
36. Habermas (2001), 'A Constitution for Europe?'; (1999) 'The European Nation–State and the Pressures of Globalization'; and (1992), 'Citizenship and National Identity: Some Reflections on the Future of Europe'. Held (1995), *Democracy and the Global Order: from the Modern State to Cosmopolitan Governance*; Held and McGrew (eds) (2003), *The Global Transformations Reader*.
37. Linklater (1998), 'Cosmopolitan Citizenship', p. 32.
38. Lord and Harris, *Democracy in the New Europe*, p. 165.
39. Linklater, 'Cosmopolitan Citizenship', p. 32.
40. Lord and Harris, *Democracy in the New Europe*, p. 183.
41. Beardsworth (2008), 'Cosmopolitanism and Realism: Towards a Theoretical Convergence?', p. 92.

Conclusion: New Questions and Old Answers

A man may travel far, but his heart may be slow to catch up.[1]

In the preceding chapters I have examined nationalism from both the historical and the contemporary perspectives. To capture the spirit and politics of nationalism at play today, I have explored the traditional approaches to nationalism in the light of these new developments. The aim has been to identify gaps in traditional approaches to nationalism and suggest avenues through which to develop more fruitful approaches. In this conclusion I shall sum up the foregoing discussions, emphasise the shortcomings of the existing approaches to nations and nationalism, and conclude with seven arguments that emerged from it which I believe could offer the foundations for new theorising about nationalism.

There are some old insights, but many new questions, about nationalism. One old insight is that ethnic affiliation matters to people and politics just as much as it ever did. If it were not the case, the normative considerations of cosmopolitan discourses based on humanity would not be constrained by cultural differences and we would probably not live in a world of nation states. The classical nation state is the pinnacle of the elevation of ethnic identity into a political organisation. The political process by which the belonging to a community of some shared and some could-be shared cultural attributes becomes an invitation into history[2] and by which cultural identity is institutionalised in the form of a territorially bound political unit is nationalism. It can be peaceful, it can be honourable, but usually it is not. This is for the rather banal reason that the identification with one culture necessarily requires the identification of 'the other'. And if a nationalist programme is to deliver the consolidation of a culturally distinct group into a nation and offer it a place in the world in the form of the nation state, it must act for and on behalf of one group. It is not a fault, it is not a misinterpreted historical mission, but a function of nationalism which it acquired in modern times. While human desire for self-esteem, belonging and sharing 'common forms of life' and 'intimate communication' with people who understand one's language[3] may be as old as humanity itself, the politicisation of this identity, even its elevation into a political status with attached rights of a citizen (and obligations, but nationalism is less emphatic on those) and a sovereignty, result from modernity. There is a number of scholarly answers to the rise of nations, their historical authenticity or their constructed character and the role of nationalism in the nation's formation. I have discussed the main schools of thought that deal with the phenomenon of nationalism at relative length in Chapter 2 and I pointed to their shortcomings when viewed from the contemporary perspective. These approaches to nationalism are important because they reveal nationalism as a modern political ideology, rooted in the Age of Enlightenment. 'The nation' became an answer to the challenges of societies finding themselves at the crossroads of tradition and modernity, when new ideas about democracy were emerging and traditional societal structures were breaking down and were, in turn, accelerated by industrialisation and secularisation. The fact that this ideology, rooted in reason and democratic thought, ended up at the gates of Auschwitz adds to the many ironies and paradoxes of nationalism whose ability to appeal across historical, ideological, spatial and temporal boundaries makes it a phenomenon of baffling endurance and political consequence. The concern in this book, however, has been with new questions about nationalism, its political manifestations in our time, its strategies and methods, its relevance in the globalising world of flattening boundaries and unprecedented movement of people. It is about rising incidents of ethnic violence deriving from the cultural incomprehension between peoples and the extent to which these new questions can be answered by the existing theories of nationalism.

I am not offering a new theory of nationalism. At this stage, when it is clear that the classical nation state is changing but not clear to what, it is more important to acknowledge the deficiency of the contemporary nation state in providing answers for questions contemporary societies need urgent answers to and to clarify the issues that are relevant to the study of nationalism in our time. Ethnicity, nationhood and statehood were always different categories but successfully merged into the nation state. It is obvious that, in a time of complex transnational ethnic networks and shifting geographies, this 'merger' is severely disrupted and that nationalism operates as much within the state as beyond and across the state boundaries. Hence, I have taken a more international perspective on the nationalist phenomenon than is usual. All theories of nations, from Smith's *ethnie*, through the Gellnerian constructed nation to Habermas's constitution suffer from the lack of reflection on the precarious position of the contemporary state, even if the last much less so: under the pressure from beyond and within but with a substantially reduced ability to influence either. The pressures from beyond the state come in the form of globalisation – including the polarisation between those in receipt and those in denial of its benefits – social interaction, non-state actors' intervention into political and security spheres, increasing concern for human rights, and the rising legitimacy of regional and other organisations. The pressures from within and below the state come from an ever-increasing diversity, with a reduced ability of the state to homogenise the population, a general demise in citizens' commitment to political participation but increased forms of 'ethnic activism'.[4] This can be observed in transnational fundamentalist movements, the pursuit of autonomy and self-rule by subnational groups and minorities, and trans-border galvanisation of co-ethnic relations. Nationalism is activated on behalf of the beleaguered state, in an attempt to unify the population behind its political aims, and on behalf of ethnic groups that are resisting this attempt, often by violent means. Given the general internationalisation of ideas and political influences, their appeals spread beyond the relevant states to co-ethnics everywhere and their plight is defended by the plethora of international organisations and non-governmental organisations (NGOs). Can we assume that this 'new' nation state should be the subject of the same identity and the same theorising as the classical nation state? My answer is No.

The contemporary nation state produces new forms of

nationalism. The arguments advanced in this book are exemplified by an examination of a number of contradictory processes taking place simultaneously: the diminishing legitimacy of the state on the one hand but paradoxically increasing demands for national self-determination on the other (Chapter 7); further, by the general blurring of boundaries between national and international, accompanied by fear of homogenisation and thus the creation of new cultural and symbolic boundaries across the physical boundaries of the states (Chapters 3, 5 and 6). The main questions of our time concern the forging of solidarity across ethnic divides and the reinvention of human community, if necessary, beyond the political frameworks of the nation state. Therefore, the implicit and explicit thread running through this book is that the theorising of nationalism today, if it is to reflect the new conditions in which it arises, should shift its state-centric focus, accept the strength of ethnic affiliation and look to the forces of democratisation and transnationality for solutions. New nationalism is the meeting ground of modern and pre-modern, democracy and exclusion, perceived past and aspirations for the future. When put this way, it is the same nationalism as it was in the nineteenth century but practised in the twenty-first century which surely requires a change of tools, assumptions and solutions, and thus also new avenues through which to examine the nationalist phenomenon.

The first questions I posed in the introduction was when and why did the nation assume the relevance that can be, at best, considered important to human existence and, at worst, set against it? I hope that the introduction and the first chapter conveyed clearly that the importance of the nation in human existence rests on the combination of emotional sustenance, enhancement of self-esteem and external protection that the nation provides on individual and collective levels, and the political power in the form of the sovereign nation state. Nationalism is about political legitimacy awarded to a culturally distinct group and, since the eighteenth century, all our cultural and political points of references are intimately linked to national cultures and symbolism based on those cultures. Modernity is the merging of culture, politics and social development.

The second question proposed in the introduction is whether the challenges faced by societies in our time can be found in that classical nation state? The question is inspired by theories of nationalism which, while not in agreement on the origins of nations, are nevertheless in agreement that nationalism was an answer to the changing social, political and techno-administrative conditions and challenges thereof which traditional societies faced. The centralised and ethnicised nation state appeared to provide those answers. It is important to reiterate that, in its origins, nationalism emerged as a movement for emancipation and that, even today when we have experienced two hundred years of conflict among national groups seeking the emancipation promised by the national self-determination doctrine, nationalism remains linked to the emancipation of 'the people'. This is its political appeal, and the underestimation of this 'democratic' aspect of nationalism leads only to more nationalism. The case study of the disintegration of the Austro-Hungarian Empire served as an example of national movements emerging among all ethno-national groups within the empire, inspired by the French Revolution. Thus, officially equipped with popular sovereignty and the 'soul' which nationalism reinforced, the nation could be 'civic' if it was willing to share that soul with all people living on its territory, or 'ethnic' if it excluded people not born to it. In fact, that distinction has always been a label by which the inherently particularistic trait of nationalism could be accommodated in view of its equally inherent democratising and unifying qualities; I have argued that this distinction obscures more than it explains (Chapters 1 and 2). The story of nationalism is embedded in an account of the development of Western civilisation; it began with civic intentions but the response to Rousseau's democratic nation, when spread in conditions where the only shared commonality among people was the language or religion and where their aspirations were met with hostility, was ethnic. This dynamic has not changed to this day.

Binary concepts tend to pervade the theories of nations and nationalism. According to modernists, nations are a modern construction, imagined, invented, their ideas are mistaken, they are a response to industrialisation, they are tools for elites to pursue their aspirations and resist the existing political order or legitimise a new order. To primordialists they are a natural progression of ancient ethnic cores, propelled into history faster by modernity but nationalism is the expression of their existence and not the other way round as the modernists claim. I have argued that all those approaches to nationalism are persuasive – some more than others – but, on the whole, they reflect the past and even that not always convincingly. From a contemporary perspective, the most relevant and enduring explanation of national(ist) aspirations is that it is a principle of political legitimacy and that it had a function strongly connected to the erosion of traditional social structures and the emergence of industrialisation and political modernisation. The functionalism of nationalism in modernist approaches, however, poses something of a problem: if it served societies in challenging times in the past, does it perform the same function today when we are facing different challenges? The answer is probably negative, because nationalism's intrinsic love affair with the past and with the exclusivity of ethnicity appears atavistic today and not very constructive for a world in need of different forms of solidarity. As I argued, primordialists and other ethno-symbolists no longer appear so outdated when viewed via the persistence of the idea of the nation. The case study of Arab nationalism illustrated that nationalism can arise in non-industrial societies, and I have also argued that modernisation can inspire resentment and inwardness rather than progress, as we are witnessing in the current revival of fundamental Islam.

My most important critique of the Gellnerian approach is the failure of modernists (with the exception of modern-day modernists, such as Michael Mann) to link political legitimacy to democratisation. Industrialisation did not just modernise societies, it changed the expectations and structure of societies, and necessarily brought democracy into the realm of politics. Today, democracy and political legitimacy cannot be separated. We cannot explain post-communist nationalism, as I did in Chapter 4, without taking into account that the legitimacy gap left by the collapsing states and discredited regimes would be filled by nationalism. The same applies for all collapsing and dismantled states (the best example being post-Saddam Iraq). It would seem that neither the cynicism of modernists nor the romanticism of others can really answer the rise of nations and the role of nationalism in our world. A possible way forward is to investigate what nationalism does to humanity as well as for humanity.

Where in those traditional approaches to nationalism do we find the explanation to the mistreatment of minorities, the ferocity of ethnic conflicts and the will to resolve them? What is the role of the international community in the formation of nations? In our societies, when nationalism and ethnic mobilisation are on the rise, it is perhaps wise to approach nationalism through, first, its democratic thrust and, secondly, by recognising that contemporary debates in studies of nationalism need to reinvent approaches to nationalism. This reinvention should shift its state-centric focus. It should look beyond the state, explore spaces where the ethnic revival of various diasporic and other groups is activated, to the solution of minority problems and political participation of immigrants. It should incorporate new urban spaces shared by an amalgamation of numerous mutually incomprehensive cultures living in stressful conditions, and attempt to find regional arrangements to inter-ethnic relations and other similar situations where collective identities operate.

In Chapter 3 I have approached the 'grey area' where the cultural and political nation do not overlap, which is the case of nearly all states. Consequently, one of the most important themes in contemporary politics today is how to reconcile cultural diversity and political unity within the state. The contemporary nation state is increasingly less capable of insulating its borders from the influx of immigrants and therefore, now more than ever, the role of citizenship and national narratives need to be re-evaluated. I suggested that we find out more about nationalism when investigating the 'grey areas' than we do when focusing on the presumed congruence between the political and cultural nation, and that theories of nationalism give us little in the way of solutions to this very contemporary predicament of nation states and their peoples. Cultural diversity is an irrefutable and permanent fact of our political and social reality. That is not an historical novelty; the novelty, however, is the challenge to the state and to its cultural and political authority. If the state is losing its unassailable image, logically, the relationship between the state and society is changing, too, and we can safely say that the most visible among those changes is the relationship between majorities and minorities. The clue to the relationship between majorities and minorities is actually in the intensity of the homogenising policies of the state which can range from an accommodation of minorities to mild attempts at the appropriation of state power by the dominant national group to the exclusion of minorities. The issue of citizenship and the idea of national identity need redeveloping in view of the evident fact that there is no future for the nation state without an increasing number of immigrants and that many minorities and migrants will never become 'nationals' in the traditional sense because they do not wish to and because the ties to their home countries are too strong. The case study of multicultural Britain suggested that multiculturalism cannot mean the integration of an immigrant population into the dominant culture, but the integration of the whole society, including the British people, into the new Britain with a new corresponding national identity in which all can partake but do not have to. When viewed from this perspective, our contemporary nation state bears less and less relation to its nineteenth-century ideal, and the challenges it faces find fewer and fewer answers in theorising about the origins of nationalism.

In Chapter 4 I have explored post-communist nationalism and the disintegration of Yugoslavia. Post-communism, more than any other period in recent history, illustrated the close connection between democracy and nationalism. The combination of politics, democratisation, ethnic mobilisation and the creation of new states in early post-communism was, indeed, as Hroch argued, analogous to nineteenth-century nationalism. In this respect, a number of classical theories could be applied to post-communist nationalism, namely: the ethno-symbolist use of historical markers in elite mobilisation; Hobsbawm's invention of traditions; and, possibly most appropriately, the strongly politically founded Breuilly's theory of nationalism. Overall, as in nearly all nationalisms, the post-communist version was also too multifactorial to be grasped by one theory. The civic/ethnic dichotomy looked somewhat meaningless when demands of all national groups were simultaneously civic and ethnic. Importantly, though, these democratisation processes involved a whole new aspect: European integration as the final objective. The national rhetoric in the newly independent states took on an unusually international guise in its appeals to the nation and showed the effectiveness of nationalism even in this most international of efforts. Classical theories of nationalism have little, if anything, to say about this form of 'internationalising' nationalism. Post-communist nationalism also showed the dynamism of the relationship between majorities and minorities which, at all times, responds to the opportunities and constraints of institutional processes within the state and to the geopolitical processes beyond it. All of those factors were in flux in post-communist states, and the implication I sought to draw was that nationalism, for all its state-centric appeals, is affected by politics from beyond the state's boundaries and that ethnic mobilisation reaches across them, too.

Ethnic conflicts, which were the subject of Chapter 5, allow for the worst of humanity to emerge. It would be a mistake, however, to class all conflicts as 'identity' conflicts and neglect the political power which remains decisive to ethnic violence. Ethnic violence is truly a 'dark side of democracy', and I have illustrated the extreme of the nation state's misconception of democracy as the appropriation of the state by a dominant *ethnos* by the case of Israel and its Palestinian minority. I have also argued that the ethno-national bond has dangerous implications, but that the acknowledgement of it is woefully unhelpful. The solution could possibly be found in finding a convincing form of solidarity among peoples which could offer an identity meaningful enough to fulfil the sense of uniqueness and offer protection without the exclusion of others. It is clear where my argument is heading: while we are conflating ethnicity and politics, politically motivated, identity-driven violence remains the dark side not only of democracy but of humanity.

In the Chapter 6 I approached the dispora as the most symbolic identity of our fractured world of complex affiliations, deriving from shifting geographies and global economies and communications. I argued that, theoretically, diasporas defy many conventions of democratic theory, international relations and nationalism because none of the underlying assumptions applies: the world is not divided into nation states that embody distinct nations; the sovereign state is no longer the only political actor; and there are various new forms of partial citizenship in which it is not clear where political interests and participation lie. Diasporas can, and increasingly do, actively influence the homeland's foreign policies. This contradicts the state-centrically preoccupied foundations of international relations theory because diasporas reside outside the state but claim a stake within it. The tightly connected trinity of the nation, its territory and the state is disturbed as are the arguments about citizenship, civic nations and political community because the boundaries of who is 'in' and who is 'out' are very blurred. We are entering a murky area of the de-territorialized nation where civic equality is subordinated to ethnic solidarity reaching beyond the state's boundaries. The case of the Hungarian diaspora in Central Europe illustrated my arguments but also showed that the issue of dual affiliation is less problematic in more de-territorialized regions, such as the European Union. I have also argued that diasporas are a triumph of ethnicity and homeland territory but also a sign that the geopolitical space of the nation state is no longer a sacred territory of and for its nationals. The point of the chapter on diasporas and transnationalism has been to describe a phenomenon of collective identity operating within and beyond the nation-state which is not easily explained by any theory of nationalism but nevertheless is a phenomenon inspired by ethno-national identity. The discussion about diasporas and transna-tionalism, as represented by the case of the Hungarian minority, endorsed my argument advanced throughout and emphasised in the concluding Chapter 7 that binary concepts of ethnic or civic identity, and primordial or modernist approaches to national-ism, no longer satisfactorily answer complex questions relating to various forms of ethno-political affiliations and mobilisation in our world. Hence, our theoretical imagination ought to follow spaces beyond and above states and official cultures where these forms of ethnic activities are located.

In the final, seventh chapter I have intensified the 'interna-tional' dimension in contemporary nationalism. I have argued that nationalism, in the form of its defining national self-determination principle, is problematical for both peace and sovereignty in the international system because it remains difficult to juggle the justice of this not necessarily peaceful principle in the international arena, and sometimes the self-determination of one group must be set against the international order. Staying with dilemmas of the national self-determination doctrine, I have argued that the history of state formation in the past and in the present shows that the attainment of nationhood depends on more than the strengths of its national movement, the intensity of patriotic fervour or even on the level of industrialisation; it depends on politics and on the con-stellation of power in the international system. The case of Kosovo and its still unclear status shows that nationalism, in civic or ethnic form, may claim that 'the people' are both bearers and receivers of history but, in truth, 'the people' are participants at best and often victims of the dramas played out elsewhere.

Theories of nationalism are at their weakest when it comes to cap-turing the internationalisation of national struggles. I have debated the constructivist theory of international relations in order to show that, even if the constructivist approach has not been thought out for the purpose of ethnic conflict, as a social theory it can teach us something about the resolution of conflicts which, similarly to states, arise from the interaction among ethno-national groups locked in a cycle of mistrust and historically accumulated hostili-ties. Nationalists believe in territorially based sovereignty, and they want either to control the state or to create one they can control in the name of the nation or, as is currently the case, in the name of a religion. This alone does not make contemporary nationalism new. The new aspects of some nationalisms are the intense invocation of a mythical past combined with very modern methods and the monstrous violence that accompanies these extreme forms of cultural self-righteousness. We ought to ask ourselves what makes our post-modern, but still nationally constructed, world so disappointing to ethnic militants that they use all benefits of modernity to humiliate and reject it.

Some may seek answers in cosmopolitan endeavour which is quite rightly asking whether the territorial sovereign nation state can remain the only moral community when there is so much interdependence but also confusion and injustice deriving from it. It is obvious that the territorial nation state has emerged in different conditions in order to answer different questions, and that it is time to acknowledge its deficiencies in providing answers for our time. The tenacity of the nation state, however, suggests that it is not going anywhere soon but I have argued throughout that it cannot continue in the same form either. The violence we are witnessing partially derives from the confusion about how our world should be organised, if the nation state has consistently failed to provide the answers to challenges within and without.

A number of arguments has thus emerged from the foregoing chapters which I believe could offer the foundations for new theorising about nationalism:

1. There is an inherent tension between nationalism and democracy which is exemplified by the national self-determination doctrine as the fundamental principle of nationalist endeavour. Nationalism makes democratic claims but its actions are exclusivist. There is no answer to this dilemma within the classical nation state which is based on the national self-determination of the dominant national group.

2. The nation state has not been very successful in reconciling the inner conflict of the contemporary state: the need for political unity and the fact of cultural diversity. Policies of nation states, including liberal states, tend towards a preferential treatment of the dominant nation which leaves minorities, if not subordinated, then having to seek special measures to protect their identity and interests. Classical approaches to nationalism are inattentive to this dynamic which is then studied as a separate issue when it is actually the fundamental issue at the heart of the nation state design.

3. The approaches to nationalism stress either the modernity of the nation or the durability of the ethnic affiliation. The former

blinds us to the power of ethnicity, the latter to the political consequences of it, but the past, territory, myths, perceptions, belonging,
modernity and the future are all parts of the same nation. There are
no other nations, all affinities are constructed, but that does not
make them unreal.

4. The studies of nationalisms suffer from too many binary
concepts, such as ethnic and civic nationalism, modern and primordial, national and ethnic identity, homogeneity, multiculturalism, accommodation, conflict, and so on which only obscures
the fact that nationalism thrives on ambiguities and dilemmas.[5]
Nationalism is simultaneously modern and pre-modern, ethnic
with some civic features, democratic and exclusivist, and, in spite
of the continued relevance of the nation state, increasingly more
international.

5. Contemporary nationalism cannot be understood through
traditional approaches because its manifestations have escaped the
confines of the traditional nation state for which these approaches
have been developed. 'New' nationalism is not new in the claims
it is making; in fact, it is increasingly more atavistic but it is new
in the strategies it employs, its geopolitical scope and its global
significance. This is where we ought to look for some answers to
Islamic terrorism.

6. Democratisation and the internationalisation of inter-ethnic
relations are the most important aspects of the analysis of contemporary nationalisms. Therefore, solutions to some ethnic conflicts
have to be sought in the combination of measures above and
beyond the politics of the state, such as regional settlements and
international agreements.

7. There is no traditional approach nor a theory of nationalism that is wrong and does not explain one or more aspects of all
nationalisms. On the other hand, there is not one approach that
encompasses the emerging issues in contemporary nationalism
which appears to have adapted better to shifting geographies and
the complexities of our simultaneously fracturing and globalising
world than approaches to it. We are living in a transitional period
between the classical nineteenth-century nation state and something yet unformed; this 'new' nation state cannot be subject to
similar theorising as the classical nation state.

Whether one believes, as most nationalists do, that nationalism
emerges from cultural identity, or that cultural identity is strengthened by the politics of nationalism, as I believe, does not change its

political influence. The explicit and implicit thread throughout this book has been that, if nationalism is to be understood in our time, its appeal must be sought in the democratic notion of 'the people' which does not mean that this notion is always about freedom or emancipation; it can be, and often is, about resentment, fear, intolerance of others and the elevation of one's own nation. It may not be how nationalism entered our world in the nineteenth century but, for the twenty-first century, we must reconsider the meaning of democracy, what are the consequences and benefits of nationalism are, what the appeals of cultural affinity are, and how it can be maintained without being institutionalised. Ethnic affiliation has been the answer to the solidarity and political organisation of our world for the last two hundred years. It has achieved momentous successes and produced solidarity among people who have otherwise had little in common. But, it has produced wars and conflicts that may not outweigh the benefits and, moreover, may no longer produce greatness either. Forging solidarity beyond and above ethnic affinities remains the challenge of our time, thus far unanswered by the nation state, even in its civic form. Perhaps we ought to continue to question the whole idea of the nation state and its ability to answer new societal and political challenges. We should not assume that the continued proliferation of nation states suggests its success.[6] It suggests the success of nationalism and it is time to approach ethnic identities, political solidarity and political power in different ways.

Notes

1. Rose Tremain (2008), *The Road Home*, London: Vintage, p. 31.
2. Nairn (1975), 'Modern Janus', p. 12.
3. Ignatieff (1998), quoting Isaiah Berlin in *A Life of Isaiah Berlin*, p. 292.
4. Waterbury (2006), 'Ideology, Organization, Opposition: How Domestic Political Strategy Shapes Hungary's Ethnic Activism', pp. 65–86, refers to official and unofficial policies by a state using the diaspora for domestic political goals as 'ethnic activism'. I find this term very suitable for all forms of nationalism which operates beyond and between states whether on behalf of a state or an ethno-national group.
5. Roshwald (2006), *The Endurance of Nationalism*, pp. 1–2.
6. Bauman (1992), 'Soil blood and identity', p. 690.

Bibliography

AbuKhalil, As'ad (1992), 'A new Arab Ideology?: Rejuvenation of Arab Nationalism', *Middle East Journal* 46: 1, pp. 22–36.

Ágh, Attila, (1998), *The Politics of Central Europe*, London: Sage.

Anderson, Benedict (1983), *Imagined Communities*, London: Verso.

Ankersen, Christopher (ed.) (2007), *Understanding Global Terror*, Cambridge: Polity Press.

Appadurai, Arjun (2006), *Fear of Small Numbers*, Durham and London: Duke University Press.

Armstrong, John (1982), *Nations Before Nationalism*, Chapel Hill, NC: University of North Carolina Press.

Balakrishnan, Gopal (1996), *Mapping the Nation*, London: Verso.

Balibar, Ettienne (2004), *We, the People of Europe?*, Princeton: Princeton University Press.

Barnard, Frederick, M. (1983), 'National Culture and Political Legitimacy: Herder and Rousseau', *Journal of the History of Ideas* XVIV: 2, pp. 231–53.

Barnard, Frederick, M (1984), 'Patriotism and Citizenship in Rousseau: A Dual Theory of Public Willing', *The Review of Politics*, 46: 2, pp. 244–65.

Barnett, Michael (2005), 'Social Constructivism', in J. Baylis and S. Smith, *The Globalization of World Politics*, Oxford: Oxford University Press, pp. 251–70.

Bauman, Zygmunt (1992), 'Soil, blood and identity', *Sociological Review*, 40: 2, pp. 675–701.

Beardsworth, Richard (2008), 'Cosmopolitanism and Realism: Towards a Theoretical Convergence?', *Millenium: Journal of International Studies*, 37: 1, pp. 69–96.

Behar, Moshe (2005), 'Do Comparative and Regional Studies of Nationalism Intersect?', *International Journal of Middle East Studies*, 37, pp. 587–612.

Beissinger, Mark (2008), 'A New Look at Ethnicity and Democratization', *Journal of Democracy*, 19: 3, pp. 85–97.

Ben-Ami, Shlomo (2006), *Scars of War, Wounds of Peace: The Israeli–Arab Tragedy*, Oxford: Oxford University Press.

Ben-Ami, Shlomo (2008), 'A War to Start all Wars', *Foreign Affairs*, accessed 28 August 2008 at http://www.foreignaffairs. org/20080901fareviewessay87511/shlomo. . .

Benner, E. (2001), 'Is there a core national doctrine?', *Nations and Nationalism*, 7: 2, pp. 155–74.

Berezin, Mabel and Schain, Martin (eds) (2003), *Europe Without Borders*, Baltimore: Johns Hopkins University Press.

Berezin, M. (2004), 'Re-asserting the National: The Paradox of Populism in Transnational Europe', CSES Working paper #21, Department of Sociology, Cornell University, Ithaca.

Berghe, Pierre van den (1979), *The Ethnic Phenomenon*, New York: Elsevier.

Berlin, Isaiah (1972), 'The bent twig', *Foreign Affairs*, 51: 1, pp. 11–31.

Booth, Ken (1995), 'Human wrongs and international relations', *International Affairs*, 71: 1, pp. 103–26.

Bozóki, András (1999), *Intellectuals and Politics in Central Europe*, Budapest: Central European University Press.

Braziel, Jana and Mannur, Anita (2003), *Theorizing Diaspora*, Malden, MA and Oxford: Blackwell.

Breuilly, John (1993), *Nationalism and the State* (2nd ed.), Manchester: Manchester University Press.

Breuilly, John (1996), 'Approaches to Nationalism' in 'Balakrishnan, G., *Mapping the Nation*, London: Verso, pp. 146–74.

Brown, Archie (2000), 'Transitional Influences in the Transition from Communism', *Post Soviet Affairs*, 16: 2, pp. 177–200.

Brown, David (1999), 'Are there good and bad nationalisms?, *Nations and Nationalism*, 5: 2, pp. 281–302.

Brubaker, Rogers (1996), *Nationalism Reframed*, Cambridge: Cambridge University Press.

Brubaker, R. and Cooper, F., (2000), 'Beyond "identity"', *Theory and Society* 29, pp. 1–47.

Caspersen, Nina (2008), 'Intragroup divisions in ethnic conflicts: from popular grievances to power struggles', *Nationalism and Ethnic Politics*, 14: 2, pp. 239–65.

Cerutti, Furio and Rudolph, Enno (eds) (2001), *A Soul for Europe*, Leuven: Peeters.

Chen, Cheng (2007), *The Prospects for Liberal Nationalism in Post-Leninist States*, University Park, PA: Pennsylvania State University Press.

Choueiri, Yousseff (2000), *Arab Nationalism, A History*, Oxford: Blackwell.

Cohen, Lenard (1993), *Broken Bonds*, Oxford: Westview Press.

Connor, Walker (1972), 'Nation-Building or Nation-Destroying', *World Politics* XXIV: 3, pp. 319–55.

Connor, Walker (1984), *The National Question in Marxist–Leninist Theory and Strategy*, Princeton: Princeton University Press.

Connor, Walker (1993), 'Beyond reason: the nature of the ethnonational bond', *Ethnic and Racial Studies*, 16: 3, pp. 373–89.

Connor, Walker (2001), 'Homelands in a World of States', in M. Guibernau and J. Hutchinson (eds), *Understanding Nationalism*, Cambridge: Polity Press.

Deets, Stephen (2006), 'Reimagining the Boundaries of the Nation: Politics and the Development of Ideas on Minority Rights', *East European Politics and Societies*, 20: 3, pp. 419–46.

Deets, Stephen and Stroschein, Sherrill (2005), 'Dilemmas of Autonomy and Liberal Pluralism: examples involving Hungarians in Central Europe', *Nations and Nationalism*, 11: 2, pp. 185–305.

Delanty, Gerard and Kumar, Krishan (2006), *The Sage Handbook of Nations and Nationalism*, London: Sage Publications.

Delanty, Gerard (2006), 'Borders in Changing Europe: Dynamics of Openness and Closure', *Comparative European Politics*, 4: 2/3, pp. 183–202.

Diamond, Larry and Plattner, Marc (eds) (1994), *Nationalism, Ethnic Conflict, and Democracy*, Baltimore and London: Johns Hopkins University Press.

Diamond, Larry (2002), 'Elections without Democracy: Thinking about Hybrid Regimes', *Journal of Democracy*, 13: 2, 21–35.

Diaz, Thomas, Stetter, Stephen and Albert, Mathias (2006), 'The European Union and Border Conflicts: The Transformative Power of Integration', *International Organization*, 60: pp. 563–93.

Dimitras, Panayote (2004), 'Nationalism of Majorities and Minorities in the Balkans', in M. Kovács and P. Lom (eds), *Studies on Nationalism*, Budapest: Central European University Press, pp. 35–42.

Dimitrijević, Nenad (1999), 'Words and Death: Serbian Nationalist Intellectuals', in Dragojević, Mila (2005), 'Competing Institutions in National Identity Construction: the Croatian Case', *Nationalism and Ethnic Politics*, 11, pp. 61–87.

Eley, Geoff and Suny, Ronald (1996), *Becoming National*, Oxford: Oxford University Press.

Elster, Jon, Offe, Claus and Preuss, Ulrich, K. (1998), *Institutional Design in Post-communist Societies*, Cambridge: Cambridge University Press.

Freeman, Michael (1999), 'The right to self-determination in international Politics: six theories in search of a policy', *Review of International Studies*, 25, pp. 355–70.

Fukuyama, Francis (1989), 'The End of History?', *National Interest*, summer 1989, pp. 3–18.

Fukuyama, Francis and Avineri, Shlomo (1994), 'Comments on Nationalism and Democracy' in Diamond, Larry and Plattner, Marc, *Nationalism, Ethnic Conflict, and Democracy*, Baltimore and London: Johns Hopkins University Press, pp. 23–34.

Geddes, Andrew (2005), 'Europe's Border Relationships and International Migration Relations', *Journal of Common Market Studies*, 43: 4, pp. 787–806.

Gellner, Ernest (1964), *Thought and Change*, London: Weidenfeld and Nicolson.

Gellner, Ernest (1994 [1983]), *Nations and Nationalism*, Oxford: Blackwell.

Glenny, Misha (1999), *The Balkans 1804–1999*, London: Granta Books.

Goldmann, Kjell, Hannerz, Ulf and Westin, Charles (eds) (2000), *Nationalism and Internationalism in the Post-Cold War Era*, London: Routledge.

Greenfeld, Liah (1992), *Nationalism: Five Roads to Modernity*, Cambridge, MA: Harvard University Press.

Guibernau, Monserat and Hutchinson, J. (2001), *Understanding Nationalism*, Cambridge: Polity Press.

Habermas, Jürgen (1992), 'Citizenship and National Identity: Some Reflections on the Future of Europe', *Praxis International*, 12: 1, pp. 1–19.

Habermas, Jürgen (1999), 'The European Nations – State and the Pressures of Globalization', *New Left Review*, 235, pp. 46–56.

Habermas, Jürgen (2001), 'A Constitution for Europe?' *New Left Review*, 11, pp. 5–26.

Hajdinjak, Marko (2004), 'Tolerantly Ethnic and Aggressively Civic?' in M. Kovács and P. Lom (eds), *Studies on Nationalism*, Budapest: Central European University Press, pp. 247–58.

Hall, John (1998), *The State of the Nation*, Cambridge: Cambridge University Press.

Halliday, Fred (1999), *Revolution and World Politics*, London: Macmillan.

Halliday, Fred (2005), 'Nationalism' in J. Baylis and S. Smith *The Globalization of World Politics*, Oxford: Oxford University Press, pp. 521–38.

Hardt, Michael and Negri, Antonio (2000), *Empire*, Cambridge, MA: Harvard University Press.

Harris, Erika (2002), *Nationalism and Democratisation: Politics of Slovakia and Slovenia*, Aldershot: Ashgate Publishing.

Harris, Erika (2004), 'Europeanization of Slovakia', *Comparative European Politics* 2, pp. 185–211.

Harris, Erika (2007), 'Moving Politics Beyond the State: The Hungarian Minority in Slovakia', *Perspectives: The Central European Review of International Affairs* 27, pp. 43–62.

Hearn, Jonathan (2006), *Rethinking Nationalism*, Basingstoke: Palgrave Macmillan.

Hechter, Michael (2000), *Containing Nationalism*, Oxford: Oxford University Press.

Held, David (1995), *Democracy and the Global Order: from the Modern State to Cosmopolitan Governance*, Cambridge: Polity Press.

Held, David and McGrew, Anthony (eds) (2003), *The Global Transformations Reader*, Cambridge: Polity Press.

Hobsbawm, Eric (1990), *Nations and Nationalism since 1780: Programme, Myth and Reality*, Cambridge: Cambridge University Press.

Hobsbawm, Eric and Ranger, Terence (1983) (eds), *The Invention of Tradition*, Cambridge: Cambridge University Press.

Horowitz, Donald (1985), *Ethnic Groups in Conflict*, Berkeley: University of California Press.

Horowitz, Donald (1994), 'Democracy in Divided Societies' in Diamond, Larry and Plattner, Marc, *Nationalism, Ethnic Conflict, and Democracy*, Baltimore and London: Johns Hopkins University Press, pp. 35–54.

Hribar, Tine (1987), 'The Slovenes and European Transnationality' in the special issue 'Prispevki za Slovenski Nacionalni program' in *Nova Revija* VI: 57, pp. 33–6.

Hroch, Miroslav (1993), 'From National Movement to the Fully-Formed Nation', *New Left Review* 198, pp. 3–20.

Huntington, Samuel (1993), 'The Clash of Civilizations?', *Foreign Affairs* 72: 3, pp. 22–49.

Hutchinson, John (2005), *Nations as Zones of Conflict*, London: Sage Publications.

Hyde-Pryce, Adrian (1996), *The International Politics of East/Central Europe*, Manchester: Manchester University Press.

Ignatieff, Michael (1998), *Isaiah Berlin: a Life*, London: Random House.

Ignatieff, Michael (2005), *The Lesser Evil*, Edinburgh: Edinburgh University Press.

Isaac, Jeffrey (1996), 'The Meanings of 1989', *Social Research*, 63: 2, pp. 291–334.

Jankowski, James and Gershoni, Israel (1997), *Rethinking Nationalism in the Arab Middle East*, New York: Columbia University Press.

Judt, Tony (2007), *Postwar: A History of Europe since 1945*, London: Pimlico.

Kafka, Petr (2004), 'A critique of David Miller's model of ethno-cultural justice', in Kovács, Mária and Lom, Peter (eds), *Studies on Nationalism*, Budapest: Central European University Press, pp. 237–46.

Kaldor, Mary (2004), 'Nationalism and Globalisation', *Nations and Nationalism*, 10: pp. 1–2 and 161–77.

Kaldor, Mary (2006), *New and Old Wars: Organized Violence in a Global Era*, Cambridge: Polity Press.

Kann, Robert, A. (1973), *The Habsburg Empire*, New York: Octagon Books.

Kaufmann, Eric (2004), *Rethinking Ethnicity*, London, New York: Routledge.

Kaufmann, Eric (2008), 'Debate on John Hutchinson's Nations as Zones of Conflict', *Nations and Nationalism* 14: 1, pp. 1–28.

Keating, Michael (1998), 'Territory and Politics', in *The New Regionalism in Western Europe: territorial restructuring and political change*, Cheltenham: E. Elgar.

Keating, Michael (2004), 'European Integration and the Nationalities Question', *Politics and Society*, 32: 3, pp. 367–88.

Keating, Michael and McGarry, John (2001), *Minority Nationalism and the Changing International Order*, Oxford: Oxford University Press.

Kedourie, Elie (1960), *Nationalism*, London: Hutchinson.

Kedourie, Elie (1971), *Nationalism in Asia and Africa*, London: Weidenfeld and Nicolson.

Keitner, Chimène (1999) 'The False Premise of Civic Nationalism', *Journal of International Studies* 28: 2, pp. 341–51.

Kimmerling, Baruch and Migdal, Joel S. (1994), *Palestinians: The Making of a People*, Cambridge, MA: Harvard University Press.

Kohn, Hans (2005 [1944]), *The Idea of Nationalism*, New Brunswick, NJ: Transaction Publishers.

Kováč, Dušan (2005), 'Nacionalizmus a politická kultúra v Rakúsko-Uhorsku v období dualizmu', *Historický časopis* 53: 1, pp. 45–55.

Kovács, Mária and Lom, Peter (eds), *Studies on Nationalism*, Budapest: Central European University Press.

Kupchan, Charles, A. (1995), *Nationalism and Nationalities in the New Europe*, Ithaca and London: Cornell University Press.

Kymlicka, Will (1995), *The Rights of Minority Cultures*, Oxford: Oxford University Press.

Kymlicka, William (2003),'Immigration, Citizenship, Multiculturalism: Exploring the Links', *The Political Quarterly*, 74: Supplement 1, pp. 195–208.

Kymlicka, William (2004), 'Justice and Security in the Accommodation of Minority Nationalism: Comparing East and West', in M. Kovács and P. Lom (eds), *Studies on Nationalism*, Budapest: Central European University Press, pp. 5–34.

Kymlicka, William and Opalski, Magda (2001), *Can Liberal Pluralism be Exported?*, Oxford: Oxford University Press.

Laborde, Cecile (2002), 'From Constitutional to Civic Patriotism', *British Journal of Political Studies*, 32, pp. 591–612.

Laitin, David (2007), *Nations, States, and Violence*, Oxford: Oxford University Press.

Lapid, Yosef and Kratochvil, Friedrich (eds) (1997), *The Return of Culture and Identity in IR theory*, Boulder: Lynne Rienner Publishers.

Leško, Marián (1998), 'Príbeh sebadiskvalifikácie favorita' in M. Bútora and F. Šebej (eds) (1998), *Slovensko v šedej zone*, Bratislava: IVO, pp. 15–80.

Lijphart, Arend (1995), 'Self-Detemination versus Pre-Determination of Ethnic Minorities in Power-Sharing Systems', pp. 275–99 in Kymlicka, W., *The Rights of Minority Cultures*, Oxford: Oxford University Press.

Linklater, Andrew (1998), 'Cosmopolitan Citizenship', *Citizenship Studies* 2: 1, pp. 23–42.

Linz, Juan and Stepan, Alfred (1996), *Problems of Democratic Transition and Consolidation*, Baltimore: Johns Hopkins University Press.

Lipták, L'ubomír (1998), *Slovensko v 20.storočí* , Bratislava: Kalligram.

Lom, Peter (2004), 'The Limits of European Identity', in M. Kovács and P. Lom (eds), *Studies on Nationalism*, Budapest: Central European University Press, pp. 141–7.

Lord, Christopher and Harris, Erika (2006), *Democracy in the New Europe*, Basingstoke: Palgrave Macmillan.

McGrew, Anthony (2003), 'Models of Transnational Democracy', in D. Held and A. McGrew (eds), *The Global Transformations Reader*, Oxford: Blackwell Publishing Ltd.

Maier, C. S. (1992), 'Democracy since the French Revolution', in J. Dunn (ed.), *Democracy the Unfinished Journey*, Oxford: Oxford University Press.

Malešević, Siniša (2004), '"Divine ethnies" and "Sacred nations": Anthony. D. Smith and neo-Durkhemian theory of nationalism', *Nationalism and Ethnic Politics*, 10: 4, pp. 561–93.

Mann, Michael (1995), 'A Political Theory of Nationalism and its Excesses', in Sukumar Periwal (ed.), *Notions of Nationalism*, Budapest: Central European University Press, pp. 44–64.

Mann, Michael (1999), 'The Dark Side of Democracy: The Modern Tradition of Ethnic and Political Cleansing', *New Left Review* 235, pp. 18–45.

Mann, Michael (2004), *The Dark Side of Democracy: Explaining Ethnic Cleansing*, Cambridge: Cambridge University Press.

Marin, Ruby (2005), 'Transnational Politics and the Democratic Nation-State: Challenges and Prudential Considerations', paper prepared for 'Citizens, non-citizens and voting rights in Europe', conference 3–4 June 2005 at the University of Edinburgh.

Mason, Andrew (1999), 'Political Community, Liberal Nationalism, and the Ethics of Assimilation', *Ethics*, 109, pp. 261–86.

Migdal, Joel, (2004), 'State Building and the Non-Nation-State', *Journal of International Affairs*, 58: 1, pp. 17–46.

Mill, John Stuart (1991), *On Liberty*, Oxford: Oxford University Press.

Miller, David (1995), *On Nationality*, Oxford: Clarendon Press.

Miller, David (2000), *Citizenship and National Identity*, Oxford: Clarendon Press.

Miodownik, Dan and Cartrite, Britt (2006), 'Demarking Political Space: Territoriality and the Ethnoregional Party Family', *Nationalism and Ethnic Politics* 12: pp. 53–82.

Modood, Tariq (2003), 'Muslims and Politics of Difference', *The Political Quarterly*, 74: Supplement 1, pp. 100–15.

Moore, Margaret (2001), 'Normative justification for liberal nationalism: justice, democracy and national identity', *Nations and Nationalism*, 7: 1, pp. 2–19.

Nairn, Tom (1975), 'Modern Janus', *New Left Review* 94, pp. 3–31.

Nairn, Tom (1981 [1977]), 2nd ed., *The Break-up of Britain: Crisis and Neo-Nationalism*, London: Verso.

Nairn, Tom (1997), *Faces of Nationalism*, London: Verso.

Nodia, Ghia (1994), 'Nationalism and Democracy' in Diamond, Larry and Plattner, Michael (eds), *Nationalism, Ethnic Conflict, and Democracy*, Baltimore and London: The Johns Hopkins University Press, pp. 3–22.

Offe, Claus (1991), 'Capitalism by Democratic Design?', *Social Research* 58: 4, pp. 865–92.

Ogden, Chris (2008), 'Diaspora Meets IR's Constructivism: An Appraisal', *Politics* 28: 1, pp. 1–11.

O'Leary, Brendan (1998), 'Ernest Gellner's diagnosis of nationalism: a critical overview, or, what is living and what is dead in Ernest Gellner's philosophy of nationalism?' in J. Hall, *The State of the Nation*, Cambridge: Cambridge University Press.

Özkirimli, Umut (2000), *Theories of Nationalism*, Basingstoke: Macmillan Press.

Özkirimli, Umut (2005), *Contemporary Debates on Nationalism*, Basingstoke: Palgrave Macmillan.

Parekh, Bhikhu (2000), *Rethinking Multiculturalism*, London: Macmillan Press.

Pearson, Raymond (1994), *The Longman Companion to European Nationalism 1789–1920*, London: Longman.

Peleg, Ilan (2007), *Democratizing the Hegemonic State: Political Transformation in the Age of Identity*, Cambridge: Cambridge University Press.

Periwal, Sukumar (ed.) (1995), *Notions of Nationalism*, Budapest: Central European University Press.

Poole, Ross (1999), *Nation and Identity*, London: Routledge.

Pridham, Geoffrey (2001), 'Uneasy Democratisations – Pariah Regimes, Political Conditionality and Reborn Transitions in Central and Eastern Europe', *Democratisation*, 8: 4, pp. 65–94.

Pritzel, Ilya (1998), *National Identity and Foreign Policy*, Cambridge: Cambridge University Press.

Ramet, Sabrina P. (1994), 'The Yugoslav Crisis and the West: Avoiding "Vietnam" and Blundering into "Abyssinia"', *East European Politics and Societies*, 8: 1, pp. 189–219.

Ramet, Sabrina P. (2002), *Balkan Babel*, Boulder, Colorado: Westview Press.

Ramet, Sabrina P. (2004), 'Explaining the Yugoslav meltdown, 1 "For a charm of pow'erful trouble, Like a hell-broth boil and bubble": Theories about the Roots of the Yugoslav Troubles', *Nationalities Papers*, 32: 4, pp. 731–63.

Ramet, Sabrina P. (2005), *Thinking about Yugoslavia*, Cambridge: Cambridge University Press.

Ramet, Sabrina P. (2007), 'The denial syndrome and its consequences: Serbian political culture since 2000', *Communist and Postcommunist Studies*, 40, pp. 41–58.

Reitz, Jeffrey G. (2002), 'Host Societies and the Reception of Immigrants: Research Themes, Emerging Theories and Methodological Issues', *International Migration Review*, 36: 4, pp. 1005–19.

Roshwald, Aviel (2006), *The Endurance of Nationalism*, Cambridge: Cambridge University Press.

Rumford, Chris (2006), 'Rethinking European Spaces: Territory, Borders, Governance', *Comparative European Politics*, 4-2/3, pp. 127–40.

Safran, William (1991), 'Diasporas in Modern Societies: Myths of Homeland and Return', *Diaspora: A Journal of Transnational Studies*, 1: 1, pp. 83–99.

Sartori, Giovanni (1995), 'How Far Can Free Government Travel?', *Journal of Democracy*, 6: 3, pp. 101–11.

Sasse, G. and Thielemann, E. (2005), 'A Research Agenda for the Study of Migrants and Minorities in Europe', *Journal of Common and Market Studies*, 43: 4, pp. 655–71.

Schedler, Andreas (1998), 'What is Democratic Consolidation', *Journal of Democracy*, 9: 2, pp. 91–103.

Schwarzmantel, John (1991), *Socialism and the Idea of the Nation*, Hemel Hempstead: Harvester Wheatsheaf.

Sen, Amartya (2006), *Identity and Violence*, London: Penguin Books.

Shain, Yossi and Barth, Aharon A. (2003), 'Diaspora in International Relations Theory', *International Organization*, 57: 3, pp. 449–79.

Shami, Setenyi (2000), 'The little nation: minorities and majorities in the context of shifting geographies', in K. Goldmann et al., *Nationalism and Internationalism in the Post-Cold War Era*, pp. 103–26.

Simms, Brendan (2002), *Unfinest Hour: Britain and the Destruction of Bosnia*, London: Penguin Books.

Shulman, Stephen (2002), 'Challenging the civic/ethnic and West/East dichotomies in the study of nationalism', *Comparative Political Studies*, 35: 5, pp. 554–86.

Silber, Laura and Little, Allan (1996), *The Death of Yugoslavia*, London: Penguin Books.

Snyder, Jack (2000), *From Voting to Violence: Democratisation and Nationalist Conflict*, New York: W. W. Norton.

Smith, Anthony D. (1983) (2nd ed.), *Theories of Nationalism*, London: Duckworth, and New York: Holmes and Meier.

Smith, Anthony D. (1986), *The Ethnic Origins of Nations*, Oxford: Blackwell.

Smith, Anthony D. (1991), *National Identity*, London: Penguin Books.

Smith, Anthony D. (1998), *Nationalism and Modernism*, London: Routledge.

Smooha, Sammy (2002), 'Types of democracy and modes of conflict management in ethnically divided societies', *Nations and Nationalism* 8: 4, pp. 423–31.

Soysal, Yaasemin (1998), 'Toward a postnational model of membership' in Gershon Shafir (ed.), *The Citizenship Debates: a Reader*, Mineapolis, Minn.: University of Minnesota Press, pp. 189–220.

Steiner, George (2008), *My Unwritten Books*, London: Weidenfeld and Nicolson.

Tamir, Yael (1993), *Liberal Nationalism*, Princeton: Princeton University Press.

Tibi, Bassam (1997), *Arab Nationalism Between Islam and the Nation-State*, Basingstoke: Macmillan Press.

Tønnesson, Stein (2004), 'Globalising national states', *Nations and Nationalism*, 10: 1–2, pp. 179–94.

Vermeersch, Peter (2007), 'A Minority at the Border: EU Enlargement and the Ukrainian Minority in Poland', *East European Politics and Societies*, 21: 3, pp. 475–502.

Wakefield, J. and Yuval-Davis, N. (eds). *Power and the State*, London: Croom Helm, pp. 52–71.

Walters, W. (2006), 'Rethinking Borders Beyond the State', *Comparative European Politics*, 4–2/3, pp. 141–59.

Warleigh, Alex (2006), 'Learning from Europe? EU Studies and the Re-thinking of "International Relations"', *European Journal of International Relations*, 12: 1, pp. 31–51.

Waterbury, Myra (2006), 'Internal Exclusion, External Inclusion: Diaspora Politics and Party-Building Strategies in Post-Communist Hungary', *East European Politics and Societies*, 20: 3, pp. 483–515.

Waterbury, Myra (2006), ' Ideology, Organization, Opposition: How

Domestic Political Strategy Shapes Hungary's Ethnic Activism', *Regio-Minorities, Politics, Society*, Issue 1, pp. 65–86, available at: http://www.ceeol.com/aspx/issuedetails.aspx?issueid=8f8fabe4-15ee-4b23-900c-46ad85eaa265&articleId=d3332431-2cb1-49f3-b843-f8324c96ac52

Wendt, Alexander (1992), 'Anarchy is what states make of it: social construction of power politics', *International Organization* 46, pp. 395–421.

Wimmer, Andreas (2002), *Nationalist Exclusion and Ethnic Conflict*, Cambridge: Cambridge University Press.

Yiftachel, Oren (2001), 'The Homeland and Nationalism', in A. Motyl (ed.), *Encyklopedia of Nationalism*, Volume 1, San Diego: Academic Press.

Yiftachel, Oren (2002), 'Territory as the kernel of the nation: Space, Time and Nationalism in Israel/Palestine', *Geopolitic* 7: 2.

Yiftachel, Oren (2006), *Ethnocracy: land and identity politics in Israel/Palestine*, Philadelphia: University of Pennsylvania Press.

Yiftachel, Oren and Ghanem, As'ad (2004), 'Towards a theory of ethnocratic regimes', in E. Kaufmann (2004), *Rethinking Ethnicity*, London, New York: Routledge.

Zakaria, Fareed (2003), *The Future of Freedom: Illiberal Democracy at Home and Abroad*, New York: W. W. Norton.

Zehfuss, Maja ((2001), 'Constructivism and Identity: A Dangerous Liaison', *European Journal of International Relations* 7: 3, pp. 315–48.

Žižek, Slavoj (1997), 'Multiculturalism, or the Cultural Logic of Multinational Capitalism', *New Left Review* 225, pp. 28–52.

Zubaida, Sami (1978), 'Theories of Nationalism', in Littlejohn, G., Smart, B., Wakefield, J. and Yuval-Davis, N. (eds), *Power and the State*, London: Croom Helm, pp. 52–71.

Zubaida, Sami (2004), 'Islam and nationalism: continuities and contradictions', *Nations and Nationalism*, 10: 4, pp. 407–20.

Index